A Research Agenda for Mergers and Acquisitions

Elgar Research Agendas outline the future of research in a given area. Leading scholars are given the space to explore their subject in provocative ways, and map out the potential directions of travel. They are relevant but also visionary.

Forward-looking and innovative, Elgar Research Agendas are an essential resource for PhD students, scholars and anybody who wants to be at the forefront of research.

For a full list of Edward Elgar published titles, including the titles in this series, visit our website at www.e-elgar.com.

A Research Agenda for Mergers and Acquisitions

Edited by

DAVID R. KING

Higdon Professor of Management, Florida State University, USA

OLIMPIA MEGLIO

Associate Professor of Management, University of Naples Federico II, Italy

Elgar Research Agendas

Edward Elgar
PUBLISHING

Cheltenham, UK • Northampton, MA, USA

Published by
Edward Elgar Publishing Limited
The Lypiatts
15 Lansdown Road
Cheltenham
Glos GL50 2JA
UK

Edward Elgar Publishing, Inc.
William Pratt House
9 Dewey Court
Northampton
Massachusetts 01060
USA

A catalogue record for this book
is available from the British Library

Library of Congress Control Number: 2024932700

This book is available electronically in the **Elgar**online
Business subject collection
http://dx.doi.org/10.4337/9781035319077

MIX
Paper from
responsible sources
FSC
www.fsc.org   FSC® C013056

ISBN 978 1 0353 1906 0 (cased)
ISBN 978 1 0353 1907 7 (eBook)

Printed and bound in Great Britain by
TJ Books Limited, Padstow, Cornwall

To Carlo,
with love and remembrance, beyond life.
O.M.

Contents

Figures

Tables

Contributors

Editors

David R. King is the Higdon Professor of Management at Florida State University where he teaches undergraduate and graduate business strategy, and undergraduate cross-cultural management. Before joining academia, Dave managed aircraft procurement for the U.S. Air Force. While in the military, he earned his Ph.D. in Strategy and Entrepreneurship from Indiana University's Kelley School of Business. Dave's research focuses on complementary resources, M&A integration and performance, technology innovation, and defense procurement.

Olimpia Meglio is currently Associate Professor at the University of Naples "Federico II" where she teaches managing alliances and acquisition at master level. She is affiliated to the European M&A institute. Olimpia's research interests revolve around growth strategies with a focus on mergers and acquisitions. Her works are regularly presented at international conferences and are published in leading academic journals.

Contributors

Florian Bauer is a Professor of Strategic Management at the University of Bristol Business School. His research focuses on strategic and organizational transformation and particularly on M&A. Florian is also co-founder and Chief Research Officer of MADiscover, a firm specializing in target screening with AI-based algorithms. Since 2023, he has been a board member of the federal German M&A Association.

Kyeong-Seop Choi is a doctoral student at Florida State University where he is studying business strategy and mergers and acquisitions. KS has a Ph.D. in Philosophy from the University of Wurzburg.

Paige Costanzo is an undergraduate at Florida State University (FSU). Paige is a finance major who participated in FSU's undergraduate research opportunity program (UROP). UROP identifies high achieving undergraduates and matches them with faculty working on research projects.

Mai Anh Dao received her Ph.D. from the University of Innsbruck, and then co-founded MADiscover, a consultant firm using a target screening algorithm for acquiring firm managers, where she is CEO.

Joana Geraldi is an Associate Professor at the Copenhagen Business School. Her research sheds light on how projects organize, and how they are organized in firms and society. Joana has published in leading journals, is senior editor of *Project Management Journal* and she has led several Special Issues on project studies.

Svetlana N. Khapova is Professor of Organisational Behaviour at the Vrije Universiteit Amsterdam. She is Past Division Chair of the Careers Division of the Academy of Management. Her research focuses on strategic leadership topics, including leadership development, career mobility, emotions in organizations, and board dynamics. Her research has been published in top-tier journals. She is author (together with M. B. Arthur and J. Richardson) of the book *An Intelligent Career: Taking Ownership of Your Work and Your Life* published by Oxford University Press in 2017.

Christine Kirkland is a doctoral student at Florida State University. She returned to FSU to pursue her Ph.D. in Business Administration with a major in Strategy after working in non-profits, starting a consulting firm and doing research with entrepreneurs. Her research is focused on entrepreneurial skills and resource acquisition through investigation of the business–society interface and the microfoundations of management and entrepreneurship.

David Kroon is Associate Professor of Strategy and Organisation at the Vrije Universiteit Amsterdam and affiliate member of the European M&A Institute. He received his Ph.D. from Tilburg University, the Netherlands. His current research focuses on inter-organizational collaborations, organizational change, and post-M&A integration with a particular emphasis on identity/identification, justice, culture, communication/language, emotions, and trust. His research has been published in various top-tier journals and edited books.

Nicola Mirc holds a Ph.D. in Economics and Business from Ecole Polytechnique in France and is Professor of Strategy at Toulouse School of Management (University of Toulouse, CNRS, France). Her research interests lie in the study of post-acquisition integration and innovation management. Her work addresses in particular the dynamics of social structures and relations underlying synergy creation and knowledge transfer processes in innovation- and knowledge-intensive sectors. Her research has been published in thought-leading journals.

Gonzalo Molina-Sieiro earned his Ph.D. from Florida State University, and he is an Assistant Professor at University of Nevada, Las Vegas. His research interests are international business strategy, including acquisitions, with a focus on how contextual factors influence firm-level strategy.

Thi Nguyen is a Ph.D. candidate in International Management at the Toulouse School of Management, Université Toulouse Capitole (France). As part of her studies, she completed research stays at Turku School of Economics (Finland) and Vrije Universiteit Amsterdam (the Netherlands). Her research interests include external stakeholders in M&A and how they cope with challenges. She is a member of the eM&Ai Institute, where she served as track chair at the 2022 eM&Ai conference. Thi has presented her work at several leading management conferences, including EURAM, EGOS, and AIMS.

Christina Öberg is Professor in Marketing at Karlstad and Linnaeus Universities, and associated with the Ratio Institute, Sweden. She has been a visiting scholar at Harvard University, Stanford University, the University of Florence, the University of Exeter, the University of Bath, and Manchester University. Her research interests include mergers, acquisitions, business relationships, networks and new ways to pursue business. She has published in leading journals.

Timo Paumen started to pursue a Ph.D. program at the Vrije Universiteit Amsterdam parallel to working in the M&A advisory section at KPMG in Cologne, Germany. After three years of M&A consulting experience, he joined the M&A department of the REWE Group, one of Germany's leading retail and tourism groups, as a project manager. His research focuses on M&A failure and whether there are factors impacting the outcomes of M&A transactions. His research particularly evolves around private equity funds' processes and operations, as well as M&A team roles and structures.

Audrey Rouziès is Professor of Strategic Management. Her work focuses on the management of mergers and acquisitions, more specifically on the organizational and human issues involved in the implementation of these operations. She uses qualitative and mixed methods, preferably longitudinal, to understand the research areas she studies. Her research has been published in top-tier journals in management. Her latest research projects deal with resilience and sustainable M&A in a post-growth economy. Audrey is the co-founder of the European M&A Institute (eM&Ai).

Mehdi Samimi earned his Ph.D. from Iowa State University, and he is an

Assistant Professor at the City College of New York. His research focuses on CEOs, including their influence on mergers and acquisitions, and innovation.

David Santana is a Ph.D. candidate in Strategy at the Toulouse School of Management. His research centers on Mergers and Acquisitions, specifically the valuation of targets by external M&A advisors. He employs a combination of qualitative and quantitative methods, including experiments, in his studies. David has presented his findings at several conferences, including the EURAM and AIMS conferences in Europe. He serves as the program coordinator for the SIG 13 Strategic Management of EURAM, where he was a part of the Online Task Force that made possible two online conferences during the COVID-19 pandemic. In 2021, he was selected for the CEFAG program in France. He has also had the opportunity to visit and conduct research at universities in Lancaster and Valencia.

Svante Schriber earned his Ph.D. from the Stockholm School of Economics on Synergies in M&A. He is Professor of Management at Stockholm Business School, Stockholm University. His research centers on corporate and business strategy, and how firms compete in dynamic industries using organic and non-organic growth. His research has contributed to research on M&A, inter-firm synergies, competitive dynamics, dynamic capabilities, organizational routines, and values in M&A.

Satu Teerikangas is Professor of Management and Organization at University of Turku, Finland. Her research focuses on the sociocultural dynamics of integration following mergers and acquisitions, as well as sustainability agency. She is the editor of the *Oxford Handbook of Mergers & Acquisitions*.

Preface

Despite over a century of research much remains unknown about what motivates and influences the performance of acquisitions. In parallel with the relevance measured in terms of value and frequency of deals across the globe, substantial research still leaves a fragmented picture of this complex phenomenon. Existing reviews and meta-analyses largely cover different angles or acquisition phases. This book provides a unique collection of novel research questions to answer or new theoretical lenses to employ to generate fresh perspectives for impactful research on mergers and acquisitions. Instead of reviewing topics of past research, the focus of the current book is to summarize and identify emerging topics offering new paths of investigation. Contributions come from a mix of established and emerging scholars from across the globe.

Acknowledgments

Any acknowledgment of those influencing this book is inherently incomplete, as a book requires a community effort, including people not directly involved. For example, prior research offers inspiration for additional inquiry. Still, we would like to thank the publisher for taking on the project. Additionally, in addition to the contributors of chapters who also served as reviewers, we would like thank Sina Amiri, Gustavo Birollo, Katia De Melo Galdino, Kaitlyn DeGhetto, Yves Felker, Massimo Picone, Elio Shijaku, Ana Sniazhana Sniazhko, Andres Strobl, and Matt Thomas for serving as reviewers of chapters. As a result, all chapters were both edited and blind reviewed.

Introduction: moving acquisition research forward

David R. King and Olimpia Meglio

Introduction

Firms typically achieve multiple goals with acquisitions, such as expanding their reach, increasing their market share, or gaining access to new technologies and resources (Bauer and Matzler, 2014). The frequency and volume of acquisitions explains a growing interest in studying what drives them, as well as their implications on firms, employees, investors, and society at large. After a century of research starting with Dewing (1921), a huge volume of academic articles has been produced, primarily looking at acquisition performance, often displaying inconsistent results (King et al., 2004, 2021; Meglio and Risberg, 2011). Taken together, these studies highlight that acquisitions are complex and unique events that are surrounded by ambiguity and uncertainty. The heterogeneity of acquisition activity explains the lack of a grand theory on acquisitions and the continuous interest in finding additional, novel research questions, perspectives, theoretical lenses, and research methods (Risberg, King and Meglio, 2015).

Traditionally, acquisition activity is viewed as a tool for achieving financial growth with a focus on shareholders. More recently, increasing awareness of stakeholder implications has extended research to consider effects on employees, customers, suppliers, and society. As a result, there are unanswered questions about how acquiring firms can be cognizant of a multitude of effects they produced from an acquisition. Moreover, enlarging the number of actors under investigation identifies unexamined relationships and theoretical perspectives.

With this book, we build upon what we have already seen to envision a path forward. Our research agenda aims to be a platform for the next decade of merger and acquisition (M&A) research. Our goal is to provide fresh perspectives that innovate the way we investigate acquisitions and outline new areas of research that can help address these questions and provide insights for improving acquisition success. Accordingly, this chapter is ideally divided into three parts. We first review existing knowledge of acquisitions to identify common threads in acquisition research and spot gaps. Next, we summarize themes associated with the collected chapters. Finally, we challenge conventional wisdom to discern paths for future M&A research (Meglio, 2022).

State of acquisition research

Research does not take place in a vacuum, and it reflects a collective journey. A journey that started most likely with the first publication on acquisitions (Dewing, 1921) and has progressed thanks to multiple scholars, conferences and workshops, and publications, including books (King, Bauer and Schriber, 2018; Meglio and Schriber, 2020), edited books (Faulkner, Teerikangas and Joseph, 2012, Risberg et al., 2015), the Advances in Mergers and Acquisitions book series, special issues (Angwin et al., 2023; Thanos et al., 2020), or research initiatives, such as the European M&A Institute. Over time, multiple conversations on acquisitions have developed on different facets of such an intriguing, yet elusive, phenomenon. In the following paragraphs, we summarize existing research with a focus on meta-analyses and reviews.

Broad reviews of acquisition research are less common given the amount of research, but there are exceptions. Haleblian et al. (2009) identify four key areas of research: (1) understanding the antecedents of M&A activity; (2) examining the M&A process from initiation to integration; (3) investigating the impact of M&A on organizational outcomes; and (4) developing a better understanding of the factors that moderate the M&A process and outcomes. King et al. (2018) also provide a comprehensive overview of the research exploring the evolution of acquisition activity, as well as the theories and frameworks developed to understand M&A. The authors also discuss the role of corporate governance, culture, and leadership in M&A activities.

It is more common to summarize research at different phases of an acquisition, such as pre-acquisition decisions (Welch et al., 2020), completion (King et al., 2021), and integration (Graebner et al., 2017; Steigenberger, 2017). As a result, we now turn to summarizing recent research findings from reviews and meta-analyses for each phase of an acquisition, as well as reviews focused on more specific topics in acquisition research. For example, fragmentation of M&A research has led to reviews that are focused on specific research domains, such as behavioral aspects (Devers et al., 2020), cross-border acquisitions (Xie, Reddy and Liang, 2017), or family business (King et al., 2022).

Pre-acquisition

In a review of research pre-acquisition, Welch et al. (2020) provide a review of research examining the pre-deal phase before an acquisition is announced and completed. Associated negotiation, due diligence, and deal structuring can be critical for the success of M&A activities, and they highlight the need for further research to understand relationships from this phase on later phases of an acquisition. Additionally, they underscore the importance of understanding the cultural and social factors, such as trust, communication, and power dynamics.

Completion

Focusing largely on acquisition characteristics at completion, King et al. (2021) present a meta-analytic integration of acquisition performance prediction using data from 220 primary studies. They find that the most consistent predictor of performance across financial measures was the use of stock as a method of payment, and it is reliably associated with lower performance across different measures. Still, in better understanding the impact of other commonly studied variables, the paper highlights the need for more research on the role of contextual factors, such as industry and country, in predicting acquisition performance.

Integration

Post-acquisition integration has been recognized as important, and extent research is summarized in three reviews. Graebner et al. (2017) review the post-merger integration (PMI) process, and they identify several key factors, including integration strategy, integration management, integration tactics, and integration outcomes. Next, a review by Steigenberger (2017) focuses on integration challenges and factors that influence integration success. The authors identify several challenges, including cultural integration, communication, leadership, and employee engagement. For implementation, they highlight the importance of understanding the role of power and politics in integration, and the need for effective project management during the integration process. This relates to a meta-analytic examination of executive turnover post-acquisition by Bilgili et al. (2017) who find that executive turnover is a common occurrence in M&As and is primarily driven by power dynamics, clashing cultures, and performance issues. Further, the timing of executive turnover plays a critical role in post-acquisition performance with early turn-over having a more significant negative effect than turnover that occurs later.

Specific domains or topics

Devers et al. (2020) review behavioral acquisition literature to identify the key themes and trends. The paper identifies four main themes in the emerging behavioral acquisition literature: (1) the role of emotions and affect in M&A decision-making; (2) the importance of cognitive biases and heuristics in M&A activities; (3) the impact of social networks and power dynamics on M&A outcomes; and (4) the importance of leadership and organizational culture in post-merger integration.

Xie et al. (2017) review country-specific determinants of cross-border acquisitions (CBA) and outline a need for a more comprehensive and nuanced understanding of the country-specific determinants of these activities. The paper identifies four main categories of country-specific determinants: (1) institutional factors, such as legal and regulatory frameworks, cultural norms, and political stability; (2) economic factors, such as market size, growth potential, and infrastructure; (3) industry-specific factors, such as technology and innovation capabilities, and market competitiveness; and (4) firm-specific factors, such as strategic motives, organizational capabilities, and financial resources.

King et al. (2022) review research on family business restructuring that faces unique challenges, such as the interplay between family dynamics and business considerations, and balancing family interests with other stakeholders. The paper identifies four main categories of family business restructuring: (1) strategic restructuring, such as diversification, internationalization, and innovation; (2) financial restructuring, such as debt restructuring and capital-raising; (3) ownership restructuring, such as succession planning and family governance; and (4) operational restructuring, such as process improvement and organizational design.

Additional reviews have focused on specific constructs, such as acquisition experience (Langosch and Tumlinson, 2022; Schweizer et al., 2022), and diversification (Schommer, Richter and Karna, 2019). For acquisition experience, Langosch and Tumlinson (2022) find that experience alone does not necessarily lead to better acquisition performance. Instead, the impact of experience depends on the complexity of the acquisition and the level of uncertainty in the environment, and acquisition experience is most beneficial for improving acquisition performance when the acquisition is complex, and the environment is highly uncertain. Meanwhile, in a meta-analysis, Schweizer et al. (2022) find that experiential learning positively affects M&A performance. However, the post-acquisition integration strategy moderates the relationship between experiential learning and M&A performance. While a proactive integration strategy enhances the positive effects of experiential learning on M&A performance, a reactive integration strategy weakens the positive effects of experiential learning on M&A performance.

In an examination of diversification, Schommer et al. (2019) conduct a meta-analytical review and they find that the relationship between diversification and firm performance has changed over time. While the relationship between diversification and firm performance is negative and statistically significant, the magnitude of this relationship has declined over time, indicating that the negative impact of diversification on firm performance has weakened. Further, the negative impact was isolated to unrelated diversification, as related diversification has a positive effect on acquiring firm performance.

Emerging themes

Taken together, this book presents collected research from established and emerging M&A scholars who have contributed ten chapters. Table I.1 provides a synopsis of topics covered, types of chapters (conceptual, empirical, literature review), theoretical underpinnings, a summary of their content, the contribution to future research avenues, and the connections to other chapters in this book. Instead of summarizing each chapter, we discuss four themes.

Pre-merger uncertainty

Due to a lack of visibility by researchers, there has been relatively little attention on pre-merger decisions and target selection. The success of an M&A activity depends largely on the selection of the right target, requiring a thorough understanding of the target's capabilities, strengths, weaknesses, and potential synergies with the acquirer. However, the process of target selection is often complex and challenging, as it involves a wide range of factors, including financial, strategic, and cultural considerations. Chapters 1 and 2 highlight that this process is less rational than generally assumed to highlight the use of heuristics by top managers.

Research can explore the use of big data and advanced analytics to help identify potential targets more accurately and efficiently. For example, machine learning algorithms can be used to analyze large amounts of data on companies'

Table I.1   Summary of book chapters

Chapter/ topic	Type of chapter	Theory/ perspective	Chapter summary	Contribution	Connections to other chapters
1/ Heuristics in Pre-Merger Process	Conceptual	Cognitive/ heuristics	Examines the pre-deal process in M&As from a cognitive perspective, offering a novel examination of the role of heuristics employed by involved actors, such as managers, consultants, and legal advisors. The study investigates the use of heuristics across various sub-phases of the pre-deal process, develops the antecedents and outcomes of heuristics in these stages, and identifies several relationships and potential research avenues. The potential benefits of efficient decision-making and communication and the risks associated with biases and oversimplification are highlighted.	Heuristics can enable acquisition research to identify ways to increase M&A success.	2 – target screening. 3 – role of managers. 6 & 10 – multiple actors surrounding acquisitions (advisors; competitors/ suppliers).

Chapter/ topic	Type of chapter	Theory/ perspective	Chapter summary	Contribution	Connections to other chapters
2/Target Screening	Empirical (qualitative)	Heuristics	Assesses the target screening phase of an acquisition. During target screening, an acquirer can translate the strategy into screening criteria and after an evaluation of potential targets, creates an actionable shortlist. However, while this process appears to be straightforward or textbook like, findings from a qualitative research highlight that the practices managers employ during target screening give rise to heuristics and cognitive simplifications that trigger cognitive biases. This offers a novel explanation for why many acquisitions fall short in creating value.	Need to dig deeper into the acquisition decision and target screening processes.	1 – heuristics in pre-deal phase. 3 – role of executives in acquisitions. 9 – explanation of acquisition failure.
3/Top Executives	Literature review	Summary of different theories (upper echelon, agency, behavioral, market power, real options, RBV, resource dependence, TCE)	Executives and the decisions they make during acquisitions are often overlooked or treated in isolation by research. Theories studying executives in acquisitions could benefit from integration. When covered, theory applied to research tends to focus just on executives. To foster a more comprehensive understanding of how executives drive and lead acquisitions, more research needs to consider the people conceiving and implementing acquisitions.	Need to study top managers formulating and implementing acquisitions.	2 – role of managers in target selection.

Chapter/topic	Type of chapter	Theory/perspective	Chapter summary	Contribution	Connections to other chapters
4/Analysts	Empirical (quantitative)	Information asymmetry	Acquisitions present an information asymmetry problem for external stakeholders. Analyst coverage that decreases information asymmetry also increases stock price volatility for the acquiring firm when an acquisition is announced. This aligns with information economics, or more information available about a previously less-known target firm from analysts can reduce information asymmetry for investors and contribute to market efficiency.	Identifies overlooked influence of analysts on acquisitions.	10 – actors surrounding acquisitions.
5/Social Media	Literature review	Information asymmetry	Social media is an increasingly common tool to disclose information and engage with shareholders, but research on whether social media impacts firm performance remains limited. A review of research firm performance finds evidence that social media activity internal and external to a firm can impact performance. While reviewed research identifies a positive effect of social media on firm performance, it is mostly based on internal firm and positive or informational messages.	Need to consider the impact of modern communication channels on acquisitions.	10 – actors surrounding acquisitions.

Chapter/ topic	Type of chapter	Theory/ perspective	Chapter summary	Contribution	Connections to other chapters
6/Networks and M&As	Literature review	Ecosystem	By conceptualizing business transactions within a network framework, a deeper understanding of how M&A are influenced by and influence other business transactions is possible. For example, network effects exist across the M&A process, as power dynamics influence negotiations with suppliers or positioning an acquiring firm relative to its competitors. Integration also involves managing reactions that either enhance or hinder efficiency gains.	Adopting networks as analytical units in M&A studies uncovers new motives, integration challenges, and performance measures.	5 – use of social media. 10 – actors surrounding acquisitions.
7/M&As as Projects	Conceptual	Project management	Considering M&A as projects creates a broader research agenda that focuses on the transient nature of acquisitions. Applying concepts of projects, programs, and portfolio can aid organizing M&A before and after deals. As a project, M&As should be "completed" on time and within budget. As a program, M&A converge yet never reach full integration between organizations. As a portfolio, an individual M&A transaction can be considered as one among an ongoing series of M&A integrating at different tempos and degrees that together form the firm.	Offers alternative perspectives to organizing M&A.	3 – manager decisions. 8 – rational process involving people.

Chapter/topic	Type of chapter	Theory/perspective	Chapter summary	Contribution	Connections to other chapters
8/An Effectuation Lens to M&As	Conceptual	Contrasts and then integrates causation and effectuation research	Causation logic remains narrow and incomplete as acquisitions are fraught with uncertainty and ambiguity due to information asymmetries and cognitive biases. Blending goal-driven process with non-goal driven logic, an effectuation model of post-acquisition processes that combines effectuation and causation provides an agenda for future research.	Considering effectuation highlights the role of co-creators of value through processes of self-organization.	3 – theories on manager role in acquisitions.
9/Acquisition Failure	Literature review	Several disciplinary perspectives (process perspective, organization behavior, RBV, etc.)	M&A failure has various disciplinary perspectives that can be better understood from considering failure across the M&A process. Blind spots in current research are identified to inform future study.	Provides a comprehensive framework that identifies different determinants of M&A failure across M&A phases.	3 – theories on manager role in acquisitions.
10/Acquisition Ecosystem and Outcomes	Conceptual	Ecosystem	The assumption that acquisitions should primarily serve an acquiring firm's shareholders is challenged, as other actors need to be considered. Specifically, acquisition research should also consider outcomes for additional actors, or subjective and dynamic perceptions of non-financial value. This reflects that acquisitions are embedded in an ecosystem. Considering an acquisition ecosystem disentangles acquisition stakeholders and outcomes.	Integrates complementary perspectives of acquisition outcomes to inspire additional study.	6 – networks.

financial and operational performance, as well as external factors such as industry trends and market conditions, to identify targets that are most likely to be successful. Text analysis of earnings calls or news coverage of acquisitions will also likely provide new insights.

Executive decision-making

Another area of acquisition research that has received relatively little attention is the decision-making process of executives. The success of an M&A activity often depends on the quality of the decisions made by executives, including the selection of the right target, the negotiation of favorable terms, and the integration of the acquired company into the acquirer's operations. These topics are considered by Chapters 1, 2, 3, 5, and 9.

New research can explore the use of decision support systems and other tools to help executives make better decisions. For example, managers may need to be aware of potential biases in making acquisition decisions, including tendencies to deviate from rational decision-making due to emotions or heuristics.

Network relationships and actors

The impact of network relationships on acquisitions has received research attention, and Chapters 4, 6, 8, 9, and 10 begin to frame associated relationships and actors. For example, in existing research, board ties between an acquirer and a target firm can facilitate acquisitions by providing valuable information about the target firm, reducing information asymmetry, and increasing trust between the parties (e.g., Palmer and Barber, 2001; Xia et al., 2018). However, employees of the target company may face job insecurity, and employees of the acquiring company may face integration challenges. Further, both customers and suppliers of combining companies experience uncertainty due to changes in their relationships and contracts. Regulators may scrutinize the acquisition for potential antitrust violations, and the broader community may be impacted by changes in the local economy or social dynamics. Additionally, investment bankers, lawyers, consultants, and analysts play a role in shaping and facilitating acquisitions.

Chapter 5 also reviews available empirical research on social media and firm performance. Despite its ubiquity in society, the role of social media has received relatively little research attention. Social media platforms are popular, and many firms now use social media platforms to communicate with stakeholders. However, the use of social media in M&A activities is relatively unexplored, and there is little research on how it can be used effectively.

Additionally, external actors can share information on social media that can impact firms. For example, the collapse of Silicon Valley Bank in 2023 was hastened by social media (Macheel, 2023).

New research is needed to explore relationships beyond combining firms. Associated relationships are likely to be complex and depend on a variety of factors, including the nature of the relationship, the context of the acquisition, and the motivations of the parties involved.

Project management

Another potential focus for acquisition research that has received limited attention is project management, and it is the focus of Chapter 7. The success of an M&A activity depends largely on the ability of the acquirer to manage the complex and often challenging process of integrating the acquired company into its operations. This process involves a wide range of activities, including cultural integration, organizational design, and the development of new business processes and systems that new research can explore.

Discerning the future of acquisition research

The cumulative effect of the book is going beyond traditional gap spotting to generate novel lines of inquiry (cf., Alvesson and Sandberg, 2013, 2014; Meglio, 2022; Wicker, 1985). As Wicker (1985) aptly describes, studying familiar problems over time results in cognitive problems that need to be addressed (Meglio, 2022). Beyond identified themes, future research will ideally employ three strategies to avoid stagnation: (1) rethinking key constructs or topics, (2) identifying relatively neglected or even novel areas of investigation, and (3) advancing novel theoretical lenses.

Rethinking key constructs or topics

The first strategy scrutinizes key constructs. In acquisition research, there is already a significant body of research on how acquisitions perform, or what causes success and failure. However, this risks research taking outcomes for granted, or a lack of precision in linking theory with appropriate measures (e.g., Cording, Christmann and Weigelt, 2010). In Chapter 9, Paumen, Kroon and Khapova reflect on what acquisition failure is and what are the major blind spots in existing research. This complements existing studies focusing on assessing failure rates or causes (cf., Renneboog and Vansteenkiste, 2019). In a similar vein, Chapter 10 examines acquisition performance beyond financial performance by advancing the ecosystem effects of acquisitions. Associated recent research examines sources of value and synergies in acquisitions (Bauer and Friesl, 2022; Feldman and Hernandez, 2022; Meglio and Schriber, 2023).

Identifying relatively neglected or novel areas of investigation

Acquisitions are multifaceted events and as such they provide a seemingly inexhaustible soil for investigation. In this book, we have several chapters covering neglected areas of investigation. While acquisitions are recognized as process driven, there has been limited attention given to pre-merger processes and decisions that set conditions for later stages. While implementation is inarguably important, a focus on later acquisition phases has resulted in little knowledge on how acquisition decisions are made and any sources of major flaws in the pre-merger stage that are covered in Chapters 1 and 2. The first chapter provides a conceptual framework, while the second one offers insights from an empirical qualitative study. Relatedly, Chapter 3 focuses on top executives and provides fresh perspectives by integrating different research streams that have largely developed in parallel.

Identifying new areas for research also applies to Chapters 4 and 5. Both chapters deal with the information asymmetry problem, or a classic topic in acquisition research with potential remedies. Chapter 4 deals with the role of analysts, key intermediaries in the market for corporate control, and Chapter 5 reviews a role for social media in mitigating the information asymmetry problem.

Advancing novel theoretical lenses

Acquisition research can benefit from borrowing theoretical lenses from adjacent fields, and we offer three examples of how we can learn from alternative frameworks. Chapter 6 advances a network perspective to remedy a taken for granted assumption in acquisition research, that acquisitions happen in a vacuum and suggests exploring both positive and negative effects of network ties, internal and external to the merging companies to achieve a better grasp of the contextual, embedded nature of acquisitions (cf., Rouzies, Colman and Angwin, 2019). Chapter 7 looks at the project management realm and reflects on the transient nature of organizing by mobilizing projects, programs, and portfolio concepts to organize M&A before and after deals. The chapter complements conceptual (Geraldi, Teerikangas and Birollo, 2022) and empirical research (Bansal, King and Meglio, 2022; Birollo and Teerikangas, 2019) at the intersection of project management and acquisitions. Finally, Chapter 8 draws on effectuation to augment the rational portrayal of acquisitions to offer a complementary perspective that acknowledges the importance of flexibility, creativity, and adaptability in acquisition implementation.

Conclusion: what's next?

Acquisitions will continue to be part of firm strategy and economic growth, and, along with economies and industries, their use by firms will continue to adapt. As a result, while prior research on acquisitions offers insights, continued exploration of different facets and aspects of acquisitions is needed. It could be argued that acquisition research has reached maturity, and there is no room for ground-breaking research. We disagree, as acquisitions produce a multitude of outcomes beyond financial performance or competitive effects. Not only as scholars are we exposed to acquisitions, but so are competitors, customers, employees, society, and suppliers. Given the pervasiveness of acquisitions and their evolving nature, we need to expand our understanding of this complex phenomenon and its inherent ambiguities. We outline several novel areas of acquisition research that we hope will continue to inspire both seasoned and emerging acquisition scholars. By exploring new areas of research, we can gain insights and develop strategies for managers to make better decisions and improve M&A success.

References

Alvesson, M., & Sandberg, J. (2013). Has management studies lost its way? Ideas for more imaginative and innovative research. *Journal of Management Studies*, 50(1), 128–152.

Alvesson, M., & Sandberg, J. (2014). Habitat and habitus: boxed-in versus box-breaking research. *Organization Studies*, 35(7), 967–987.

Angwin, D., Kroon, D., Mirc, N., Oliveira, N., Prashantham, S., Rouziès, A., & Tienari, J. (2023). Mergers and acquisitions: time for a theory rejuvenation of the field? *Long Range Planning*, 56(3), 102398.

Bansal, A., King, D., & Meglio, O. (2022). Acquisitions as programs: the role of sensemaking and sensegiving. *International Journal of Project Management*, 40(3), 278–289.

Bauer, F., & Friesl, M. (2022). Synergy evaluation in mergers and acquisitions: an attention-based view. *Journal of Management Studies*. https://doi.org/10.1111/joms.12804.

Bauer, F., & Matzler, K. (2014). Antecedents of M&A success: the role of strategic complementarity, cultural fit, and degree and speed of integration. *Strategic Management Journal*, 35(2), 269–291.

Bilgili, T., Calderon, C., Allen, D., & Kedia, B. (2017). Gone with the wind: a meta-analytic review of executive turnover, its antecedents, and postacquisition performance. *Journal of Management*, 43(6), 1966–1997.

Birollo, G., & Teerikangas, S. (2019). Integration projects as relational spaces: a closer look at acquired managers' strategic role recovery in cross-border acquisitions. *International Journal of Project Management*, 37(8), 1003–1016.

Cording, M., Christmann, P., & Weigelt, C. (2010). Measuring theoretically complex constructs: the case of acquisition performance. *Strategic Organization*, 8(1), 11–41.

Devers, C., Wuorinen, S., McNamara, G., Haleblian, J., Gee, I., & Kim, J. (2020). An integrative review of the emerging behavioral acquisition literature: charting the next decade of research. *Academy of Management Annals*, 14(2), 869–907.

Dewing, A. (1921). A statistical test of the success of consolidations. *Quarterly Journal of Economics*, 36(1), 84–101.

Faulkner, D., Teerikangas, S., & Joseph, R. J. (eds.) (2012). *The Handbook of Mergers and Acquisitions*. New York: Oxford University Press.

Feldman, E., & Hernandez, E. (2022). Synergy in mergers and acquisitions: typology, life cycles, and value. *Academy of Management Review*, 47(4), 549–578.

Geraldi, J., Teerikangas, S., & Birollo, G. (2022). Project, program and portfolio management as modes of organizing: theorising at the intersection between mergers and acquisitions and project studies. *International Journal of Project Management*, 40(4), 439–453.

Graebner, M., Heimeriks, K., Huy, Q., & Vaara, E. (2017). The process of postmerger integration: a review and agenda for future research. *Academy of Management Annals*, 11(1), 1–32.

Haleblian, J., Devers, C., McNamara, G., Carpenter, M., & Davison, R. (2009). Taking stock of what we know about mergers and acquisitions: a review and research agenda. *Journal of Management*, 35(3), 469–502.

King, D., Bauer, F., & Schriber, S. (2018). *Mergers & Acquisitions: A Research Overview*. Abingdon: Routledge.

King, D., Dalton, D., Daily, C., & Covin, J. G. (2004). Meta-analyses of post-acquisition performance: indications of unidentified moderators. *Strategic Management Journal*, 25(2), 187–200.

King, D., Meglio, O., Gomez-Mejia, L., Bauer, F., & De Massis, A. (2022). Family business restructuring: a review and research agenda. *Journal of Management Studies*, 59(1), 197–235.

King, D., Wang, G., Samimi, M., & Cortes, A. (2021). A meta-analytic integration of acquisition performance prediction. *Journal of Management Studies*, 58(5), 1198–1236.

Langosch, M., & Tumlinson, J. (2022). Does experience improve acquisition performance? It's complicated, and that is when it helps most. *Academy of Management Discoveries*, 8(3), 414–440.

Macheel, T. (2023). Social media raises bank run risk, fueled Silicon Valley Bank's collapse. CNBC: https://www.cnbc.com/2023/04/24/social-media-raises-bank-run-risk-fueled-svbs-collapse-paper-says.html.

Meglio, O. (2022). Reshaping M&A research: strategies and tactics for a new research agenda. *European Management Journal*, 40(6), 823–831.

Meglio, O., & Risberg, A. (2011). The (mis) measurement of M&A performance: a systematic narrative literature review. *Scandinavian Journal of Management*, 27(4), 418–433.

Meglio, O., & Schriber, S. (2020). *Mergers and Acquisitions: Rethinking Key Umbrella Constructs*. Cham: Springer Nature.

Meglio, O., & Schriber, S. (2023). Towards a more inclusive notion of values in acquisition research. *Long Range Planning*, 56(6), 102331.

Palmer, D., & Barber, B. (2001). Challengers, elites, and owning families: a social class theory of corporate acquisitions in the 1960s. *Administrative Science Quarterly*, 46(1), 87–120.

Renneboog, L., & Vansteenkiste, C. (2019). Failure and success in mergers and acquisitions. *Journal of Corporate Finance*, 58, 650–699.

Risberg, A., King, D., & Meglio, O. (eds.) (2015). *The Routledge Companion to Mergers and Acquisitions*. Abingdon: Routledge.

Rouzies, A., Colman, H., & Angwin, D. (2019). Recasting the dynamics of post-acquisition integration: an embeddedness perspective. *Long Range Planning*, 52(2), 271–282.

Schommer, M., Richter, A., & Karna, A. (2019). Does the diversification–firm performance relationship change over time? A meta-analytical review. *Journal of Management Studies*, 56(1), 270–298.

Schweizer, L., Wang, L., Koscher, E., & Michaelis, B. (2022). Experiential learning, M&A performance, and post-acquisition integration strategy: a meta-analysis. *Long Range Planning*, 55(6), 102212.

Steigenberger, N. (2017). The challenge of integration: a review of the M&A integration literature. *International Journal of Management Reviews*, 19(4), 408–431.

Thanos, I., Angwin, D., Bauer, F., & Teerikangas, S. (2019). Reshaping M&A scholarship: broadening the boundaries of M&A research. *European Management Journal*, 37(4), https://doi.org/10.1016/j.emj.2019.06.003.

Welch, X., Pavićević, S., Keil, T., & Laamanen, T. (2020). The pre-deal phase of mergers and acquisitions: a review and research agenda. *Journal of Management*, 46(6), 843–878.

Wicker, A. (1985). Getting out of our conceptual ruts: strategies for expanding conceptual frameworks. *American Psychologist*, 40(10), 1094–1103.

Xia, J., Ma, X., Tong, T. W., & Li, W. (2018). Network information and cross-border M&A activities. *Global Strategy Journal*, 8(2), 301–323.

Xie, E., Reddy, K., & Liang, J. (2017). Country-specific determinants of cross-border mergers and acquisitions: a comprehensive review and future research directions. *Journal of World Business*, 52(2), 127–183.

1 Heuristics in pre-merger processes

David Santana, Thi Nguyen, Nicola Mirc and Audrey Rouziès

Introduction

Acquisitions are complex, multifaceted, and uncertain situations (Faulkner, Teerikangas and Joseph, 2012), involving different actors with varied interests (Kolasinski and Kothari, 2008). However, investigations into human factors have largely focused on the integration phase, while the pre-deal phase has been of greater interest for exploring financial and strategic factors (Calipha, Tarba and Brock, 2010). The pre-deal phase, namely the processes that happen until the moment when the ownership transfers from the target to the acquirer (Gomes et al., 2013), is a crucial part of the merger and acquisition (M&A) process and involves a variety of actors, such as an acquirer, a target firm's managers, and their advisors (e.g., investments bankers, M&A advisors, legal advisors). To reduce errors and yield an external point of view, the acquirer and target firms often seek the expertise of advisors to assist them in their decision-making. Advisors often embody the perfect rational agent for M&A researchers and practitioners alike. M&A advisors are required to deliver a professional, objective, unbiased, rational, and well-informed analysis of the target (Angwin and Karamat, 2015; Servaes and Zenner, 1996). Together with managers, advisors process large amounts of data, from different sources, reflecting different parties and interests.

However, M&A advisors and other actors may not be the perfect rational agents the field has long assumed and might exhibit bounded rationality (Simon, 1955).

To navigate the complexity of the pre-deal phase, research suggests that actors adopt heuristics to simplify decision-making due to information asymmetry, time pressure, and ambiguity (Aschbacher and Kroon, 2023). A heuristic is a mental shortcut (i.e., rule of thumb) that is quick to use for judgment under uncertainty (Kauser et al., 2015), to simplify reality, ignore information and reduce complexity, and make decisions (Mousavi and Gigerenzer, 2014; Gigerenzer and Gaissmaier, 2011; Goldstein and Gigerenzer, 2002; Serwe and Frings, 2006; Tversky and Kahneman, 1974). Research into heuristics can be broadly categorized into two camps: the heuristics-and-biases paradigm and the fast-and-frugal paradigm. The heuristics-and-biases paradigm links the use of heuristics with sub-optimal outcomes, which might create "severe and systematic errors" of judgment (Tversky and Kahneman, 1974, p. 1124). Meanwhile, the fast-and-frugal paradigm has a more positive stance and views heuristics as simple and adaptive strategies to make good decisions with minimal cognitive effort (Gigerenzer, 2008; Mousavi and Gigerenzer, 2014).

We begin to explore the use of heuristics during the pre-merger phase of M&A, and how actors successfully use them to: (1) understand the operations, (2) make efficient valuations with the information available, (3) communicate, and (4) accumulate learning. We also outline that heuristics can lead to biased assessments and wrong expectations about the future of the merged companies. This is done through delineating antecedents and outcomes of heuristics in different sub-phases of the pre-deal phase and discussing how the various actors involved might potentially employ heuristics. Building on heuristic and M&A research, we make multiple contributions. Due to bounded rationality (Simon, 1955) of actors involved in the pre-acquisition phase (Jensen and Meckling, 1976), heuristics can have positive outcomes for decision-makers recognizing potential pitfalls due to cognitive bias, as well as guide them toward more efficient decision-making. Moreover, we delineate the importance of M&A context (Rouzies, Colman and Angwin, 2019) to understand potential sources of tension and success.

Theoretical background

Heuristics and decision-making

Traditionally, decision-makers are assumed to be aware of all the potential alternatives, possess the ability to calculate the risk and return for each decision, and select the course of action that would maximize outcomes. However, scholars have observed that actual decision-making deviates from normative rational models and acknowledged the cognitive limitations of decision-makers (Kahneman, 2003; Thaler, 2016). Actors may have limited cognitive capacity (Gigerenzer and Gaissmaier, 2011) and thus consciously (Artinger et al., 2015) or unconsciously (Kahneman, 2011) simplify their decision-making with heuristics.

Research into heuristics and decision-making can be broadly categorized into two main paradigms: (1) the heuristics-and-biases paradigm, and (2) the fast-and-frugal paradigm (Kelman, 2011). First, the heuristics-and-biases paradigm links the use of heuristics with systematic biases and errors (Kahneman, 2003; Simon, 1972; Tversky and Kahneman, 1974). Heuristics may not always produce the optimal outcome and can result in cognitive biases, which might create "severe and systematic errors" of judgment (Tversky and Kahneman, 1974, p. 1124). In acquisitions, theoretical contributions have called for understanding the negative consequence of bias, such as overconfidence bias, anchoring bias, endowment, and hindsight and confirmation biases (Asaoka, 2019; Garbuio, Lovallo and Horn, 2010).

The more recent and positive fast-and-frugal paradigm considers heuristics as adaptive tools that allow individuals to make good and effort-efficient decisions under uncertainty (Gigerenzer, 2008; Mousavi and Gigerenzer, 2014). This paradigm relies on "a minimum of time, knowledge, and computation to make adaptive choices" (Gigerenzer and Todd, 1999, p. 14). Unlike the prior heuristic-and-bias paradigm, the fast-and-frugal paradigm does not view heuristics as the consequence of mental shortcomings, or that they always lead to second-best decisions (e.g., Kahneman, 2011). Rather, simple heuristics, such as recognition heuristic (Gigerenzer and Goldstein, 2011), satisficing heuristic (Simon, 1955), or take-the-best heuristic (Gigerenzer and Goldstein, 1999) allow for adaptive responses to the circumstances of uncertain environments (Artinger et al., 2015) where it is not possible to identify *ex ante* the optimal choice (Dequech, 2001). Thereby, actors posit "ecological rationality," which allows them to systematically use environmental information (Goldstein and Gigerenzer, 2002).

While both paradigms recognize that actors use heuristics in decision-making, the heuristics-and-bias paradigm tends to focus on situations where heuristics lead to systematic errors, whereas the fast-and-frugal paradigm emphasizes situations where these simple decision rules can be adaptive and lead to effective decisions. We aim to illuminate situations in the pre-merger phase, where actors could employ heuristics that fall into both paradigms; thereby, our chapter bridges the previous dichotomy. While scholars have recognized the value of heuristics at the individual level, more research is needed to fully grasp the role of heuristics at the collective, intra-, and inter-organizational levels.

Current research suggests that heuristics developed by individual actors are more prone to failure than heuristics that have been collectively developed if used in a different context (Bingham, Howell and Ott, 2019). A possible reason for that could be that collectively developed heuristics rely on a greater pool of knowledge about different contexts. Vuori, Laamanen and Zollo (2023) put forth that heuristics developed by experienced managers are more robust than those by inexperienced managers. On the contrary, Serwe and Frings (2006) showed that heuristics lead to greater predictive accuracy when non-experts apply them compared to when experts apply them, suggesting that heuristics may benefit in certain situations from ignoring expert knowledge. Hence, our chapter illuminates situations where different actors interact, which might shape the usage, outcome, and evolution of heuristics.

Heuristics and the M&A process

Different contextual factors of the pre-deal process could trigger the use of heuristics for making decisions, such as uncertainty (Bargeron et al., 2009), lack of information (Goldstein and Gigerenzer, 2002), time pressure, standardization, and emotions (Aschbacher and Kroon, 2023). We develop a simplified process where an acquirer searches for a target to fulfill a strategic need. For theoretical simplicity, the conventional view on acquisition is applied, where the pre-deal phase is divided into the following stages: exploring initiatives and setting M&A objectives, screening of companies, strategic evaluation, due diligence, and negotiation (Galpin and Herndon, 2014; Haspeslagh and Jemison, 1991). However, it should be noted that each deal is unique, and the different stages presented in this chapter can be interchanged, omitted, or combined depending on the concrete characteristics. However, there are recurrent steps that managers and M&A advisors must consider in M&A (Iannotta, 2010). The separation of each of these tasks in stages provides a clearer view of the different cognitive processes and heuristics that may be used.

Table 1.1 presents the role of the relevant actors in each phase, examples of heuristics, potential antecedents of using heuristics, and some potential M&A outcomes. The table covers until the moment when both companies agree on a price and conditions for the merger. By focusing on concrete recurrent steps of the pre-merger phase, it is possible to observe recurrent scenarios where managers and advisors of both parties are involved. Given the concrete characteristics of each phase, theoretical arguments are developed to illustrate (1) why the different recurrent steps should trigger the use of heuristics, and (2) what the impact of those heuristics according to previous research in similar contexts could be.

Table 1.1   Antecedents of heuristics and potential outcomes in the pre-merger phase

Pre-merger phase	Actors	Antecedents that trigger heuristics	Examples of heuristics	Potential positive outcomes	Potential negative outcomes	Examples of reference
Setting strategic objectives	• Acquirer managers • Consultants	• Uncertainty • Scarce information • Managers' previous acquisition experience • Consultants' previous experience in recommending acquisitions	• Buy a company to expand into a foreign market • Buy a company to acquire a key resource or capability • Buy a company to reduce competition in the market	• Managers and consultants can quickly assess the strategic challenges	• Managers and consultants may prioritize over prioritize M&A over other strategies, which could kick-off value-destroying deals	Bonaccio and Dalal (2006); Schrah et al. (2006); McDonald and Westphal (2003); Alexiev et al. (2010); Gable (1996)

Pre-merger phase	Actors	Antecedents that trigger heuristics	Examples of heuristics	Potential positive outcomes	Potential negative outcomes	Examples of reference
Search and screening	• Acquirer managers • M&A advisors specialized in target screening	• Limited information • Previous experience of managers and advisors • Managers need to communicate to M&A advisors priorities when searching candidates • M&A advisors have limited time and resources to develop a list of potential candidates • M&A advisors need an easy way to manage information about companies to compare potential candidates • M&A advisors need to communicate why they have selected certain candidates over others	• Select companies with revenues over 1M€ • Select companies producing a certain product • Select companies with little or no debt • Select companies with a market share over 5%	• Managers can efficiently communicate what is important to them • M&A advisors can efficiently select candidates • Good communication flow between advisors and managers	• M&A advisors may discard candidates that could have been interesting for the acquirer • Managers may discard good candidates for the next stages • M&A advisors and managers would prioritize known candidates	Luan et al. (2019); DeMiguel et al. (2009); Goldstein and Gigerenzer (2002); Borges et al. (2000); Serwe and Frings (2006)

Pre-merger phase	Actors	Antecedents that trigger heuristics	Examples of heuristics	Potential positive outcomes	Potential negative outcomes	Examples of reference
Strategic evaluation	• Acquirer managers • Target managers • M&A advisors	• Previous experiences of the key actors in strategic evaluations of targets • Information asymmetry between the acquirer, target, and advisors • Target managers need to create a good impression by communicating key competitive advantages of their firms • M&A advisors must find relevant clues to assess if the target company is suitable for the acquisition • Decisions on which candidate should be taken to next round must be taken after few visits and/or conversations with target managers	• Discard candidates with unfriendly managers • Discard candidates with potentially problematic employees • Show the latest innovation (target managers) • Show the company facilities and introduce visitors to charismatic personnel (target managers)	• Managers and advisors can quickly assess the potential of each candidate and make a final selection • Target managers can easily communicate the best facts about their firms	• Important indicators may pass unobserved by acquirer managers and their advisors	Luan et al. (2019); Bouwman et al. (1987, 1995); Mukherjee et al. (2004)

Pre-merger phase	Actors	Antecedents that trigger heuristics	Examples of heuristics	Potential positive outcomes	Potential negative outcomes	Examples of reference
Due diligence	• Auditors with different expertise • Target managers	• Auditors must find and analyze important amounts of data in a short period of time • Target managers need to provide required information to auditors without disturbing operations • Auditors must coordinate their research activity with the target personnel	• Confirm that the company correctly paid taxes in the last years • Confirm that there are no union disputes • Search for potential future litigations against the company	• Due diligence process can be done quickly without affecting operations	• "Red flags" may pass unobserved by the auditors	Gole and Hilger (2009); Vuori and Vuori (2014); Kummer and Sliskovic (2007); Marquardt and Zur (2015)

Pre-merger phase	Actors	Antecedents that trigger heuristics	Examples of heuristics	Potential positive outcomes	Potential negative outcomes	Examples of reference
Negotiation	• Target managers • Target advisors • Acquirer managers • Acquirer advisors • Legal advisors	• Acquirer advisors must establish an initial price for the negotiations from all the previous data • Acquirer advisors must easily explain for how much they value the target company to the acquirer managers • Acquirers need to propose an initial offer to target managers • Managers of both parties need to communicate their valuations to support their proposals	• Reference price = EBITDA * X • Calculate Discounted Cash Flow to estimate future performance • Check that agreement between parties is compliant with antitrust regulation (legal advisors)	• Reduce time spent in developing legal contracts • Reduce time spent in negotiations • Improved communication between parties	• The acquirers may propose a price that does not account for the potential synergies • Anchoring: The initial price will serve as a reference for the final acquisition price	Venema (2012); Gole and Hilger (2009); Malhotra et al. (2015); Whittington and Bates (2007)

Developing a model of heuristics' antecedents and outcomes in the pre-deal phase

In the following, we address different antecedents and outcomes that heuristics by different types of actors may induce during the pre-deal phase (Figure 1.1).

Heuristics for strategic choices

M&A can solve different strategic challenges, and the suggestion to pursue M&A may come directly from the managers or as a recommendation from external consultants. From an information-processing perspective, managers seek advice from external consultants to find solutions when their own information search is not successful (Bonaccio and Dalal, 2006) or to confirm their own preliminary thoughts (Schrah, Dalal and Sniezik, 2006). Previous research has shown that managers seek the advice of experts to support different strategic challenges, such as declines in performance (McDonald and Westphal, 2003), to pursue exploratory innovation (Alexiev et al., 2010), or to improve information systems (Gable, 1996). Acquiring companies is a possible way to acquire resources or competencies (Graebner et al., 2017), which could be employed to solve different strategic challenges. Therefore, suggesting acquisitions is one of the options that external consultants may propose to managers for different strategic challenges.

Consultants with acquisition experience might learn from experience accumulation, knowledge articulation, and knowledge codification processes (Zollo and Winter, 2002). Thus, they may have developed portfolios of heuristics that could guide their behavior toward suggesting acquisitions (Bingham and Eisenhardt, 2011), as existing acquisition experience increases the likelihood of future acquisitions (Haleblian, Kim and Rajagopalan, 2006).

Additionally, due to the sequential assessment of alternatives and satisficing heuristics (Simon, 1955), consultants would consider M&A initiatives first over other strategic choices. Therefore, when discussing with managers different strategic choices to solve strategic challenges at hand, consultants with previous involvement in acquisitions may prioritize exploring the possibility of acquiring over other strategic choices (e.g., alliances). The core argument is that some of the M&A projects that fail should not even have been considered from the very beginning, but they may have been considered due to the use of what we refer to as *experience heuristics* of external consultants.

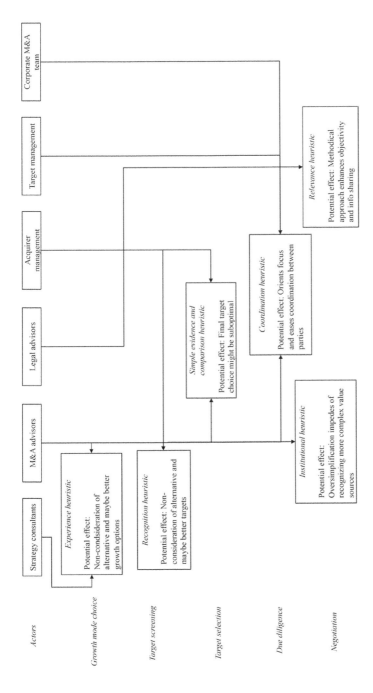

Figure 1.1   Heuristics' antecedents and outcomes in the pre-deal phase

Heuristics in the search and screening phase

Once the decision to pursue an acquisition is taken, the search for candidates starts. The potential candidate may be targeted from the beginning (i.e., a key supplier, competitor, etc.), while in other cases, it may be necessary to screen the market for candidates. M&A advisors are usually responsible for target screening due to their expertise (Kesner and Shapiro, 1994; Sharma, 1997). There are also small M&A boutiques specialized in market screening for targets in concrete industries.

Acquiring managers may explicitly give M&A advisors a set of criteria that facilitate their target screening process, such as finding companies in a concrete country, with revenues higher than a certain amount, or that produce a certain product. In this hectic phase, M&A advisors may rely on their accumulated experience in the focal industry, such as heuristics, to find and prioritize potential candidates (Bingham and Eisenhardt, 2011; Eisenhardt, Furr and Bingham, 2010). Moreover, the given set of criteria by managers could be combined with the heuristics of M&A advisors to help them develop the final list of candidates, leading to few cues (Gigerenzer, 2008). Relying on fewer cues might imply more accurate decision-making in different uncertain contexts, including personal selection (Luan, Reb and Gigerenzer, 2019) or investment portfolio allocation (DeMiguel, Garlappi and Uppal, 2009).

One of the heuristics that may drive M&A advisors' but also acquiring management's decision-making in this phase is the *recognition heuristic*. This heuristic infers that recognized options have a higher value (Goldstein and Gigerenzer, 2002). Thus, they would prioritize potential target companies that are known or familiar to them (e.g., through their prior experience or the media presence of the potential candidate).

Although relying upon some concrete criteria for selecting recognized options is efficient and accurate in different uncertain contexts (Borges et al., 2000; Goldstein and Gigerenzer, 2002; Serwe and Frings, 2006), it could have a negative effect on the target screening process. Interesting candidates may be ignored because they do not fulfill the concrete criteria or are not popular, although other business aspects could potentially be interesting for the acquirer. These other aspects would be ignored in the screening process, and only the companies that pass these first filters would be considered for an extensive analysis.

Heuristics in the strategic evaluation of target companies

Once advisors establish a list of candidates or a preferred candidate, the fit of the target company and the potential synergies must be estimated (Gomes et al., 2011). In big deals, different teams of advisors are asked to assess the potential target(s), while, in smaller deals, the advisors who helped in the target screening process may also be involved. In this stage, the understanding of the products, strategy, and organization of the company may be more relevant than other financial indicators used in the screening phase (Bouwman, Frishkoff and Frishkoff, 1987).

This stage of deep assessment is characterized by information asymmetry (Parvinen and Tikkanen, 2007). Given the high levels of uncertainty, M&A advisors might search for few relevant cues to form an opinion of the target (Luan et al., 2019) and employ heuristics that they developed over time with previous experiences (Bingham and Eisenhardt, 2011). This heuristic, which we call the *simple evidence and comparison heuristic*, might also allow M&A advisors to compare the different final candidates and communicate their findings to the managers.

Yet, relying on a set of heuristics may bias the perception of the candidates. Given those heuristics are retained and coded from previous experiences (Bingham and Eisenhardt, 2011), they might not apply to new contexts. Hence, important factors to the concrete deal at hand may be missed or underestimated. This bias would further impact advisors and managers who lack experience in the target industry. Simply, heuristics might help advisors and managers make sense of the target companies and start estimating how much they are worth. On the other hand, they could potentially lead to missing important indicators that could manifest later during the integration.

Heuristics in due diligence

Once a target is determined, due diligence starts. A letter of intent is signed at this stage, summarizing what elements are of interest to the acquirer and the proposed structure for the transaction (Marquardt and Zur, 2015). In due diligence, the objective of the acquirer and their advisors is to confirm important information about the target, such as financials, taxes, business, sales, operation, IT, human resources, and core and non-core portfolio assets (Deloitte, 2017). It allows the advisors to perform a more informed valuation, estimate the synergies, and refine the integration planning (Gole and Hilger, 2009). The effort, time, and resources employed in this stage highly depend on the nature of the target company.

Early-stage and fast-growing organizations may not document many of their practices and policies, potentially requiring more time and effort in face-to-face meetings. When the target is a large organization, the managers and advisors responsible for the due diligence need the assistance of further legal and financial advisors, as well as other experts (Gole and Hilger, 2009).

Due to the required coordination and communication efforts, M&A advisors and managers involved in large deals may develop and employ more heuristics than those working in small deals, where few people are involved. The literature on managerial heuristics shows that heuristics improve performance through coordination (Bingham and Eisenhardt, 2011; Vuori and Vuori, 2014). Therefore, *coordination heuristics* may be employed to ease communication and coordinate the individuals and teams of all parties. For example, the M&A advisor(s) who is (are) responsible for calculating synergies could have a heuristic of: "search for departments with duplicate functions and cut the expenses." The accountant advisor could have heuristics such as "check invoices and contracts and confirm that are aligned with the balance sheet and tax authorities." The impact on coordination and simplification of heuristics would thus accelerate due diligence.

During due diligence, target managers and key employees help provide the required information, while continuing with the company's activities. At this point, a virtual or physical "data room" is created, where the target deposits relevant information for due diligence (Kummer and Sliskovic, 2007). If the acquisition is friendly, their objective should be to show the key capabilities and value creation mechanism of the company, as well as to take attention away from issues that could scare the potential acquirers or worthen the acquisition terms or price. Again, target managers may employ impression management techniques to increase the perceived value of their companies (Westphal and Graebner, 2010; Yakis-Douglas et al., 2014).

Heuristics could be employed to ease the communication between managers, employees, and target advisors about what steps to follow during the due diligence process. For example, the operations manager could have the heuristic of "show production reports to inform acquirers about the production capacity of the plant." The target manager could employ heuristics such as "focus the attention to the sales numbers and take it away from the customer complaints." For the target, heuristics would allow for easing communication, improving coordination of the due diligence, reducing the time involved in the due diligence process, and increasing the perceived value.

However, "red flags" that are specific to the current target may be missed or underestimated as advisors and managers use heuristics developed in previous operations. However, given the pressure of due diligence (Marquardt and Zur, 2015), relying on rules of thumb is the most efficient mechanism to assess the huge amounts of information and attempt not to miss any "red flags."

Heuristics in the negotiation phase

From the first contact of the acquirer with a target, there is constant negotiation in different aspects. For simplicity, the formal negotiation phase is considered to start after the acquiring managers and their advisors have completed and analyzed the due diligence. At this point, there is a set of expectations for the operation, and there is a vision of what the merged company could look like. The initial integration plans can be refined with all the information gathered until this point (Venema, 2012). The objective of the negotiation is to reach the Purchase Agreement, which includes all the terms of the transaction, including the deal structure, purchase price, warranties, employment matters, and termination terms, among other key elements (Gole and Hilger, 2009). Draft versions of a Purchase Agreement may be agreed upon during the due diligence phase.

Small companies or big deals may require legal advice from specialized legal firms to assist during the negotiations and the drafting of the agreements (Gole and Hilger, 2009). These legal experts may have developed heuristics to examine the contracts and guarantee the safety of their clients. These heuristics may result from their previous experiences and their interaction with legal advisors (Bingham and Eisenhardt, 2011). What we call *institutional heuristics*, as an institutionalized mechanism to guide action, may adapt to the legal peculiarities of each deal (Eisenhardt et al., 2010). For example, legal advisors may have heuristics such as "check that agreement between parties is compliant with antitrust regulation" or "coordinate more routine contract points with seller's legal advisors." These heuristics should accelerate the creation of contracts, improving communication and coordination between the parties. Heuristics also help legal advisors focus their attention on previously relevant aspects (Gigerenzer, 2008).

Acquiring managers and their main advisors, who have been involved in previous stages, must process all the information until this point to determine which should be the best deal structure, the price that should be paid, and what contingencies to cover, among others. Managers and advisors may also employ such *relevance heuristics* to determine the purchase price. There are different methods to calculate the price of acquisitions. Common methods include:

(1) calculating the future discounted cash flows (Mukherjee, Kiymaz and Baker, 2004), (2) employing multipliers to certain accounting elements such as earnings before interest, taxes, depreciation, and amortization (EBITDA) (Whittington and Bates, 2007), and (3) comparing the estimated acquisition premium with previous similar acquisitions in the industry (Malhotra, Zhu and Reus, 2015). In bigger deals, robust assessment of the real value of the company requires various methods. However, given the uncertainty of an M&A, using a simpler heuristic could be more efficient and might be a better predictor than complex regression models (Artinger et al., 2015). At the same time, simple calculations facilitate communication among actors. It could be used as a reference point to start the price negotiations, potentially creating an anchoring effect (Malhotra et al., 2015).

Still, the simplification of heuristics may as well lead to valuation problems. For example, the EBITDA multiplier does not consider potential synergies or risks. Moreover, the actual performance of the merger and the synergy creation depends on the integration (Graebner et al., 2017); it is difficult to know if the methods for pricing were beneficial to their clients. Therefore, the heuristics employed would not improve with feedback over time, and there would be room for systematic biases in calculating the purchase price (Tversky and Kahneman, 1974), which could destroy shareholder value (Angwin, 2007).

Discussion

We shed light on the role of heuristics in the pre-deal process by conceptualizing their antecedents and potential outcomes. The pre-deal phase is a complex process, where many actors with different roles, incentives, expertise, and information frequently interact under time pressure and uncertainty (Parvinen and Tikkanen, 2007). Previous heuristics research argues that individuals employ heuristics to simplify reality and make efficient decisions (Dhami and Harries, 2001; Gigerenzer and Gaissmaier, 2011; Luan et al., 2019; Martignon, Katsikopoulos and Woike, 2008; Wübben and Wangenheim, 2008). Building on this research, we illustrate the antecedents and outcomes of using heuristics in the various pre-deal sub-phases.

Different contextual factors of the pre-deal process trigger the use of heuristics for making decisions, such as uncertainty (Bargeron et al., 2009), lack of information (Goldstein and Gigerenzer, 2002), time pressure, standardization, and emotions (Aschbacher and Kroon, 2023). Our framework suggests that heuristics can have favorable outcomes, such as focusing attention on relevant information, allowing efficient comprehension, and decision-making (Maitland and Sammartino, 2015), and facilitating communication and coordination across different actors (Bingham and Eisenhardt, 2011; Vuori and Vuori, 2014). Thus, heuristics used by the different actors in the pre-merger phase of M&A may stem from their previous process experience (Bingham and Eisenhardt, 2011). Given the different expertise of each actor involved in the pre-deal phase, actors develop portfolios of heuristics based on their past experiences and interactions with other actors. Moreover, the more experienced M&A advisors are, the larger and better their portfolio of heuristics, which might improve their analytical efficiency. However, the transmission of individual-based heuristics to the collective level needs further investigation (Vuori et al., 2023). Nevertheless, heuristics are based on prior experience and may not fit a particular situation and thus lead to the omission of critical factors (Bingham and Eisenhardt, 2011).

We contribute to our understanding of the pre-deal process in M&As from a cognitive perspective and put forth that bounded rationality and heuristics of different actors impact the M&A process both positively and negatively. By applying the concept of heuristics, well documented within the psychology and decision-making literature (Gigerenzer and Gaissmaier, 2011; Martignon et al., 2008; Wübben and Wangenheim, 2008), to various stages of the pre-deal process, this study offers fresh insights into how these simplified mental strategies can influence decision-making within the complex M&A context. Further, we broaden the use of cognitive frameworks within M&A research, emphasizing the essential role that different actors' cognitions, including managers, consultants, and legal advisors, play in the M&A process (Luan et al., 2019; Bingham and Eisenhardt, 2011; Gole and Hilger, 2009).

We also provide a structured approach to comprehend the antecedents and outcomes of heuristics in pre-deal M&A phases, offering valuable insights into how these can affect various stages, such as target identification, due diligence, and negotiation (Eisenhardt et al., 2010; Angwin, 2007). However, we acknowledge potential risks associated with using heuristics, bringing to light potential biases, oversimplification, and subsequent valuation problems that can arise (Tversky and Kahneman, 1974; Graebner et al., 2017). We want to stress that our research does not take a stand in the debate between followers of the heuristics-and-bias paradigm (Tversky and Kahneman, 1974) or the fast-and-frugal paradigm (Gigerenzer and Gaissmaier, 2011).

Limitations and future research

Our objective was to develop the existence of heuristics in the pre-acquisition phase, and it is the task of future research to confirm the positive and/or negative effects heuristics have on M&A outcomes. Specifically, our conceptual developments can be complemented with empirical research. Still, there are different possibilities to explore heuristics in the pre-deal phase, including longitudinal qualitative case studies, comparative qualitative studies, or field experiments.

Given the uniqueness of M&A processes, research needs to consider contextual factors that could impact the process, such as type of industry, size of companies, cultural and national differences, and so on. Further, M&A deals are not temporally linear and sequential. For example, financial evaluation and negotiation are often repeated (Parvinen and Tikkanen, 2007), and can occur simultaneously with different targets or acquirers. While we analyze the different roles of important actors (e.g., managers, consultants, and advisors) at different stages, research needs to consider the interactions of managers with other external stakeholders that could impact the deal, such as customers, suppliers, or competitors (Holtström, 2013; Öberg, 2013; Schriber, 2013).

As professionals navigate mergers and acquisitions, their reliance on and development of heuristics may change with time and experience (Wübben and Wangenheim, 2008). Much like the M&A process itself, heuristics are not static; they evolve based on lessons from previous deals. This leads to an interesting question: As actors gain experience, do their heuristics become more sophisticated, or do they converge toward a common set? Moreover, given that every deal is unique, there is room to develop specific heuristic portfolios tailored to certain scenarios, like industry type or regulatory environment. Customization could enhance the efficacy of decision-making to complete deals (Eisenhardt et al., 2010).

The M&A context may also be affected by recent technological advancements. With the surge in artificial intelligence tools, there is a potential interplay between traditional heuristics and AI insights. Can AI enhance human intuition, or does it complicate the decision-making process? On the one hand, combining the two could lead to better-informed decisions but, on the other, it could add a layer of complexity that professionals need to navigate (Luan et al., 2019). In a similar vein, while data and artificial intelligence play a significant role, the human aspect, especially emotional intelligence, remains essential for M&A, especially in negotiations. Future research should explore how M&A professionals leverage emotional cues to inform their decisions (Bingham and Eisenhardt, 2011).

Different sectors come with their own sets of challenges and nuances. For instance, a tech merger might have different considerations compared to a merger in the pharmaceutical sector. It's crucial to develop and understand heuristics that tackle these sector-specific needs (Öberg, 2013). Additionally, post-deal reflections on the use of heuristics may help understand their performance outcomes. By analyzing past deals and evaluating the effectiveness of the applied heuristics, professionals can reflect on what works and what doesn't, thus refining their future decision-making processes (Gigerenzer and Gaissmaier, 2011).

Prior research on M&A advisors has mainly applied agency theory (Gordon et al., 2019). Given incentive asymmetries present in the pre-deal phase (Parvinen and Tikkanen, 2007), agency theory provides an interesting avenue of research. However, better understanding acquisitions likely requires integrating theory (see Chapter 3). Future research on agency problems could incorporate cognitive perspectives to explore how actors operationalize while pursuing their own interests.

In closing, while most management research has been perceived as too complex for practitioners, research on heuristics can generate findings that are more applicable (Wübben and Wangenheim, 2008). As a result, research on heuristics can be translated into tools that aid the decision-making of managers that, in turn, might improve M&A success. We hope our summary helps to inform additional research on this topic.

References

Alexiev, A., Jansen, J., Van den Bosch, F., & Volberda, H. (2010). Top Management Team advice seeking and exploratory innovation: the moderating role of TMT heterogeneity. *Journal of Management Studies*, 47(7), 1343–1364.

Angwin, D. (2007). Motive archetypes in Mergers and Acquisitions (M&A): the implications of a configurational approach to performance. *Advances in Mergers and Acquisitions*, 6, 77–105.

Angwin, D., & Karamat, F. (2015). How does investment bank reputation influence M&A deal characteristics? A conceptual model and research propositions. In H. E. Spotts (ed.), *Marketing, Technology and Customer Commitment in the New Economy* (pp. 228–233). Cham: Springer International.

Artinger, F., Petersen, M., Gigerenzer, G., & Weibler, J. (2015). Heuristics as adaptive decision strategies in management: heuristics in management. *Journal of Organizational Behavior*, 36, S33–S52.

Asaoka, D. (2019). Behavioral analysis of mergers and acquisitions decisions. *Corporate Board Role Duties and Composition*, 15(3), 8–16.

Aschbacher, J., & Kroon, D. (2023). Falling prey to bias? The influence of advisors on the manifestation of cognitive biases in the pre-M&A phase of organizations. *Group & Organization Management*, https://doi.org/10.1177/105960112311714.

Bargeron, L., Lehn, K., Moeller, S., & Schlingemann, F. (2009). Do corporate acquisitions affect uncertainty about the value of acquiring firms? Working paper.

Bingham, C., & Eisenhardt, K. (2011). Rational heuristics: the "simple rules" that strategists learn from process experience. *Strategic Management Journal*, 32, 1437–1464.

Bingham, C. B., Howell, T., & Ott, T. E. (2019). Capability creation: heuristics as microfoundations. *Strategic Entrepreneurship Journal*, 13(2), 121–153.

Bonaccio, S., & Dalal, R. (2006). Advice taking and decision-making: an integrative literature review, and implications for the organizational sciences. *Organizational Behavior and Human Decision Processes*, 101, 127–151.

Borges, B., Goldstein, D., Ortmann, A., & Gigerenzer, G. (2000). Can ignorance beat the stock market? In G. Gigerenzer, P. M. Todd, & ABC Research Group (eds.), *Simple Heuristics That Make Us Smart* (pp. 59–72). Oxford: Oxford University Press.

Bouwman, M., Frishkoff, P., & Frishkoff, P. (1987). How do financial analysts make decisions? A process model of the investment screening decision. *Accounting, Organizations and Society*, 12(1), 1–29.

Bouwman, M., Frishkoff, P., & Frishkoff, P. (1995). The relevance of GAAP-based information: a case study exploring some uses and limitations. *Accounting Horizons*, 9(4), 22–47.

Calipha, R., Tarba, S., & Brock, D. (2010). Mergers and acquisitions: a review of phases, motives, and success factors. In C. L. Cooper & S. Finkelstein (eds.), *Advances in Mergers and Acquisitions* (Advances in Mergers and Acquisitions, Vol. 9) (pp. 1–24). Bingley: Emerald Group Publishing.

Deloitte (2017). M&A due diligence workshop. https://pdf4pro.com/amp/view/m-amp-a-due-diligence-workshop-deloitte-5daaf3.html.

DeMiguel, V., Garlappi, L., & Uppal, R. (2009). Optimal versus naive diversification: how inefficient is the 1/N portfolio strategy? *Review of Financial Studies*, 22, 1915–1953.

Dequech, D. (2001). Bounded rationality, institutions, and uncertainty. *Journal of Economic Issues*, 35, 911–929.

Dhami, M., & Harries, C. (2001). Fast and frugal versus regression models of human judgement. *Thinking & Reasoning*, 7, 5–27.

Eisenhardt, K., Furr, N., & Bingham, C. (2010). Microfoundations of performance: balancing efficiency and flexibility in dynamic environments. *Organization Science*, 21, 1263–1273.

Faulkner, D., Teerikangas, S., & Joseph, R. J. (eds.) (2012). *The Handbook of Mergers and Acquisitions*. New York: Oxford University Press.

Gable, G. (1996). A multidimensional model of client success when engaging external consultants. *Management Science*, 42, 1175–1198.

Garbuio, M., Lovallo, D., & Horn, J., (2010). Overcoming biases in M&A: a process perspective. In C. Cooper & S. Finkelstein (eds.), *Advances in Mergers and Acquisitions* (Advances in Mergers and Acquisitions, Vol. 9) (pp. 83–104). Bingley: Emerald Group Publishing.

Galpin, T., & Herndon, M. (2014) *The Complete Guide to Mergers and Acquisitions: Process Tools to Support M&A Integration at Every Level*, 3rd edn. Somerset, NJ: Jossey-Bass.

Gigerenzer, G. (2008). Why heuristics work. *Perspectives on Psychological Science*, 3, 20–29.

Gigerenzer, G., & Gaissmaier, W. (2011). Heuristic decision making. *Annual Review of Psychology*, 62, 451–482.

Gigerenzer, G., & Goldstein, D. (1999). Betting on one good reason: the take the best heuristic. In G. Gigerenzer, P. M. Todd, & ABC Research Group (eds.), *Simple Heuristics That Make Us Smart* (pp. 75–95). Oxford: Oxford University Press.

Gigerenzer, G., & Goldstein, D. G. (2011). The recognition heuristic: a decade of research. *Judgment and Decision Making*, 6(1), 100–121.

Gigerenzer, G., & Todd, P. (1999). Fast and frugal heuristics: the adaptive toolbox. In G. Gigerenzer, P. M. Todd, & ABC Research Group (eds.), *Simple Heuristics That Make Us Smart* (pp. 3–34). Oxford: Oxford University Press.

Goldstein, D., & Gigerenzer, G. (2002). Models of ecological rationality: the recognition heuristic. *Psychological Review*, 109(1), 75–90.

Gole, W., & Hilger, P. (2009). *Due Diligence: An M&A Value Creation Approach*. Hoboken, NJ: John Wiley & Sons.

Gomes, E., Angwin, D. N., Weber, Y., & Yedidia Tarba, S. (2013). Critical success factors through the mergers and acquisitions process: revealing pre- and post-M&A connections for improved performance. *Thunderbird International Business Review*, 55, 13–35.

Gomes, E., Weber, Y., Brown, C., & Tarba, S. Y. (2011). *Mergers, Acquisitions and Strategic Alliances: Understanding the Process*. London: Macmillan International Higher Education.

Gordon, J., Sieiro, G., Ellis, K., & Lamont, B. (2019). M&A advisors: padding their pockets or source of expertise? In C. Cooper & S. Finkelstein (eds.), *Advances in Mergers and Acquisitions* (Advances in Mergers and Acquisitions, Vol. 18) (pp. 27–49). Bingley: Emerald Group Publishing.

Graebner, M., Heimeriks, K., Huy, Q., & Vaara, E. (2017). The process of postmerger integration: a review and agenda for future research. *Academy of Management Annals*, 11, 1–32.

Haleblian, J., Kim, J.-Y., & Rajagopalan, N. (2006). The influence of acquisition experience and performance on acquisition behavior: evidence from the US commercial banking industry. *Academy of Management Journal*, 49, 357–370.

Haspeslagh, P., & Jemison, D. (1991). The challenge of renewal through acquisitions. *Planning Review*, 19, 27–30.

Holtström, J. (2013). Supplier relationships at stake in mergers and acquisitions. In H. Anderson, V. Havila, & F. Nilsson (eds.), *Mergers and Acquisitions: The Critical Role of Stakeholders* (pp. 168–184). Abingdon: Routledge.

Iannotta, G. (2010). *Investment Banking: A Guide to Underwriting and Advisory Services*. Cham: Springer.

Jensen, M., & Meckling, W. (1976). Theory of the firm: managerial behavior, agency costs and ownership structure. *Journal of Financial Economics*, 3, 305–360.

Kahneman, D. (2003). Maps of bounded rationality: psychology for behavioral economics. *American Economic Review*, 93, 1449–1475.

Kahneman, D. (2011). *Thinking, Fast and Slow*. New York: Farrar, Straus and Giroux.

Kauser, S., Gordon, A., Papamichail, K., & Reddy, C. (2015). Analysis and improvement of M&A decision making processes in the high-tech sector: a behavioral strategy perspective. In T. K. Das (ed.), *The Practice of Behavioral Strategy* (pp. 1–40). Charlotte, NC: Information Age Publishing.

Kelman, M. (2011). *The Heuristics Debate*. Oxford: Oxford University Press.

Kesner, I., & Shapiro, D. (1994). Brokering mergers: an agency theory perspective on the role of representatives. *Academy of Management Journal*, 37(3), 703–721.

Kolasinski, A., & Kothari, S. (2008). Investment banking and analyst objectivity: evidence from analysts affiliated with mergers and acquisitions advisors. *Journal of Financial and Quantitative Analysis*, 43(4), 817–842.

Kummer, C., & Sliskovic, V. (2007). Do virtual data rooms add value to the mergers and acquisitions process? Institute of Mergers, Acquisitions and Alliances (MANDA). https:// www .imaa -institute .org/ docs/ kummer -sliskovic _do %20virtual %20data %20rooms %20add %20value %20to %20the %20mergers %20and %20acquisitions %20process.pdf.

Luan, S., Reb, J., & Gigerenzer, G. (2019). Ecological rationality: fast-and-frugal heuristics for managerial decision making under uncertainty. *Academy of Management Journal*, 62(6), 1735–1759.

Maitland, E., & Sammartino, A. (2015). Managerial cognition and internationalization. *Journal of International Business Studies*, 46, 733–760.

Malhotra, S., Zhu, P., & Reus, T. (2015). Anchoring on the acquisition premium decisions of others: anchoring in acquisition premiums. *Strategic Management Journal*, 36, 1866–1876.

Marquardt, C., & Zur, E. (2015). The role of accounting quality in the M&A market. *Management Science*, 61, 604–623.

Martignon, L., Katsikopoulos, K., & Woike, J. (2008). Categorization with limited resources: a family of simple heuristics. *Journal of Mathematical Psychology*, 52, 352–361.

McDonald, M., & Westphal, J. (2003). Getting by with the advice of their friends: CEOs' advice networks and firms' strategic responses to poor performance. *Administrative Science Quarterly*, 48(1), 1–32.

Mousavi, S., & Gigerenzer, G. (2014). Risk, uncertainty, and heuristics. *Journal of Business Research*, 67, 1671–1678.

Mukherjee, T., Kiymaz, H., & Baker, H. (2004). Merger motives and target valuation: a survey of evidence from CFOs. *Journal of Applied Finance*, Fall/Winter, 7–24. https://papers.ssrn.com/sol3/papers.cfm?abstract_id=670383.

Öberg, C. (2013). Why do customers dissolve their business relationships with the acquired party following an acquisition? In H. Anderson, V. Havila, & F. Nilsson (eds.), *Mergers and Acquisitions: The Critical Role of Stakeholders* (pp. 259–282). Abingdon: Routledge.

Parvinen, P., & Tikkanen, H. (2007). Incentive asymmetries in the mergers and acquisitions process. *Journal of Management Studies*, 44, 759–787.

Rouzies, A., Colman, H. L., & Angwin, D. (2019). Recasting the dynamics of post-acquisition integration: an embeddedness perspective. *Long Range Planning*, 52(2), 271–282.

Schrah, G., Dalal, R., & Sniezek, J. (2006). No decision-maker is an island: integrating expert advice with information acquisition. *Journal of Behavioral Decision Making*, 19, 43–60.

Schriber, S. (2013). Managing the influence of external competitive change during integration. In H. Anderson, V. Havila, & F. Nilsson (eds.), *Mergers and Acquisitions: The Critical Role of Stakeholders* (pp. 149–167). Abingdon: Routledge.

Servaes, H., & Zenner, M. (1996). The role of investment banks in acquisitions. *Review of Financial Studies*, 9, 787–815.

Serwe, S., & Frings, C. (2006). Who will win Wimbledon? The recognition heuristic in predicting sports events. *Journal of Behavioral Decision Making*, 19, 321–332.

Sharma, A. (1997). Professional as agent: knowledge asymmetry in agency exchange. *Academy of Management Review*, 22, 758–798.

Simon, H. (1955). A behavioral model of rational choice. *Quarterly Journal of Economics*, 69, 99–118.

Simon, H. (1972). Theories of bounded rationality. *Decision and Organization*, 1, 161–176.

Thaler, R. (2016). Behavioral economics: past, present, and future. *American Economic Review*, 106, 1577–1600.

Tversky, A., & Kahneman, D. (1974). Judgment under uncertainty: heuristics and biases. *Science*, 185, 1124–1131.

Venema, W. (2012). Integration: the critical M&A success factor. *Journal of Corporate Accounting & Finance*, 23, 49–53.

Vuori, N., Laamanen, T., & Zollo, M. (2023). Capability development in infrequent organizational processes: unveiling the interplay of heuristics and causal knowledge. *Journal of Management Studies*, 60(5), 1341–1381.

Vuori, N., & Vuori, T. (2014). Comment on "Heuristics in the strategy context" by Bingham and Eisenhardt (2011). *Strategic Management Journal*, 35, 1689–1697.

Westphal, J., & Graebner, M. (2010). A matter of appearances: how corporate leaders manage the impressions of financial analysts about the conduct of their boards. *Academy of Management Journal*, 53, 15–44.

Whittington, M., & Bates, K. (2007). M&A as success. In D. Angwin (ed.), *Mergers and Acquisitions* (pp. 27–62). Hoboken, NJ: Wiley-Blackwell.

Wübben, M., & Wangenheim, F. (2008). Instant customer base analysis: managerial heuristics often "get it right." *Journal of Marketing*, 72, 82–93.

Yakis-Douglas, B., Angwin, D., Meadows, M., & Ahn, K. (2014). Voluntary disclosures as a form of impression management to reduce evaluative uncertainty during M&A. *Academy of Management Annual Meeting Proceedings*, 1364–1369.

Zollo, M., & Winter, S. (2002). Deliberate learning and the evolution of dynamic capabilities. *Organization Science*, 13, 339–351.

2 Target screening: a key strategic success factor for acquisitions

Florian Bauer and Mai Anh Dao

Introduction

Acquisitions have constituted a core strategic tool for corporate development for more than 100 years and have attracted researchers from various disciplines (Cartwright and Schoenberg, 2006). Despite the significant experience managers have in executing acquisitions, demonstrated by annual transaction volumes exceeding the GDP of large economies, the failure rates remain constantly high. Interestingly, while acquisition success is typically attributed to manager implementation, acquisition failure is attributed to cultural issues during integration (Graebner et al., 2017). This also refers to the intuitively appealing claim that all value is created during acquisition integration (Haspeslagh and Jemison, 1991, p. 13). However, this implies that an acquirer can choose the right target firm and evaluate the potential synergies correctly in the first place (Bauer and Friesl, 2022). This assumption is problematic.

Target screening has received scant research attention, but it is important to "the execution of an effective M&A strategy" (Rosner, 2006, p. 9). Despite its strategic importance, many organizations pursue ad hoc and little systematic screening approaches that often result in disappointing acquisitions. This undermines the assumption that M&A managers are rational (Jemison and Sitkin, 1986). Ideally, target screening should involve multiple steps, from initiating, to assessing, to comparing different firms with each other (Feldman and Hernandez, 2022; Rosner, 2006; Bauer, Friesl and Dao, 2022). However, it is the complexity and the sheer amount of data that can easily overwhelm managers' cognitive capacity (Simon, 1979). For example, a firm searching for a specialized machinery engineering company in Germany would have to consider more than 6,000 firms in the entire industry to assess the strategic fit. In the target screening context, the careful identification, selection, and evaluation of all potential target firms or alternatives necessary for the best decision

(Cyert and March, 1963) seems to be impossible. It is the complexity and the high stakes nature of acquisitions in general and target screening in particular that overwhelms managers, giving rise to the application of heuristics resulting in cognitive simplification. Cognitive simplification is the result of reducing challenging tasks to simpler or more manageable exercises (Simon, 1979).

Heuristics provide a problem-solving structure or a cognitive shortcut (Newell and Simon, 1972) particularly relevant for complex problems when individuals are confronted with uncertainty (Tversky and Kahneman, 1974). Research has begun recently to identify heuristics in the strategic management context (Bingham and Eisenhardt, 2011; Eisenhardt and Sull, 2001) and concluded that they can constitute an idiosyncratic feature of firms, potentially resulting in a competitive advantage. This "fast and frugal heuristics" understanding substantially differs from the "heuristics and biases" paradigm, placing heuristics in a less positive light (Ayal and Zakay, 2009). Heuristics are "highly economical and usually effective, but they lead to systematic and predictable errors" (Tversky and Kahneman, 1974, p. 1124). In the case of acquisition target screening, heuristics give rise to cognitive simplification which is the result of reducing challenging tasks to simpler or more manageable exercises (Simon, 1979). However, simplifying complex situations and engaging in cognitive simplification triggers systematic errors or biases (Barnes, 1984; Das and Teng, 1999).

While this is relevant for most strategic decisions, we argue that target screening processes that are complex by nature and require dealing with complex data, are particularly vulnerable to heuristics, cognitive simplification and, thus, to cognitive biases.

This chapter aims to shed new light on target screening practices by drawing on the "heuristics and biases" paradigm (Tversky and Kahneman, 1974). This perspective allows us to better understand why the practices managers employ during target screening are prone to systematic errors. This is a crucial point, as target screening is a core strategic task that is treated neglectfully by management practice and research likewise (Rosner, 2006) resulting in the fact that acquisitions often lose the "strategic considerations" already way before signing and closing. As such, a heuristics, cognitive simplification, and cognitive biases perspective on target screening might offer an alternative explanation for why many acquisitions fall short in creating value. Hence, we ask: *How do firms find targets and are those targets really a strategic fit?*

We apply an exploratory qualitative research design and draw on interviews with M&A managers of strategic acquirers and on insights from the daily target screening practices of a digital solution provider specializing in target screening. From 78 interviews with M&A and strategy decision-makers of large and mid-cap corporates from Germany, Austria, Switzerland, Belgium, Denmark, Finland, Italy, the Netherlands, and the U.S.A., we integrate multiple insights of ten target screening projects one of the authors was involved in. Our analysis reveals that target screening consists of three sub-processes: (1) defining the search scope and longlist development, (2) reducing the longlist to a shortlist, and (3) evaluating the shortlist and ranking development. In each of these sub-processes, managers apply a diverse range of practices. We show that different practices give rise to the application of different heuristics resulting in cognitive simplification, and ultimately triggering cognitive biases. Our findings have important theoretical and managerial implications for target screening, or the initial stage of executing an M&A strategy.

First, we show that the different practices employed in the sub-processes of target screening give rise to the application of heuristics aiming to cognitively simplify a challenging task. However, cognitive simplification triggers systematic errors such as biases (Das and Teng, 1999) and potentially satisficing behavior. Simply, individuals involved in target screening might neither search for comprehensive information nor interpret it accurately because of their limited cognitive capacity (March and Simon, 1958). To cope with limited cognitive capacity, individuals employ heuristics or simplifying strategies that trigger cognitive biases (Schwenk, 1986). Looking at the initial stage of the acquisition process that is responsible for the effective translation of an M&A strategy might offer an alternative explanation to why many acquisitions fall short in delivering their value. As such, we show that the attempt of cognitive simplification and cognitive biases (Kahneman, Slovic and Tversky, 1982; Das and Teng, 1999) in the individual sub-processes are unfortunately often only the starting point for an entire pattern in a stream of bad decisions.

Second, we combine three distinct sub-processes of target screening with the underlying practices managers employ. This approach allows us to unpack the different requirements involved in target screening and to understand why many firms deviate from an optimal search. Our focus on the practices also allows us to understand the underlying pitfalls and shortcomings and the cognitive mechanisms that commonly result in ad hoc approaches to target screening.

Target screening in M&A: theoretical background

Heuristics, cognitive simplification, and cognitive biases

How firms manage organizational processes constitutes an idiosyncratic feature of firms and might even result in a competitive advantage (Roberts, 1999; Wiggins and Ruefli, 2005). As such, organizational processes are strategically relevant (Bingham, Eisenhardt and Furr, 2007) and rare processes, such as acquisitions (Graebner, 2004; Vermeulen and Barkema, 2001), can become central to a firm's strategy. As such, the better a firm performs such processes, the better the outcome. With the increasing experience managers have with these processes, the more they can refine their understanding of cause and effect relationships (Haleblian and Finkelstein, 1999). However, the acquisition experience literature does not univocally provide evidence for a positive relationship between experience and performance but rather shows a wide range of possible effects (Graebner et al., 2017).

One reason for the inconclusive effects of acquisition experience might be the implicit assumption that all experience of managing acquisition processes that consist of multiple sub-processes (Birkinshaw, Bresman and Håkanson, 2000) piles up into one stock of accumulated experience. However, acquisition sub-processes typically involve different people and different practices that might make it difficult to first, accumulate and center all experience and second, to transfer the experience to subsequent cases. Here, heuristics that provide managers with simple problem-solving structures might be an appropriate learning outcome for firms (Bingham and Eisenhardt, 2011). Indeed, there is evidence that firms can develop a strategically relevant set or portfolio of heuristics.

However, rare strategic processes, such as acquisitions, are complex by nature. Acquisitions involve multiple decisions with far-reaching and complex consequences of a wide range of managers at different stages of the acquisition process. Here, heuristics allow managers to "simplify complex decision situations" (Das and Teng, 1999, p. 760). However, this cognitive simplification gives rise to cognitive biases that ultimately might result in systematic decision errors (Kahneman et al., 1982). This is particularly relevant for target screening, something that is complex by nature and of enormous strategic relevance not only for the acquisition process but also the acquisition outcome. Simply, you can conduct the best acquisition integration but if the target is the wrong one, all efforts might come to nothing.

Target screening

Target screening is an initial step in the acquisition process and follows or should follow the M&A strategy. After successful target screening, an initial contact at the potential target firm can be established. As such, target screening involves the development of clear criteria suitable to determine the attractiveness of a potential firm (Bauer et al., 2022). This list of criteria aims to ultimately identify a firm with the best fit to the acquisition strategy and the acquiring organization. In the second step, managers can apply this list of criteria to a comprehensive list of potentially fitting target firms resulting in a ranking or an actionable shortlist (Rosner, 2006). However, most firms do not engage in systematic target screening processes but rather follow an opportunistic or externally driven approach with consultancies or M&A boutiques. Like entrepreneurs, M&A managers are confronted with enormous complexity and ambiguity. As such, it is not surprising that they "unintentionally simplify their information processing to diminish the stress and ambiguity associated with …" (Simon, Houghton and Aquino, 2000, p. 117) strategic decisions (Hansen and Allen, 1992). As such, we focus on the target screening process and the employed practices to understand: *How do firms find targets and if those targets are really a strategic fit?*

Research context

We focus on target screening practices, corresponding heuristics, and how cognitive simplification triggers cognitive biases. This required access to M&A managers who are involved in target screening processes. Contrary to occasional acquirers that usually do not have a dedicated M&A function, we focused on serial acquirers that typically have such a function. The M&A function or M&A department is responsible for deal execution or all activities following the strategic decision to engage in an acquisition (Trichterborn, Zu Knyphausen-Aufseß and Schweizer, 2016) that is usually made by C-suite managers. As such, we aimed to reach out to M&A managers of large and mid-cap corporates for data collection purposes.

Our research mainly relies on primary data with semi-structured interviews with 78 M&A managers. The interviewees were located mainly in Germany, Austria, Switzerland, Belgium, Denmark, Finland, Italy, the Netherlands, and the U.S.A. The positions of the interviewed M&A managers included presidents of M&A, vice-presidents of M&A, and M&A managers. The interviews took place online and lasted between 40 and 120 minutes. In total, our interviews lasted 2,472 minutes. Due to the sensitivity and confidentiality of the interviews, we were not allowed to record all of them, but recorded interviews were transcribed verbatim. For the other interviews, we took notes during the meeting and made a reflective summary of the interview afterwards. In each interview, we asked about their target screening processes, the underlying practices and the challenges they experience during target screening. We always asked the interviewees to signify to specific cases to obtain a contextualized understanding of target screening practices. We also integrated multiple insights of ten target screening projects one of the authors was involved in.

For data analysis, we followed an abductive approach (Dubois and Gadde, 2002). As such, we first identified the target screening practices and heuristics managers applied inductively from our interview data. Second, we used cognitive simplification and cognitive biases to guide our analysis. Overall, our analysis followed a four-step procedure.

Step 1: In the first step, we investigated how interviewees conceptualized the target screening process. In each interview, we asked for the employed sub-processes and the key activities, practices, and difficulties involved (Table 2.1).

Step 2: In the second step, we built on the sub-processes identified in step 1 and focused on the heuristics involved in target screening and the corresponding cognitive simplification (Table 2.2).

Step 3: Building on steps 1 and 2 as the necessary inductive groundwork, we investigated cognitive biases in the sub-processes. As such, we analyzed these deductively (Table 2.3).

Step 4: Building on all previous steps, we investigated to which extent the underlying practices, cognitive simplification, and cognitive biases impact the strategic ideas of an acquisition. We summarize our results in Figure 2.1.

Results

In Figure 2.1, we summarize our results and show the effects of practices, heuristics, cognitive simplifications, and cognitive biases on the strategic considerations of an acquisition.

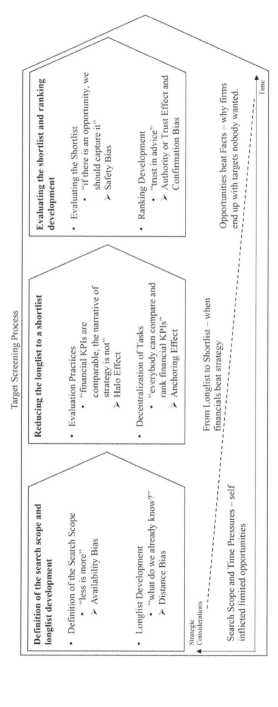

Figure 2.1   Target screening process, practices, heuristics, cognitive simplifications, and cognitive biases

Target screening sub-processes and practices

When asked about their target screening practices, most managers initially struggled with a clear answer. Target screening is a very sensitive topic for managers not only because of the level of confidentiality necessary at this stage, and managers confessed that despite being an important topic, target screening is largely neglected and lacks professionalization. However, there was also broad agreement on the importance of target screening, as illustrated by Kurt's (director of M&A) account: "Target screening is key. This is the phase where we can decide what fits best to us. This is where we can effectively translate our strategy into criteria." When asked about the target screening process, our interview partners gave us a broad range of examples of activities and the underlying practices. These activities can be organized into three different consecutive sub-processes (Table 2.1).

Definition of the search scope and longlist development

The first step of target screening is the sub-process, where initial demographic search criteria such as firm size, industry, and geographic location are defined. In some cases, this scope decision already involves technical or strategic criteria. Further, it is about the data sources managers use to create a longlist of firms. The practices firms employ in the definition of the search scope are quite similar. Most firms rely on demographic data to set the boundaries, which seems to be an objective approximation for the search scope.

However, the first complex task in target screening is to compile the longlist. Particularly managers need to decide on the source(s) they use to retrieve firm information. Despite the strategic importance of target search, most firms rely on search engines such as Google. Only a minor share of the interview partners uses comprehensive databases. Still, even when using databases, the retrieved data is perceived as too much or too complex. Anyway, this is only the first step in the target screening process and the second step seems even more labor-intense compared to the first one.

Reducing the longlist to a shortlist

The second step aims to reduce the number of potential target firms and to narrow it down to number of firms that can be processed, something managers call an "actionable shortlist." This second sub-process of target screening requires clear criteria to make firms comparable and to develop a reasoning to exclude specific firms. As this step is very labor-intensive, it is often done by novices and not M&A or industry experts, but when M&A managers evaluate

Table 2.1   Target screening sub-processes, descriptive examples, and sample evidence

Sub-process	Aggregated themes	Sample evidence
Definition of the search scope and longlist development	Definition of search scope	"We define the search scope as narrow as possible. Otherwise, we just have too many firms to screen." "We have this advanced database that allows us to create very comprehensive longlists. However, in our search fields we quickly end up with 60,000–80,000 results in our area. This is simply too much." "We search for firms with less than 25 mil Euros in revenues." (M&A manager) "We only focus on firms in our country." "We restrict our search to firms that are exactly in our industry." "With our scoping, we might exclude relevant firms that just don't fall within the boundaries." "We distinguish between core business and adjacent business, with different search logics."
	Longlist development	"We use the internet to identify companies." "We rely on Dr. Google." "We are very advanced; we have access to a database but there are too many results." "We asked around in our [internal and external] network – talking to colleagues from procurement and sales, investment bankers, industry experts, info brokers."

Sub-process	Aggregated themes	Sample evidence
Reducing the longlist to a shortlist	Evaluation practices	"We developed simple 'yes/no' criteria that everybody can make the evaluation. This is important and it would be too much work for a single person. The simplicity of our evaluation model makes it robust. Once this evaluation is done, we can add weights to the criteria as we like it." "We have a standing list that we constantly refine." "We developed simple 'yes/no' criteria that everybody is able to engage in the evaluation." "We start with those firms that are on sale, as these firms are actionable."
	Decentralization of tasks	"We always have interns doing the evaluation for us." "It would be way too time-consuming for us to do an elaborated ranking based on strategic criteria, so a quick look on the financials must be sufficient." "Research is for junior colleagues below our pay scale." "We anyway know all firms in our field." "We know our industry, we know the players and all relevant firms. As such, there are rarely or never firms in the longlist we do not know."
Evaluating the shortlist and ranking development	Evaluating the shortlist	"We only look at the top ten firms with the highest average scores." "We need to move fast to close our strategic and revenue gap. As such, we need focus on what is close to us." "An intern prepares a PowerPoint presentation for us with the best targets." "We do elaborated workshops and spent hours and hours in discussing the same companies."
	Ranking development	"There is no time for complex math, we already have our favorites, and these are the firms we know." "It is difficult to make firms comparable. Our point system helps here." "In the end, we have a small number of criteria that really matters for us."

the longlist, it is mostly only a quick look and not a thorough analysis. Finally, in many instances, managers were quite confident with their knowledge of the industry and the relevant players in it. While considered as strategically important, reducing the longlist to a shortlist is a labor-intensive activity that is typically delegated to non-M&A or non-industry experts.

Evaluating the shortlist and ranking development

The final step in target screening relates to the development of rankings within the shortlist. Again, we experienced that this is either a task that is delegated or a task that managers try to perform quickly. In the end, it is this shortlist that should be discussed with the board or the project leading business units. As the target selection is key for successful acquisitions, strategic criteria should become even more important. However, managers overwhelmingly raised concerns and identified major difficulties in making strategic matters comparable. While these steps are typically employed for an initial evaluation and ranking of target firms, they are counterfactual. Simply put, the value managers attribute to an individual firm derives from the practices employed in the target screening process. As such, we will turn now to the heuristics managers employ in the different stages of target screening and the associated cognitive simplification tactics.

Heuristics and cognitive simplification tactics

It is the complexity of the involved activities, or the amount of data needed for an objective decision, that gives rise to heuristics and cognitive simplifications. Again, we will discuss the findings of our study along the three sub-processes of target screening.

Heuristics and cognitive simplification tactics in the search scope and longlist development phase

It is the number of available options and data in combination with time constraints that somehow often forces managers to be quite restrictive with regard to the search scope. Table 2.1 exemplifies what most managers told us, which results in the heuristic: "Less is more." A narrow search scope gives managers the feeling of control and the heuristic "less is more" is a clear shortcut they employ to reduce complexity and ambiguity. Further, this heuristic has consequences on how managers develop longlists. Instead of developing comprehensive longlists, the "less is more" heuristic triggers the cognitive simplification of the task. Indeed, most managers restrict the search for potential targets to what is already known in their environment or known by others in their organization. As such, firms typically look inside and rely on information that is already there (e.g., by sales force or partnering firms).

Heuristics and cognitive simplification when evaluating the longlist

When it comes to the evaluation of the longlist and the reduction of the longlist to a shortlist, managers are suddenly confronted with enormous complexity. They must evaluate, compare, and rank firms. Simply, complex information needs to be structured and made commensurable (Kornberger, 2017). This is a particularly challenging task for strategic information that is usually captured in a narrative and not in a number.

This challenge gives rise to the next heuristic: "financial key performance indicators (KPIs) are comparable, the narrative of strategy is not." This heuristic triggers the cognitive simplification "everybody can compare and rank financial KPIs" that is rooted in the comparability of numbers, the ease of access, and the transparency it involves. As such, the focus on financial KPIs allows managers to work on reducing longlists towards an actionable shortlist in a decentral, transparent, and fast way. Simply, generally accepted KPIs based on easily comparable numbers allow them to simplify the challenging task of comparing firms. Further, this approach allows managers to hand over this task to interns or other potentially non-experts within their organization.

Heuristics and cognitive simplification when evaluating the shortlist

When evaluating the shortlist, managers recognize the shortcomings of pure financial evaluation and they find companies in their shortlist that do not provide any strategic fit.

The fact that many shortlists are not comprehensive, gives rise to the next heuristic: "if there is an opportunity, we should capture it." This also reflects the M&A market of the 2010s, when sellers had more opportunities compared to buyers. Anyway, when it is about a decision between different options, managers apply another cognitive simplification: "Trust in advice." This simplification avoids an exhausting in depth analysis and then complex comparison of different opportunities. Simply, M&A managers rely on the information of externals, authorities, or other persons they trust within their organization. Table 2.2 summarizes the heuristics and cognitive simplifications that are applied by managers throughout the target screening process. Further, we give sample evidence.

Heuristics and cognitive simplifications that trigger cognitive biases

While the application of heuristics and cognitive simplifications help managers to navigate the complexity of the target screening process, they also bear the

Table 2.2   Screening sub-processes, heuristics, cognitive
simplifications, and evidence

Sub-process	Aggregated themes	Heuristic, cognitive simplification	Sample evidence
Definition of the search scope and longlist development	Definition of search scope	"Less is more"	"We need to move fast so we have no time to broaden our search." "Let's look at those firms that are for sale at the moment."
	Longlist development	"What do we already know?"	"Our sales staff knows the market and the firms in it exactly, they support us efficiently in creating shortlists!" "We are quick in creating suitable longlists. We call our business units with a presence in the geographic market and ask them for firms that are on sale. This takes us a couple of days." "It is faster to call our partners at other locations to receive information about which firms are currently on sale or will have succession difficulties!" "Seven years ago, we have engaged a consulting firm for a market analysis and since then we're just updating this list with information from our network."

Sub-process	Aggregated themes	Heuristic, cognitive simplification	Sample evidence
Reducing the longlist to a shortlist	Evaluation practices	"Financial KPIs are comparable, the narrative of strategy is not"	"We rely on financial and some strategic information." "KPIs are hard facts, we can compare them." "Financial KPIs say a lot, we can interpret them and extrapolate to which extent we'd be able to achieve our revenue goals." "Strategic information would be relevant but how should we get to this information? In the end, we need a score and a ranking, and this is impossible with strategic information."
	Decentralization of tasks	"Everybody can compare and rank financial KPIs"	"On top of financial KPIs, which we draw quite detailed, we simplify strategic criteria such as actionability, market fit, competence fit, technology fit on a scale from 1 to 5. This allows everyone to contribute to this list." "We have multiple people working on these longlists. So the only reliable information we have is of financial nature." "This can be done by people way below my pay scale."
Evaluating the shortlist and ranking development	Evaluating the shortlist	"If there is an opportunity, we should capture it"	"Often, I have the feeling that we miss out on relevant companies as we focus too much on financials and overly rely on our network. However, we wouldn't have the capacity to start the process all over again." "We figured out that one firm is for sale, as such, a perfect opportunity." "Why engaging with other firms, if we know that this one could fit and is for sale."
	Ranking development	"Trust in advice"	"Dr. […] gave us this hint, so it must be a great firm." "Our partners abroad mentioned this firm to us; they are industry experts and know about all movements in our relevant market."

risk of giving rise to cognitive biases resulting in systematic error. In the first sub-process of target screening, we find that the "less is more" heuristic triggers "availability bias." Availability bias refers to the utilization of recent events to anticipate the likelihood of future events. This bias also results in a marginalization of in-depth analysis (Schwenk, 1988; Tversky and Kahneman, 1973). Simply, managers tend to rely dominantly on easily available information (Ahmad, Shah and Abbass, 2021). This bias has a strong imprint on the definition of the search scope. While the search scope sets the strategic direction of target screening, broadening the search scope would make later analysis and decisions more complex. As such, it is easier for decision-makers to rely on past events and experiences when defining the search scope, making the availability bias a serious issue. Simply, through a narrow search scope, many opportunities or potential target firms are not identified, as they just fall out of the narrowly set boundaries.

This bias goes hand in hand with the bias deriving from the cognitive simplification "what do we already know," namely the distance bias. Simply, when developing longlists, managers tend to focus on information that is already available or somehow available in close distance. As such, they initially try to gather information from within their organization by simultaneously ignoring other information. Typically, sales personnel are well informed about the market as they receive information from customers, but also competitors on industrial fairs. Further, there might be written-down information in customer relationship management databases that can be helpful to M&A managers. Another option is to get in contact with business units that operate in the geographic region of the search scope. While this approach might speed up the target screening process and avoid the tedious work with databases, it reduces the comprehensiveness of the longlist and leads to systematic blind spots.

Once M&A managers have developed a longlist, they need to evaluate it and make firms comparable. This is a difficult task and gives rise to heuristics and cognitive simplifications. The heuristic "financial KPIs are comparable, the narrative of strategy is not" is particularly dangerous, triggering the halo effect. With this bias, managers start drawing a conclusion from a few qualities about the entire organization (Halvorson and Rock, 2015). Here financial KPIs seem particularly relevant for them. Indeed, "company performance creates an overall impression that shapes how we perceive its strategy, leaders, employees, culture, and other elements" (Rosenzweig, 2007, p. 8). This is critical in a target screening context, as the heuristic in combination with the halo effect typically result in a "screening out" of strategically relevant targets. Further, as KPI-driven evaluation of longlists allows the decentralization and speeding up of the process, the anchoring bias becomes more pronounced. The anchoring bias is about the dominant reliance on the first information that serves as an anchor to compare all other information (Halvorson and Rock, 2015). Particularly, KPIs constitute strong anchors that also allow managers to easily rank order firms. However, this might also result in the elimination of relevant target firms that just do not meet the financial KPI anchor.

When managers proceed and evaluate the shortlist of companies, we could observe the heuristic "if there is an opportunity, we should capture it." This refers to a safety bias or the tendency of individuals to avoid losses. Having gone through a target screening process with all the associated efforts and costs triggers the desire of managers to continue with the process and to avoid any corresponding (emotional) losses. This highlights the presence of a safety bias, or the tendency to avoid any losses along the acquisition process. The final step in the target screening process, the ranking development, is affected by two biases triggered through the cognitive simplification "trust in advice." The first bias that comes into play is the authority or trust effect and describes the reliance of individuals on authorities or persons from higher positions within their organization.

Next to hierarchical differences, we also find that for example academic titles like a Ph.D. or job experience in consulting or private equity trigger authority and trust bias. Further, confirmation bias might result in decision errors. We find that once managers made up their preferences, they only search for evidence confirming their initial idea and simultaneously ignore or disconfirm other evidence (Schwenk, 1988). Combined, a reflection of the practices, heuristics, cognitive simplifications, and the presence of these biases during target screening processes suggests that many firms might not be able to identify the potentially best fitting target.

The strategic idea of an acquisition considering target screening practices, heuristics, cognitive simplifications, and biases

Building on all previous steps, we investigated to which extent the underlying practices, heuristics, cognitive simplifications, and cognitive biases impact target screening (Table 2.3). Now we turn to our research question: *How do firms find targets and if those targets are really a strategic fit?* The idea described in the rare literature (Rosner, 2006) that firms should initiate target screening with a comprehensive list of companies, clear search criteria such as industry or technology, followed by an evaluation of each company resulting in a transparent ranking and a suitable shortlist, is something we cannot find in our data. We find that each sub-process of the target screening process has the potential to result in a drift away from the initial strategic idea.

When looking at the "definition of the search scope and longlist development," we find that this sub-process often results in self-inflicted limited opportunities. By applying the heuristic "less is more" and the cognitive simplification "what do we already know," managers give rise to availability and distance biases. Both biases initially reduce the search field resulting in narrow search boundaries that might make it already difficult from the start to identify an appropriate target and acquire it at a later stage. Simply by setting narrow boundaries, many relevant target firms might be screened-out from the very beginning, while multiple non-relevant targets or less suitable targets are carried on into the target screening process. One manager told us:

> M&A target screening is all about being flexible and fast – less about being exact. Company names, what they're doing, or the business cluster and some size relations are sufficient for execution.

This statement reflects that a major share of managerial attention is devoted to execution and probably not to identify the best fitting target. This is in line with Peter who told us:

> In a small market, M&A target screening is *a flat exercise, the toughest part is to get access to the decision-maker.*

Ultimately, Lisa's comment is symptomatic for multiple firms we interviewed:

> A shorter list of targets is better and, thus, we need to restrict the search scope.

On the other hand, multiple managers in our study also reported that "Target screening is about access to data" or that "the one who has the better information base and data wins." This is in line with several firms spending serious financial resources on databases. However, the sheer amount of data available makes the development of an initial longlist a challenging exercise and a core question is "How well can I narrow down the field anyway?" (Tomi, M&A manager). Further, managers also raise doubts when using databases as illustrated by the comment of Jeff (head of M&A): "Database xxx – contrary to the promise that the data are max. 2 weeks old, we found out that some of them

Table 2.3   Screening sub-processes, heuristics and cognitive
             simplifications, and biases

Sub-process	Aggregated themes	Heuristic, cognitive simplification	Resulting cognitive biases
Definition of the search scope and longlist development	Definition of search scope	"Less is more"	Availability bias "Transaction experience cannot be replaced. We know what we do, we did this recently."
	Longlist development	"What do we already know?"	Distance bias "What we do in target screening is relationship management." "Our blind spots are in geographies, where we do not have any subsidiaries, or which are just too large to be screened systematically." "We have always searched in our close context. This is something where we can be very confident, we know the industry, our region, and most firms in it, etc. This all helps us to develop good longlists. Searching in another region is overly complex."
Reducing the longlist to a shortlist	Evaluation practices	"Financial KPIs are comparable, the narrative of strategy is not"	Halo effect "The ROA says everything in our industry." "If a firm is good with working capital, they have a good strategy and good management."
	Decentralization of tasks	"Everybody can compare and rank financial KPIs"	Anchoring effect "An ROA of 11% is good, no need to look below."

Sub-process	Aggregated themes	Heuristic, cognitive simplification	Resulting cognitive biases
Evaluating the shortlist and ranking development	Evaluating the shortlist	"If there is an opportunity, we should capture it"	Safety bias "We need a target, and this seems reasonable." "This Brazilian target fits well from a strategic standpoint; however, it's too far away, so we'll move on with a firm in our home country." "We have come so far, now we want to go on. This target [...] is available and we should go for it and not slow down the process."
	Ranking development	"Trust in advice"	Authority or trust effect/confirmation bias "As I suggested, great ROI, great target." "As expected, the head of sales was right, a good candidate." "This shortlist has been created by XX [renowned strategy consulting firm]." "Our CEO is in love with this particular firm, so it must be good; he is in the business for so long and has always been successful." "As I told you, this is a great target, look at their financials and also their technology" (Manager A). "But there might be a serious risk with regard to [...]" (Manager B). "Come on, really, that is nothing to worry about. This is, as I always said, a great firm" (Manager A).

are older." To improve reliability, some firms engage in complex processes as Michael (director M&A) told us:

Dealsourcing is all about data integration from various sources. Thereby, data access and transparency are key.

However, due to the complexity, the responsibility for longlist development is often outsourced to consultants or boutiques as Hans (vice-president M&A) says:

> A qualified target list is one that fits to our individual/specialized search field. This can be generated by M&A boutiques only.

Only in some cases, firms are looking for technological solutions: "Technology is decisive for being more systematic and comprehensive" (Luis, M&A manager). Combined, our research suggests that already in the initial stage of the target screening process, multiple potential targets are not even considered, as they either fall out of the narrowly defined boundary conditions, or they are not captured by databases.

When taking a closer look at the sub-process "reducing the longlist to a short-list" we find that firms strongly engage in heuristics and cognitive simplifications. Both relate to the reliance on financial KPIs. The heuristic "financial KPIs are comparable, the narrative of strategy is not" gives the direction for the evaluation of the longlist. It is the belief in so-called "hard facts" that gives priority to financial evaluation instead of strategic relevance. As Christine (president M&A) highlights:

> KPIs are hard facts, we can compare them. They don't leave room for interpretation and discussion. Simply, they matter.

Further, it is the organization of this sub-process that triggers simplification. The evaluation of the longlist is a task typically executed by interns or in some cases by consulting firms. Additionally, it can be pursued in a decentral way and simultaneous working on this sub-process allows firms to speed up the process. As such, a focus on KPIs reduces complexity and ambiguity, and time; however, it also gives rise to detrimental biases.

Anyway, some firms are aware of the shortcomings of KPI-driven target evaluation and see more responsibilities within the business units. Lars (head of M&A) told us:

> Longlist evaluation is a collaborative effort between the M&A department and the business units.

This approach aims to ensure that the ultimate responsibility for the evaluation is within the eventually integrating organizational entity. However, most interviewed firms relied on financial KPIs to reduce the longlist to a shortlist. This is problematic, as financial KPIs refer to a standalone past of an individual company. Acquisitions, however, are a tool to execute strategy and thus, target screening should consider the future entity and the synergetic effects between acquiring and acquired organization. Combined, the sub-process of reducing a longlist to a shortlist seems to be the phase when financials beat strategy in acquisitions.

Finally, in the last sub-process "evaluating the shortlist and ranking development" we find that managers rely on the heuristic "if there is an opportunity, we should capture it." This heuristic triggers a "safety bias" indicating that managers perceive it as more important to ultimately engage with a target, then engaging with the best fitting target or disengaging with a non-fitting target. The perceived loss of disengaging seems at this stage higher than the potential future losses when continuing the process with the wrong target. This safety bias also triggers a cognitive simplification, namely to "trust in advice." It refers to "authority or trust effects and confirmation biases." While the first one indicates an over-reliance on specific informants, the second one suggests that once a preference has established, managers only search for confirming evidence and ignores that which disconfirms one. Combined, this sub-process is a phase when "opportunities beat facts" or a possible explanation why firms often end up with targets nobody wanted.

Conclusion

We took a closer look at target screening during acquisitions, a part of the acquisition process that has received only little research attention (Rosner, 2006). Interestingly, target screening seems also a topic that receives too little managerial attention. Indeed, it is a decisive part for the further acquisition process, as finding and selecting a fitting target is essential for the strategic ideas of an acquisition. However, we find that most firms fail in identifying the best fitting targets. This is not the result of a single wrong or poor decision; it is the result of applied practices that trigger the heuristics and cognitive simplifications. While per se heuristics and cognitive simplifications can be valuable and even constitute competitive advantages (Bingham and Eisenhardt, 2011), they can also result in systematic errors. We find that the heuristics and cognitive simplifications applied during target screening give rise to multiple cognitive biases, ultimately obscuring initial strategic considerations.

Managers aim to reduce the complexity of the consecutive steps in target screening. By defining a narrow search scope, the initial longlist can be kept short. This allows them to speed up the process and arrive quicker at an execution stage. While several firms understand that they restrict their opportunities through these practices, they are struggling to develop better or more suitable practices. For example, the use of databases, which should allow firms to broaden their scope, also involves several drawbacks that particularly relate to the processing of information. In the second sub-process of target screening, strategic considerations often get lost and financial analysis becomes more important. This is in line with research showing the increasing dominance of functional synergies and the marginalization of strategic synergies through evaluation practices in the pre-acquisition stage (Bauer and Friesl, 2022). Ultimately, we find that the last sub-process of target screening mirrors the focus on execution from the first sub-process. The fear of losing an acquisition opportunity is greater that the potential losses through an acquisition of an unsuitable target firm, resulting in many firms making acquisitions with non-fitting target firms. This is a novel explanation for acquisition failure (see also Chapter 9), and we hope our research encourages future work in this fascinating field.

References

Ahmad, M., Shah, S., & Abbass, Y. (2021). The role of heuristic-driven biases in entrepreneurial strategic decision-making: evidence from an emerging economy. *Management Decision*, 59(3), 669–691.

Ayal, S., & Zakay, D. (2009). The perceived diversity heuristic: the case of pseudodiversity. *Journal of Personality and Social Psychology*, 96(3), 559–573.

Barnes Jr., J. (1984). Cognitive biases and their impact on strategic planning. *Strategic Management Journal*, 5(2), 129–137.

Bauer, F., & Friesl, M. (2022). Synergy evaluation in mergers and acquisitions: an attention-based view. *Journal of Management Studies*. https://doi.org/10.1111/joms.12804.

Bauer, F., Friesl, M., & Dao, M. A. (2022). Run or hide: changes in acquisition behaviour during the COVID-19 pandemic. *Journal of Strategy and Management*, 15(1), 38–53.

Bingham, C., & Eisenhardt, K. (2011). Rational heuristics: the 'simple rules' that strategists learn from process experience. *Strategic Management Journal*, 32(13), 1437–1464.

Bingham, C., Eisenhardt, K., & Furr, N. (2007). What makes a process a capability? Heuristics, strategy, and effective capture of opportunities. *Strategic Entrepreneurship Journal*, 1(1–2), 27–47.

Birkinshaw, J., Bresman, H., & Håkanson, L. (2000). Managing the post-acquisition integration process: how the human integration and task integration processes interact to foster value creation. *Journal of Management Studies*, 37(3), 395–425.

Cartwright, S., & Schoenberg, R. (2006). Thirty years of mergers and acquisitions research: recent advances and future opportunities. *British Journal of Management*, 17(S1), S1–S5.

Cyert, R., & March, J. (1963). *A Behavioral Theory of the Firm*. Englewood Cliffs, NJ: Prentice Hall.

Das, T., & Teng, B. (1999). Cognitive biases and strategic decision processes: an integrative perspective. *Journal of Management Studies*, 36(6), 757–778.

Dubois, A., & Gadde, L. (2002). Systematic combining: an abductive approach to case research. *Journal of Business Research*, 55(7), 553–560.

Eisenhardt, K., & Sull, D. (2001). Strategy as simple rules. *Harvard Business Review*. https://hbr.org/2001/01/strategy-as-simple-rules#:~:text=%E2%80%9CStrategy%20as%20simple%20rules%E2%80%9D%20makes,without%20constraining%20them%20in%20straitjackets.

Feldman, E., & Hernandez, E. (2022). Synergy in mergers and acquisitions: typology, life cycles, and value. *Academy of Management Review*, 47(4), 549–578.

Graebner, M. (2004). Momentum and serendipity: how acquired leaders create value in the integration of technology firms. *Strategic Management Journal*, 25(8–9), 751–777.

Graebner, M., Heimeriks, K., Huy, Q., & Vaara, E. (2017). The process of postmerger integration: a review and agenda for future research. *Academy of Management Annals*, 11(1), 1–32.

Haleblian, J., & Finkelstein, S. (1999). The influence of organizational acquisition experience on acquisition performance: a behavioral learning perspective. *Administrative Science Quarterly*, 44(1), 29–56.

Halvorson, H., & Rock, D. (2015). Beyond bias. *Strategy+ Business (PWC)*, 80, 1–10.

Hansen, E., & Allen, K. (1992). The creation corridor: environmental load and pre-organization information-processing ability. *Entrepreneurship Theory and Practice*, 17(1), 57–65.

Haspeslagh, P., & Jemison, D. (1991). *Managing Acquisitions: Creating Value through Corporate Renewal*. New York: Free Press.

Jemison, D., & Sitkin, S. (1986). Corporate acquisitions: a process perspective. *Academy of Management Review*, 11(1), 145–163.

Kahneman, D., Slovic, P., & Tversky, A. (eds.) (1982). *Judgment Under Uncertainty: Heuristics and Biases*. Cambridge: Cambridge University Press.

Kornberger, M. (2017). The values of strategy: valuation practices, rivalry and strategic agency. *Organization Studies*, 38(12), 1753–1773.

March, J., & Simon, H. (1958). *Organizations*. New York: John Wiley & Sons.

Newell, A., & Simon, H. (1972). *Human Problem Solving*. Englewood Cliffs, NJ: Prentice Hall.

Roberts, P. (1999). Product innovation, product–market competition and persistent profitability in the US pharmaceutical industry. *Strategic Management Journal*, 20(7), 655–670.

Rosenzweig, P. (2007). Misunderstanding the nature of company performance: the halo effect and other business delusions. *California Management Review*, 49(4), 6–20.

Rosner, S. (2006). Screening for success: designing and implementing a strategic M&A screening process. *Corporate Finance Review*, 10(4), 9–15.

Schwenk, C. (1986). Information, cognitive biases, and commitment to a course of action. *Academy of Management Review*, 11(2), 298–310.

Schwenk, C. (1988). The cognitive perspective on strategic decision making. *Journal of Management Studies*, 25(1), 41–55.

Simon, H. (1979). Rational decision making in business organizations. *The American Economic Review*, 69(4), 493–513.

Simon, M., Houghton, S., & Aquino, K. (2000). Cognitive biases, risk perception, and venture formation: how individuals decide to start companies. *Journal of Business Venturing*, 15(2), 113–134.

Trichterborn, A., Zu Knyphausen-Aufseß, D., & Schweizer, L. (2016). How to improve acquisition performance: the role of a dedicated M&A function, M&A learning process, and M&A capability. *Strategic Management Journal*, 37(4), 763–773.

Tversky, A., & Kahneman, D. (1973). Availability: a heuristic for judging frequency and probability. *Cognitive Psychology*, 5(2), 207–232.

Tversky, A., & Kahneman, D. (1974). Judgment under uncertainty: heuristics and biases: biases in judgments reveal some heuristics of thinking under uncertainty. *Science*, 185(4157), 1124–1131.

Vermeulen, F., & Barkema, H. (2001). Learning through acquisitions. *Academy of Management Journal*, 44(3), 457–476.

Wiggins, R., & Ruefli, T. (2005). Schumpeter's ghost: is hypercompetition making the best of times shorter? *Strategic Management Journal*, 26(10), 887–911.

3 Top executives and acquisitions

Gonzalo Molina-Sieiro and Mehdi Samimi

Introduction

The role of corporate executives in mergers and acquisition (M&A) decision-making is fundamental, as they are charged with identifying and appraising potential targets, orchestrating deals, and supervising post-merger integration. Recognizing the impact of executive decision-making in M&A necessitates understanding the factors that sway their choices and behaviors. This recognition starts with acknowledging that CEOs may have multiple motivations for acquisitions beyond improving firm performance. These include elevated pay, expanded discretion, and diversified employment risk. For instance, a CEO's envy of peers with higher compensation may drive acquisitions (Goel and Thakor, 2010).

However, executive outcomes are not consistently positive. For instance, a CEO-driven acquisition may encounter the issue of escalating commitment that could disregard problems unearthed during due diligence, contributing to acquisition failure. Thus, acquisition failure is frequently ascribed to executives, and problems associated with acquisitions are observed to engender higher CEO turnover (Bilgili et al., 2017; Krug, Wright and Kroll, 2014). In this context, we underscore the crucial role of top managers in acquisitions and propose research directions.

We underscore the need for research on the role of corporate executives in M&A decisions. A reward of studying this area is improving the success rate of acquisitions. While previous research has acknowledged the importance of top managers in acquisitions, there remains a scarcity of research on what influences managerial decisions regarding acquisitions and their consequent impact on acquisition performance. Simply, the field requires greater research focus on the individuals who conceptualize and execute acquisitions. We summarize theories utilized to elucidate acquisition decision-making, and we offer some thoughts on where scholars might direct research efforts.

Theory

The prevailing rationale for acquisitions hinges on the concept of synergy, the belief that combined entities will yield greater efficiency (Sirower, 1997). However, existing research persistently highlights that acquisitions often fail to deliver on promised synergies, resulting in volatile and even negative returns for companies and their shareholders over the long term (King et al., 2021; King et al., 2004; Moeller, Schlingemann and Stulz, 2005; Renneboog and Vansteenkiste, 2019). The continued use of acquisitions despite disappointing acquirer performance (King et al., 2021) has triggered a diverse range of explanations from scholars across various disciplines, including managerial motives propelling these transactions.

Executives play a critical role in shaping the many decisions tied to acquisitions, such as target selection (see also Chapter 2), payment method, decision to proceed or withdraw from the deal at various stages, and overall leadership during pre- and post-acquisition phases. The consequences of these decisions significantly influence firm performance. Thus, we present a survey of various theoretical frameworks examining managers' decision-making processes in acquisitions, along with the factors that inspire and affect acquisition outcomes. By understanding the theories underpinning managerial decisions in M&A transactions, we can delve deeper into the drivers of these decisions and their implications for the success or failure of M&As. While a portion of the theories discussed primarily focus on examining executive behaviors (e.g., upper echelons, agency theory), others with a broader scope explain firm behavior. These wider-ranging theories (e.g., resource-based view, transaction costs) can offer valuable insights into the landscape of acquisitions and potentially the role of executives within this context. An overview of summarized theories is shown in Table 3.1.

Agency theory

Agency theory proposes that managers may prioritize their own interests over those of the company or its shareholders, leading them to decisions that might not align with the company's best interests (Eisenhardt, 1989; Jensen and Meckling, 1976). As such, this theory offers a resolution to the paradox of acquisition motives. Scholars, utilizing agency theory, have primarily focused on examining how executive incentives (such as compensation) and ability (such as power) influence their pursuit of self-interests in M&A ventures.

Table 3.1   Summary of theories on executive strategic decisions

	Summary	Perspective	Focus	Application
Agency Theory	Separation of ownership and management creates divergent goals and information asymmetry (Jensen and Meckling, 1976)	Economic	Conflicts of interest	Corporate governance
Behavioral Theory	Managers perform problemistic search triggered when performance falls below benchmarks, and they exhibit satisficing behavior in decision-making (Cyert and March, 1963)	Psychology	Observable behavior	Individual and firm decisions
Firm Resources	Performance results from competitive advantages from firm resources and capabilities (Barney, 1991)	Organizational	Competitive advantage	Strategic decisions
Market Power	Ability of firm(s) to set the price of goods through manipulating supply or demand to control its profits (Landes and Posner, 1981)	Economic	Industry structure and competitive dynamics	Industry dynamics

	Summary	Perspective	Focus	Application
Real Options	Applies options from finance to corporate investment decisions under conditions of uncertainty (Trigeorgis, 1996)	Financial	Value of investments	Strategic decisions under uncertainty
Resource Dependence	Managers work to increase autonomy from their environment by controlling access to needed resources (Pfeffer and Salancik, 2003)	Inter-organizational	Resource scarcity and power asymmetry	Access to critical resources
Transaction Costs	Firm organization focuses on efficiency or the lowest cost (Williamson, 1975)	Economic	Efficient allocation of resources	Organiz-ational boundaries
Upper Echelons	Firms are reflections of their strategic leaders (Hambrick and Mason, 1984)	Cognition	Unobserv-able behavior	Strategic decisions

Managers, for instance, may aim to increase their compensation, prestige, and/or mitigate employment risk (Martin and Sayrak, 2003). In relation to acquisitions, agency problems can escalate commitment to an acquisition (Sleesman et al., 2012). This necessitates the implementation of corporate governance mechanisms to: (1) align managers' interests with those of share-holders (Dalton et al., 2007), and (2) ensure oversight (Aguilera et al., 2015). Nevertheless, research indicates that monitoring can engender additional problems (Goranova et al., 2017). For instance, controls derived from agency theory can amplify CEO risk-taking (Martin, Wiseman and Gomez-Mejia, 2016).

We identify at least three potential areas for research. First, research should investigate alternative governance mechanisms beyond monitoring. While monitoring is a crucial governance mechanism to align managers' interests with shareholders, there may be other effective mechanisms, such as shareholder lawsuits related to acquisitions, which could assist in bridging the agency–principal gap. Shareholders could directly monitor management by initiating legal action if they perceive that management is making an unfavorable acquisition (Chung et al., 2020). Researchers could analyze these alternative alignment mechanisms and the corresponding executive responses.

Second, research should scrutinize the role of emotions and cognitive biases in M&A decision-making within an agency theory framework. Conventionally, agency theory assumes that managers, even when pursuing self-interest, are rational (Bloom and Milkovich, 1998). However, emotions can significantly influence decision-making, especially in the context of high-stakes decisions like M&A. Research on upper echelons emphasizes the effect individual executives' cognitive frames have on decision-making, but less attention has been given to transient or state constructs like emotions. Additionally, the behavioral agency model (Wiseman and Gomez-Mejia, 1998) offers a nuanced perspective on how incentives impact executives' risk-taking behavior, contingent on the framing of strategic problems. However, even the behavioral agency model does not formally recognize individual executives' attributes and the role of their emotions. Research could investigate how emotions such as envy, fear, or excitement and executive characteristics, such as their personality and cognitive attributes, might influence executive decision-making in M&A. Further, it could explore how these factors interact with agency problems and governance mechanisms. Transient states like emotions may closely intertwine with principal–agent conflicts, such as the fear of disappointing the board or the emotional burden of failure when facing the board and shareholders (e.g., represented by proxies like analysts in investment banks). This could provide insights into why executives may choose to conceal failures from their monitors (e.g., the board of directors and outside investment analysts).

Third, agency theory and the upper echelons perspective often provide complementary and, in some cases, contradictory explanations for executives' impact on firm behavior, particularly in the field of acquisitions. For instance, while one study demonstrated that a CEO's career horizon affects M&A activities – with a longer CEO career horizon being associated with more risk-seeking behavior and a higher likelihood of international acquisitions (Matta and Beamish, 2008) – another study showed that this effect might not persist in certain situations and is moderated by CEO characteristics such as founder status and family membership (Strike et al., 2015). Agency theorists generally depict executives as rational opportunistic agents who prefer not to risk their wealth. For example, Ordu and Schweizer (2015) advanced the notion that top executives demonstrate a motive for hedging, as evidenced by their pre-merger put option trading. Conversely, another study showed that

CEOs' personal trading performance is positively related to the short-term performance of their mergers, indicating consistency between their personal and corporate investment decisions (Leung, Tse and Westerholm, 2019). Both the upper echelons and agency perspectives provide valuable insights into executive behavior, yet their combination may yield a more comprehensive explanation of their M&A-related activities.

Behavioral theory

Based on Cyert and March (1963), the behavioral theory of the firm examines firm behavior and factors influencing interfirm relationships (Gavetti et al., 2012). For acquisitions, behavioral theory posits that managers may overestimate benefits and undervalue costs, or undertake risker actions when performance falls (Santulli et al., 2022) A review of acquisition research using behavioral theory by Devers et al. (2020) identifies four main themes: (1) the role of emotions in M&A decision-making, (2) the significance of cognitive biases and heuristics in M&A activities, (3) the effect of social networks and power dynamics on M&A outcomes, and (4) the importance of leadership during post-merger integration. Suboptimal outcomes in acquisitions are often attributed to managerial biases such as overconfidence, confirmation bias, or groupthink. As a result, behavioral theory underscores the importance of understanding the psychological and organizational factors that influence M&A decision-making. For instance, research suggests that male and younger CEOs are more likely to finalize acquisitions (Devers et al., 2020). Moreover, previous acquisition experience shapes subsequent actions by establishing routines that can become self-reinforcing (Ellis et al., 2011; King, Shijaku and Urtasan, 2023).

Two research directions emerge regarding how executives function within behavioral theory. First, in line with our suggestions regarding upper echelons and agency approaches to study executives' impact in M&As, scholars could delve deeper into the impact of cognition and emotions on M&A decision-making as well as the role of performance signals and aspiration levels. It would be worthwhile to investigate how executives with varying characteristics or incentives respond to M&A activities when performance falls below or exceeds their aspiration levels. Alternatively, research should concentrate on exploring how executives form performance aspirations specifically concerning M&A outcomes and their response to unforeseen consequences of acquisitions.

Second, scholars should investigate the effect of social networks on M&A outcomes and how these shape aspirations. Research has emphasized the importance of social networks and power dynamics in M&A outcomes, but there is potential for further exploration of this topic. For instance, research could investigate which types of networks most heavily influence M&A decision-making, and how executives can leverage their networks to improve outcomes. Additionally, research could examine the impact of power dynamics within a firm undergoing post-merger integration, and how these dynamics can be managed to boost acquisition performance.

Firm resources

Resource-based theory (RBT) posits that firms create value and gain competitive advantage through the utilization of their unique resources. For acquisitions, this theory suggests that managers seek acquisitions to gain control over valuable, rare, and non-replicable resources (Barney, 1986, 1991). The theory emphasizes that companies pursue acquisitions to obtain resources they cannot easily develop internally, such as advanced technology, talented personnel, or well-established brands. In addition, companies may aim to acquire resources that complement their existing capabilities, thereby expanding their product range, penetrating new markets, or reducing costs through economies of scale. For instance, King, Slotegraaf and Kesner (2008) demonstrate improved acquisition performance when the acquiring and target firms have complementary resources. Similarly, Makri, Hitt and Lane (2010) establish a positive impact on post-acquisition innovation when the acquiring and target firms have complementary technologies.

Although the importance of RBT in elucidating acquisitions cannot be overstated, studies focusing on executives' perspectives in this area seldom incorporated this framework. Nevertheless, executives hold a vital position in the decision-making process concerning which resources to acquire and the approaches to adopt for obtaining them. Research should explore acquisitions within the context of strategic factor markets. The RBT asserts that firms acquire resources in strategic factor markets (Barney, 1986). However, sometimes these resources are embedded in potential targets and cannot be easily extracted from their existing structures. In such scenarios, acquisitions become a crucial method for firms to access these resources as part of their resource management process (Sirmon, Hitt and Ireland, 2007). Accordingly, scholars should investigate the role of top executives in acquisitions as part of the resource management process. Potential research questions could include: What motivates top executives to pursue these resources via M&A? How do they identify and evaluate potential targets possessing valuable resources?

Market power

Firms possessing market power can manipulate their profits by increasing prices without losing sales (Landes and Posner, 1981). Through acquisitions or mergers, companies can gain synergies from an enlarged market share, reduced competition, and access to new markets or customers (Feldman and Hernandez, 2020). These objectives align with the market power explanations for acquisitions that can contribute to increased profitability and shareholder value (Ferrier, Smith and Grimm, 1999). However, this perspective also underscores the potential negative impacts of increased market power, such as stifled innovation, elevated consumer prices, and decreased market choice (e.g., Devers et al., 2013; Martin and Sayrak, 2003; Ornaghi, 2009). Therefore, regulatory and antitrust considerations become critical when evaluating acquisition activities and the subsequent market power of the combined entities.

Three potential areas of research regarding executive decision-making in the pursuit of market power stand out. First, the role of top executives in managing the antitrust risks associated with acquisition activities could be explored further. Given the potential adverse effects of increased market power on consumers and the market, regulatory and antitrust considerations are crucial in assessing acquisition activities. However, these considerations can significantly impact top executives' decision-making processes. Research could probe how top executives evaluate and manage the antitrust risks tied to acquisition activities, including their strategies to mitigate these risks and how these affect the success of their acquisition strategies. Understanding the types of managers who opt for different strategic actions is a promising area for research.

Second, it is worth investigating the impact of increased market power on executive compensation further. Market power explanations of acquisitions suggest that companies can gain synergies from increased market share, reduced competition, and expanded markets or customers, leading to greater profitability and shareholder value. This may also result in elevated compensation for top executives. Research could examine the impact of increased market power on executive compensation, including the kinds of compensation packages top executives in firms with increased market power receive, and whether these packages incentivize executives to prioritize short-term benefits over long-term growth and innovation. Crucially, deciphering the sources of executive compensation growth (i.e., whether it is due to market power, innovation, or organic firm growth) seems like a worthy pursuit for research.

Third, in studies focusing on executive power and M&As, CEO power is often measured using proxies such as duality, ownership, family membership, and founder status (Chikh and Filbien, 2011), or by assessing excess pay (Dutta, MacAulay and Saadi, 2011). Although these proxies capture an executive's power within their own firm, they fail to capture their power relative to executives in other firms. Thus, it would be valuable for research to investigate the impact of a firm's growth and increased market power on the power of its executives. Existing studies can provide insights and inform research inquiries in this area. For instance, Chick and Filbien (2011) discovered that well-connected CEOs have a higher likelihood of completing deals despite negative market reactions to acquisition announcements. Research can delve into the same question by examining the influence of market power, specifically investigating whether CEOs of larger firms with increased market power demonstrate differing levels of responsiveness to market reactions and external feedback, including analyst recommendations.

Real options

Real options theory posits that M&A decisions can be framed as investment choices characterized by uncertainty and flexibility (Trigeorgis, 1996). Managers can employ real options thinking to evaluate potential M&A prospects, accounting for the potential value of the target company across different scenarios and the strategic adaptability to changing market conditions (McGrath, Ferrier and Mendelow, 2004; McGrath and Nerkar, 2004). Research has indicated that managers apply a "real options" heuristic in investment decisions, and smaller investments can help to mitigate risk (Chung et al., 2013; O'Brien, Folta and Johnson, 2003). This perspective sees other investments (e.g., R&D) and corporate activities (e.g., alliances) as synergistic with acquisitions (Folta and Miller, 2002; Porrini, 2004). Thus, real options theory can provide insights into the timing of acquisitions (Shi and Prescott, 2011; Shi, Sun and Prescott, 2012).

Going forward, research could delve deeper into the role of real options thinking in the M&A decision-making process. Studies could examine how managers leverage real options thinking when evaluating M&A opportunities, as well as the influencing factors that prompt managers to adopt this mindset. Additionally, research could seek to understand how managers identify and evaluate various scenarios and potential returns associated with a specific acquisition. Valuable insights can be gained through studies employing experimental designs, with a specific focus on the existing body of research in behavioral decision-making and behavioral economics.

Resource dependence

Resource dependence theory, a prominent framework for explaining acquisitions (Hillman, Withers and Collins, 2009), posits that firms engage in M&A activities to lessen their reliance on external resources and gain enhanced control over essential resources and capabilities (Pfeffer and Salancik, 2003). For instance, firms require access to resources such as capital, technology, and skilled labor to compete effectively, yet these necessary resources are often controlled by external entities like suppliers, customers, and competitors. Casciaro and Piskorski (2005) expand on this concept, noting that resource dependence can result from power imbalance or mutual dependence, a perspective that can help reconcile conflicting research findings. By executing acquisitions or mergers, firms can attain greater control over these pivotal resources, reducing their reliance on external entities. Finkelstein (1997) examined resource dependence as a factor explaining acquisitions and found it to be a strong predictor of M&A activity, as firms tend to acquire companies in industries where they have significant dependence. Moreover, acquisitions can prompt additional actions from suppliers and customers due to increased dependence (Rogan and Greve, 2015), suggesting links between resource dependence and transaction cost economics (Casciaro and Piskorski, 2005).

There are several research directions to extend the literature on executives' role in acquisitions from a resource dependence perspective. First, scholars should explore the role of top executives in managing resource dependence. While resource dependence theory proposes that firms undertake M&A to acquire greater control over crucial resources and diminish dependence on external entities, it remains unclear how top executives perceive and manage resource dependence. Research could delve into how top executives identify key resources, evaluate their reliance on external entities, and determine suitable M&A strategies to reduce dependence. Second, researchers could probe into how top executives navigate power imbalances or mutual dependence with external parties, and how they negotiate acquisition terms to secure more control over resources during acquisitions. Third, scholars should investigate the impact of resource dependence on post-acquisition integration. Given that resource dependence theory suggests acquisitions can incite additional actions from suppliers and customers due to increased dependence, it is unclear how this dependence influences post-acquisition integration. Research can examine how resource dependence affects the integration process and how top executives can effectively manage dependencies to ensure successful integration. Finally, executives' networks are anticipated to have a crucial influence in explaining firms' approaches to handling resource dependencies. For instance, a CEO with a wide-ranging and influential network may perceive decreased dependence on a specific supplier, resulting in a reduced need for vertical integration. Scholars should explore this further by studying the impact of executives' network attributes on M&As.

Transaction costs

Transaction cost economics suggests that firms engage in M&A activities to circumvent market failures (Williamson, 1975). By acquiring another firm, costs related to market transactions (e.g., search, bargaining, monitoring, and enforcement) can be sidestepped through acquiring control over essential assets and resources. This theory presumes that coordination costs from internalizing transactions in an acquisition are lower than the cost of market transactions, accounting for contractual and governance mechanisms. Thus, transaction cost economics' explanations for acquisitions revolve around enhanced efficiency (Leiblein, 2003). However, an acquiring firm typically possesses less information about a target, which in turn elevates transaction costs in acquisitions (Chakrabarti and Mitchell, 2016).

Scholars should probe the impact of transaction costs on post-merger integration. While transaction cost economics proposes that M&A can bolster efficiency by reducing transaction costs, it also suggests that the increased coordination costs of internalizing transactions could pose a challenge to post-merger integration. Research could explore the role of top executives in managing post-merger integration and how they can mitigate the impact of transaction costs on the success of M&A. For instance, they might employ their leadership skills to harmonize the objectives and values of the acquiring and target firms, or put into place effective communication strategies to ease the transfer of knowledge and resources between the companies. In essence, what specific managerial attributes may alleviate the impact of transaction costs?

Upper echelons theory

The upper echelons perspective focuses on understanding collective behavior of top managers, including the context of acquisitions (Hambrick and Mason, 1984; Hambrick, 2007). Leaders situated in a firm's upper echelons can provide a unique competitive edge (Chaganti, 2013). Their backgrounds, experiences, and personal traits, in conjunction with organizational processes, inform their decision-making, thereby significantly influencing their firms (Barnard, 1938; Hambrick and Mason, 1984; Hambrick, 2007; Wang et al., 2016). These elements shape the cognitive lens through which executives interpret information and make decisions, including strategic ones like acquisitions. For instance, organizations and executives with prior acquisition experience are often more inclined to pursue additional acquisitions (Devers et al., 2020; Meyer-Doyle, Lee and Helfat, 2019; Welch et al., 2020). Research has also explored how personal traits, such as narcissism, influence a company's acquisition behavior (Chatterjee and Hambrick, 2007; Holmes et al., 2021).

The paradox of acquisition motives, often addressed by upper echelons scholars, invokes the concept of executives' personal states. For example, hubris embodies overconfidence and optimistic assumptions that dismiss conflicting information and overlook red flags (Rumelt, 1995). It is commonly suggested that managers, driven by overconfidence or a desire to boost their egos and reputations, are responsible for value-destroying acquisitions (Sanders, 2001; Hayward and Hambrick, 1997). Hubris posits that managers may engage in M&A activities due to personal ambition and self-interest, despite a propensity to overlook acquisition pitfalls and make suboptimal decisions. Managers exhibiting hubris are often more prone to poor acquisition decisions, such as overpayment (Hayward and Hambrick, 1997) or excessive cost-cutting during integration (Krishnan, Hitt and Park, 2007). In the realm of international M&As, CEO overconfidence has been linked to the propensity to make offers, the frequency of acquisitions, and the use of cash for merger financing (Ferris, Jayaraman and Sabherwal, 2013). Another study indicated that CEO overconfidence increases the likelihood of cross-industry M&A activity (Yang, Bai and Yang, 2021) or diversifying acquisitions (Malmendier and Tate, 2008). While hubris alone cannot fully explain acquisition activity (Roll, 1986), it holds more relevance for larger corporations (Moeller, Schlingemann and Stulz, 2005).

Beyond hubris, executives exhibit a variety of characteristics that influence their M&A decisions. For example, research has utilized the political orientation of executives as a proxy for risk-seeking behavior. Elnahas and Kim (2017) found that Republican CEOs are less likely to engage in M&A activities. When they do participate, they tend to prefer cash as the payment method and target public firms within their industry. Further, Republican CEOs often avoid acquisitions with high information asymmetry that incorporate "earnout" clauses. Gada, Goyal and Popli (2021) also found a positive relationship between the acquiring firm CEO's dispositional prevention focus and the use of earnouts as a risk-mitigating tool.

A significant subset of upper echelons research related to M&A activity focuses on the influence of executives' experiences and backgrounds. Scholars have investigated the effect of factors like executives' tenure, education, and functional background on their M&A activities. A key recurring theme among these studies highlights the critical role of CEOs' experience and familiarity with target firms' businesses in facilitating successful acquisitions. For example, Custódio and Metzger (2013) posited that CEOs with industry-specific knowledge can extract a greater share of the merger surplus by negotiating deals effectively and minimizing the premium paid for the target. Their findings suggest that acquisitions led by CEOs with prior experience in the target industry yield higher abnormal announcement returns compared to those led by CEOs without such experience. Another study finds that CEOs with a longer tenure are more likely to acquire private target firms and pursue acquisitions within the same industries. Further, these long-tenured CEOs typically generate greater shareholder value in M&A deals compared to their short-tenured counterparts (Zhou, Dutta and Zhu, 2020). Tenure also facilitates better coordination within the acquiring firm, contributing to improved M&A performance (Garrow and Awolowo, 2022). This line of research suggests that even seemingly minor aspects of executives' background might enhance their M&A-related decisions. For instance, a study found that CEOs were significantly more likely to acquire target firms located in the states where they obtained their undergraduate and graduate degrees (Wang and Yin, 2018). These acquisitions, termed "education–state deals," tend to be larger in scale with higher completion rates and lower premiums, resulting in positive cumulative abnormal announcement returns.

To contribute to acquisition research within the upper echelons perspective, research should explore a few key areas. First, the impact of CEO characteristics on M&A activity presents numerous potential facets for further exploration. Given the pivotal role of top management teams (TMTs) in determining firm decisions, it would be insightful to investigate how underexplored specific CEO characteristics (such as elite education or ethnicity) along with other TMT members influence a firm's propensity to engage in M&A activity and its acquisition performance. Prior research has indicated that younger CEOs are more likely to pursue M&As (Welch et al., 2020), but it would be beneficial to explore how the attributes of TMT, such as their accumulated experiences or diversity moderate the effect of CEO attributes. Second, researchers should examine how CEO attributes that affect M&A engagement influence understudied M&A outcomes such as the likelihood of post-acquisition divestitures. Prior research suggests that hubristic managers may be more inclined to pursue value-destroying acquisitions. However, it remains unclear whether these managers are also more likely to divest underperforming businesses post-acquisition.

Considering manager cognition contrasts with economic explanations of firm strategic actions (Nadkarni and Barr, 2008). Aspects of manager cognition that can be explored are sensing opportunity, mobilizing resources, and/or reconfiguration (Durán and Aguado, 2022; Teece, 2007). Additionally, research can continue to study temporal focus (Gamache and McNamara, 2019), regulatory focus (Gamache et al., 2015), intuition (Kopalle, Kuusela and Lehmann, 2023), and overconfidence (Lee, Park and Chen, 2023) in M&A decisions. Expanding strategic leadership to investigate individual, dyadic, or teams (Samimi et al., 2022), enables examining the influence of cognitive characteristics on M&A. For example, research could explore whether hubristic CEOs are more inclined to divest poor-performing businesses following an acquisition, and whether this divestiture decision is influenced by factors such as reputation concerns or other agency-related factors.

Discussion

More research attention is needed on the people (managers) formulating and implementing acquisitions. We summarize theoretical perspectives that can illuminate factors associated with how executives influence acquisitions. Better insights can come from delving into the role of managers and integrating theories that encompass their decision-making processes in acquisitions. Because each theory is grounded in different perspectives, a multifaceted approach can unlock valuable insights. For example, executives make acquisition decisions shaped by mechanisms understood through behavioral theory, transaction costs, real options, firm resources, and/or resource dependence theory. Still, different theories enable different insights. For example, while behavioral theory upper echelons accept bounded rationality, upper echelons is more restrictive to groups and top managers. Therefore, research should use appropriate theories when studying acquisitions and framing implications.

We outline areas of future research in Table 3.2. Foremost, we need a better understanding of the motivations and decision-making processes of top executives in M&A. Given the pivotal role that top executives play in M&A, gaining insights into their motivations and decision-making processes is essential for improving the success rate of acquisitions. Second, research needs to consider both financial and non-financial motivations of executives for M&A. CEOs may have multiple motivations for pursuing M&A beyond just financial gains, such as increased compensation, greater decision-making autonomy, and diversified employment risk. Therefore, it is important to evaluate M&A decisions in the context of both financial and non-financial motivations. Third, there are several potential risks associated with CEO-driven M&A that warrant a deeper understanding. CEOs may be prone to overpaying for target companies or to escalating their commitment to an acquisition, which could lead

Table 3.2   Future research needs

Theory	Future research
Agency theory	- Alternative governance mechanisms - Study emotions and cognitive biases (behavioral agency model (BAM)) - Integrate with upper echelons and consider individual differences
Behavioral theory	- Study executives' emotion and cognition along with performance signals - Investigate the effect of executives' social networks and power dynamics
Firm resources	- Study acquisitions in the context of strategic factor markets - Study executives' role in identifying and handling resource gaps
Market power	- Study the management of antitrust risks - Explore the effect of market power on executive compensation - Expand the notion of CEO power to incorporate firm market power
Real options	- Study when and how managers adopt a real option mindset - Draw from behavioral economics and adopt experimental designs
Resource dependence	- Explore how executives perceive and manage resource dependence - Study executives' strategies in navigating power imbalances - Investigate the impact of resource dependence on post-acquisition integration - Examine the effect of executives' networks
Transaction costs	- Probe the impact of transaction costs on post-merger integration - Study how executives mitigate the impact of transaction costs in M&As
Upper echelons	- Expand the focus from CEO to TMT - Study executives' role in understudied M&A outcomes - Study managerial cognition

to acquisition failure. Thus, it is critical to be mindful of the potential risks of CEO-driven M&A.

Acknowledging the susceptibility of acquisition decisions to various cognitive biases adds a layer of importance to understanding managerial cognition. Although the examination of managerial cognition in acquisitions is in its early stages, scholars can build upon extensive research on individual- and team-level executive cognition (Durán and Aguado, 2022) to explore how cognitive factors, alongside determinants like corporate governance and leaders' demographic attributes, influence acquisition decisions.

A limitation of our review is that it is not exhaustive. For example, acquisition integration likely depends on manager sensemaking (Bansal, King and Meglio, 2022). Cultural integration also requires forming a shared identity, and different acquirer and target firm identities may create clashes from different organizational cultures that can be exacerbated in serial acquirers (Colman and Lunnan, 2022). A related area of study is the role of emotion in acquisitions (e.g., Khan et al., 2020; Klok, Kroon and Khapova, 2023). The role of emotions can involve managers or employees, but both create issues that impact manager decisions in acquisitions.

In closing, there is a need to investigate the paradox in acquisition performance and motives, as firms increasingly make large acquisitions in the face of poor acquisition performance. This paradox has been examined through several theoretical lenses. Agency theory, with the principal–agent issue, allows for the consideration of managerial motives. However, management research and practice can benefit from more comprehensive theoretical perspectives that incorporate executive characteristics, such as cognition or transaction costs, along with incentives.

References

Aguilera, R., Desender, K., Bednar, M., & Lee, J. (2015). Connecting the dots: bringing external corporate governance into the corporate governance puzzle. *Academy of Management Annals*, 9(1), 483–573.

Bansal, A., King, D., & Meglio, O. (2022). Acquisitions as programs: the role of sensemaking and sensegiving. *International Journal of Project Management*, 40(3), 278–289.

Barnard, C. (1938). *The Functions of the Executive*. Boston, MA: Harvard University Press.

Barney, J. (1986). Strategic factor markets: expectations, luck, and business strategy. *Management Science*, 32(10), 1231–1241.

Barney, J. (1991). Firm resources and sustained competitive advantage. *Journal of Management*, 17(1), 99–120.

Bilgili, T., Calderon, C., Allen, D., & Kedia, B. (2017). Gone with the wind: a meta-analytic review of executive turnover, its antecedents, and postacquisition performance. *Journal of Management*, 43(6), 1966–1997.

Bloom, M., & Milkovich, G. (1998). Relationships among risk, incentive pay, and organizational performance. *Academy of Management Journal*, 41(3), 283–297.

Casciaro, T., & Piskorski, M. (2005). Power imbalance, mutual dependence, and constraint absorption: a closer look at resource dependence theory. *Administrative Science Quarterly*, 50(2), 167–199.

Chaganti, R. (2013). Upper-echelons theory. In Kessler, E. (ed.), *Encyclopedia of Management Theory* (pp. 919–921). Los Angeles, CA: SAGE Publications.

Chakrabarti, A., & Mitchell, W. (2016). The role of geographic distance in complet-ing related acquisitions: evidence from U.S. chemical manufacturers. *Strategic Management Journal*, 37(4), 673–694.

Chatterjee, A., & Hambrick, D. (2007). It's all about me: narcissistic chief executive officers and their effects on company strategy and performance. *Administrative Science Quarterly*, 52(3), 351–386.

Chikh, S., & Filbien, J. (2011). Acquisitions and CEO power: evidence from French networks. *Journal of Corporate Finance*, 17(5), 1221–1236.

Chung, C., Kim, I., Rabarison, M., To, T., & Wu, E. (2020). Shareholder litigation rights and corporate acquisitions. *Journal of Corporate Finance*, 62, 101599.

Chung, C., Lee, S., Beamish, P., Southam, C., & Nam, D. (2013). Pitting real options theory against risk diversification theory: international diversification and joint ownership control in economic crisis. *Journal of World Business*, 48(1), 122–136.

Colman, H., & Lunnan, R. (2022). Pulling together while falling apart: a relational view on integration in serial acquirers. *Journal of Management*. https://doi.org/10.1177/01492063221121788.

Custódio, C., & Metzger, D. (2013). How do CEOs matter? The effect of industry expertise on acquisition returns. *The Review of Financial Studies*, 26(8), 2008–2047.

Cyert, R., & March, J. (1963). *A Behavioral Theory of the Firm*. Englewood Cliffs, NJ: Prentice Hall.

Dalton, D., Hitt, M., Certo, S., & Dalton, C. (2007). The fundamental agency problem and its mitigation: independence, equity, and the market for corporate control. *Academy of Management Annals*, 1(1), 1–64.

Devers, C., McNamara, G., Haleblian, J., & Yoder, M. (2013). Do they walk the talk? Gauging acquiring CEO and director confidence in the value creation potential of announced acquisitions. *Academy of Management Journal*, 56(6), 1679–1702.

Devers, C., Wuorinen, S., McNamara, G., Haleblian, J., Gee, I., & Kim, J. (2020). An integrative review of the emerging behavioral acquisition literature: charting the next decade of research. *Academy of Management Annals*, 14(2), 869–907.

Durán, W., & Aguado, D. (2022). CEOs' managerial cognition and dynamic capa-bilities: a meta-analytical study from the microfoundations approach. *Journal of Management & Organization*, 28(3), 451–479.

Dutta, S., MacAulay, K., & Saadi, S. (2011). CEO power, M&A decisions, and market reactions. *Journal of Multinational Financial Management*, 21(5), 257–278.

Eisenhardt, K. (1989). Agency theory: an assessment and review. *Academy of Management Review*, 14(1), 57–74.

Ellis, K., Reus, T., Lamont, B., & Ranft, A. (2011). Transfer effects in large acquisitions: how size-specific experience matters. *Academy of Management Journal*, 54(6), 1261–1276.

Elnahas, A., & Kim, D. (2017). CEO political ideology and mergers and acquisitions decisions. *Journal of Corporate Finance*, 45, 162–175.

Feldman, E., & Hernandez, E. (2020). Synergy in mergers and acquisitions: typology, lifecycles, and value. *Academy of Management Review*, 47(4), 549–578.

Ferrier, W., Smith, K., & Grimm, C. (1999). The role of competitive action in market share erosion and industry dethronement: a study of industry leaders and challeng-ers. *Academy of Management Journal*, 42(4), 372–388.

Ferris, S., Jayaraman, N., & Sabherwal, S. (2013). CEO overconfidence and inter-national merger and acquisition activity. *Journal of Financial and Quantitative Analysis*, 48(1), 137–164.

Finkelstein, S. (1997). Interindustry merger patterns and resource dependence: a replication and extension of Pfeffer (1972). *Strategic Management Journal*, 18(10), 787–810.

Folta, T., & Miller, K. (2002). Real options in equity partnerships. *Strategic Management Journal*, 23(1), 77–88.

Gada, V., Goyal, L., & Popli, M. (2021). Earnouts in M&A deal structuring: the impact of CEO prevention focus. *Journal of International Management*, 27(1), 100825.

Gamache, D., & McNamara, G. (2019). Responding to bad press: how CEO temporal focus influences the sensitivity to negative media coverage of acquisitions. *Academy of Management Journal*, 62(3), 918–943.

Gamache, D., McNamara, G., Mannor, M., & Johnson, R. (2015). Motivated to acquire? The impact of CEO regulatory focus on firm acquisitions. *Academy of Management Journal*, 58(4), 1261–1282.

Garrow, N., & Awolowo, I. (2022). Mergers and acquisitions and the CEO: tenure and outcomes. *Corporate Board: Role, Duties and Composition*, 18(1), 47–61.

Gavetti, G., Greve, H., Levinthal, D., & Ocasio, W. (2012). The behavioral theory of the firm: assessment and prospects. *Academy of Management Annals*, 6(1), 1–40.

Goel, A., & Thakor, A. (2010). Do envious CEOs cause merger waves? *The Review of Financial Studies*, 23(2), 487–517.

Goranova, M., Priem, R., Ndofor, H., & Trahms, C. (2017). Is there a "dark side" to monitoring? Board and shareholder monitoring effects on M&A performance extremeness. *Strategic Management Journal*, 38(11), 2285–2297.

Hambrick, D. (2007). Upper echelons theory: an update. *Academy of Management Review*, 32(2), 334–343.

Hambrick, D., & Mason, P. (1984). Upper echelons: the organization as a reflection of its top managers. *Academy of Management Review*, 9(2), 193–206.

Hayward, M., & Hambrick, D. (1997). Explaining the premiums paid for large acquisitions: evidence of CEO hubris. *Administrative Science Quarterly*, 42(1), 103–127.

Hillman, A., Withers, M., & Collins, B. (2009). Resource dependence theory: a review. *Journal of Management*, 35(6), 1404–1427.

Holmes, R., Hitt, M., Perrewe, P., Palmer, J., & Molina-Sieiro, G. (2021). Building cross-disciplinary bridges in leadership: integrating top executive personality and leadership theory and research. *The Leadership Quarterly*, 32(1), 101490.

Jensen, M., & Meckling, M. (1976). Theory of the firm: managerial behavior, agency costs and ownership structure. *Journal of Political Economy*, 3(4), 305–360.

Khan, Z., Soundararajan, V., Wood, G., & Ahammad, M. F. (2020). Employee emotional resilience during post-merger integration across national boundaries: rewards and the mediating role of fairness norms. *Journal of World Business*, 55(2), 100888.

King, D., Dalton, D., Daily, C., & Covin, J. (2004). Meta-analyses of post-acquisition performance: indications of unidentified moderators. *Strategic Management Journal*, 25(2), 187–200.

King, D., Shijaku, E., & Urtasan, A. (2023). Are acquirers different? Identifying firm precursors to acquisitions. *Journal of Strategy and Management*, 16(3), 554–575.

King, D., Slotegraaf, R., & Kesner, I. (2008). Performance implications of firm resource interactions in the acquisition of R&D-intensive firms. *Organization Science*, 19(2), 327–340.

King, D., Wang, G., Samimi, M., & Cortes, A. (2021). A meta-analytic integration of acquisition performance prediction. *Journal of Management Studies*, 58(5), 1198–1236.

Klok, Y., Kroon, D., & Khapova, S. (2023). The role of emotions during mergers and acquisitions: a review of the past and a glimpse into the future. *International Journal of Management Reviews*, 25(3), 587–613.

Kopalle, P., Kuusela, H., & Lehmann, D. (2023). The role of intuition in CEO acquisition decisions. *Journal of Business Research*, 167, 114139.

Krishnan, H., Hitt, M., & Park, D. (2007). Acquisition premiums, subsequent workforce reductions and post-acquisition performance. *Journal of Management Studies*, 44(5), 709–732.

Krug, J., Wright, P., & Kroll, M. (2014). Top management turnover following mergers and acquisitions: solid research to date but still much to be learned. *Academy of Management Perspectives*, 28(2), 147–163.

Landes, W., & Posner, R. (1981). Market power in antitrust cases. *Harvard Law Review*, 94(5), 937–996.

Lee, J., Park, J., & Chen, G. (2023). A cognitive perspective on real options investment: CEO overconfidence. *Strategic Management Journal*, 44(4), 1084–1110.

Leiblein, M. (2003). The choice of organizational governance form and performance: predictions from transaction cost, resource-based, and real options theories. *Journal of Management*, 29(6), 937–961.

Leung, H., Tse, J., & Westerholm, P. J. (2019). CEO traders and corporate acquisitions. *Journal of Corporate Finance*, 54, 107–127.

Makri, M., Hitt, M., & Lane, P. (2010). Complementary technologies, knowledge relatedness, and invention outcomes in high technology mergers and acquisitions. *Strategic Management Journal*, 31(6), 602–628.

Malmendier, U., & Tate, G. (2008). Who makes acquisitions? CEO overconfidence and the market's reaction. *Journal of Financial Economics*, 89(1), 20–43.

Martin, G., Wiseman, R., & Gomez-Mejia, L. (2016). Bridging finance and behavioral scholarship on agent risk sharing and risk taking. *Academy of Management Perspectives*, 30(4), 349–368.

Martin, J., & Sayrak, A. (2003). Corporate diversification and shareholder value: a survey of recent literature. *Journal of Corporate Finance*, 9(1), 37–57.

Matta, E., & Beamish, P. W. (2008). The accentuated CEO career horizon problem: evidence from international acquisitions. *Strategic Management Journal*, 29(7), 683–700.

McGrath, R., Ferrier, W., & Mendelow, A. (2004). Real options as engines of choice and heterogeneity. *Academy of Management Review*, 29(1), 86–101.

McGrath, R., & Nerkar, A. (2004). Real options reasoning and a new look at the R&D investment strategies of pharmaceutical firms. *Strategic Management Journal*, 25(1), 1–21.

Meyer-Doyle, P., Lee, S., & Helfat, C. (2019). Disentangling the microfoundations of acquisition behavior and performance. *Strategic Management Journal*, 40(11), 1733–1756.

Moeller, S., Schlingemann, F., & Stulz, R. (2005). Wealth destruction on a massive scale? A study of acquiring-firm returns in the recent merger wave. *Journal of Finance*, 60(2), 757–782.

Nadkarni, S., & Barr, P. (2008). Environmental context, managerial cognition, and strategic action: an integrated view. *Strategic Management Journal*, 29(13), 1395–1427.

O'Brien, J., Folta, T., & Johnson, D. (2003). A real options perspective on entrepreneurial entry in the face of uncertainty. *Managerial and Decision Economics*, 24(8), 515–533.

Ordu, U., & Schweizer, D. (2015). Executive compensation and informed trading in acquiring firms around merger announcements. *Journal of Banking & Finance*, 55, 260–280.

Ornaghi, C. (2009). Mergers and innovation in big pharma. *International Journal of Industrial Organization*, 27(1), 70–79.

Pfeffer, J., & Salancik, G. (2003). *The External Control of Organizations: A Resource Dependence Perspective*. Stanford, CA: Stanford University Press.

Porrini, P. (2004). Can a previous alliance between an acquirer and a target affect acquisition performance? *Journal of Management*, 30(4), 545–562.

Renneboog, L., & Vansteenkiste, C. (2019). Failure and success in mergers and acquisitions. *Journal of Corporate Finance*, 58, 650–699.

Rogan, M., & Greve, H. (2015). Resource dependence dynamics: partner reactions to mergers. *Organization Science*, 26(1), 239–255.

Roll, R. (1986). The hubris hypothesis of corporate takeovers. *Journal of Business*, 59, 197–216.

Rumelt, R. (1995). Inertia and transformation. In C. A. Montgomery (ed.), *Resource-based and Evolutionary Theories of the Firm: Towards a Synthesis* (pp. 101–132). Boston, MA: Springer.

Samimi, M., Cortes, A., Anderson, M., & Herrmann, P. (2022). What is strategic leadership? Developing a framework for future research. *The Leadership Quarterly*, 33(3), 101353.

Sanders, W. (2001). Behavioral responses of CEOs to stock ownership and stock option pay. *Academy of Management Journal*, 44(3), 477–492.

Santulli, R., Gallucci, C., Torchia, M., & Calabrò, A. (2022). Family managers' propensity towards mergers and acquisitions: the role of performance feedback. *Journal of Small Business and Enterprise Development*, 29(2), 293–310.

Shi, W., & Prescott, J. (2011). Sequence patterns of firms' acquisition and alliance behaviour and their performance implications. *Journal of Management Studies*, 48(5), 1044–1070.

Shi, W., Sun, J., & Prescott, J. (2012). A temporal perspective of merger and acquisition and strategic alliance initiatives: review and future direction. *Journal of Management*, 38(1), 164–209.

Sirmon, D., Hitt, M., & Ireland, R. (2007). Managing firm resources in dynamic environments to create value: looking inside the black box. *Academy of Management Review*, 32(1), 273–292.

Sirower, M. (1997). *The Synergy Trap: How Companies Lose the Acquisition Game*. New York: Simon and Schuster.

Sleesman, D., Conlon, D., McNamara, G., & Miles, J. (2012). Cleaning up the big muddy: a meta-analytic review of the determinants of escalation of commitment. *Academy of Management Journal*, 55(3), 541–562.

Strike, V., Berrone, P., Sapp, S., & Congiu, L. (2015). A socioemotional wealth approach to CEO career horizons in family firms. *Journal of Management Studies*, 52(4), 555–583.

Teece, D. (2007). Explicating dynamic capabilities: the nature and microfoundations of (sustainable) enterprise performance. *Strategic Management Journal*, 28(13), 1319–1350.

Trigeorgis, L. (1996). *Real Options: Managerial Flexibility and Strategy in Resource Allocation*. Cambridge, MA: MIT Press.

Wang, G., Holmes, R., Oh, I., & Zhu, W. (2016). Do CEOs matter to firm strategic actions and firm performance? A meta-analytic investigation based on upper echelons theory. *Personnel Psychology*, 69(4), 775–862.

Wang, Y., & Yin, S. (2018). CEO educational background and acquisition targets selection. *Journal of Corporate Finance*, 52, 238–259.

Welch, X., Pavićević, S., Keil, T., & Laamanen, T. (2020). The pre-deal phase of mergers and acquisitions: a review and research agenda. *Journal of Management*, 46(6), 843–878.

Williamson, O. (1975). *Markets and Hierarchies: Analysis and Antitrust Implication: A Study of the Economics of Internal Organization*. New York: The Free Press.

Wiseman, R., & Gomez-Mejia, L. (1998). A behavioral agency model of managerial risk taking. *Academy of Management Review*, 23(1), 133–153.

Yang, G., Bai, X., & Yang, S. (2021). Chief executive officer proactive personality and acquisitions: a fuzzy set qualitative comparative analysis of China's listed firms. *Frontiers in Psychology*, 12. https://www.frontiersin.org/articles/10.3389/fpsyg.2021.703678.

Zhou, B., Dutta, S., & Zhu, P. (2020). CEO tenure and mergers and acquisitions. *Finance Research Letters*, 34, 101277.

4 The impact of analysts on acquirer stock price volatility

Kyeong-Seop Choi

Introduction

Research tends to focus on whether acquisitions create synergy (e.g., Barkema and Schijven, 2008; Haleblian et al., 2009; Graebner et al., 2017; Welch et al., 2020), and not on the impacts of market information around acquisition announcements (Schijven and Hitt, 2012). Information serves as a universal medium connecting economic agents and it plays a role in driving the market's function and growth. Further, information is the cornerstone of mutual trust that is needed to establish and nurture an efficient market. If information is unavailable or distorted, it can lead to market failures (Akerlof, 1978). Advances in information technology have corresponded to an exponential growth in the availability of information. The amount of data available has facilitated a role for financial analysts as intermediaries that produce and share information on covered companies.

Analysts actively engage in earnings conference calls, where they interact with CEOs and top executives, asking questions and providing insights. Additionally, they conduct on-site visits to company facilities for in-depth research and assist institutional clients in executing large-scale block securities transactions. Further, information from analysts (i.e., earnings forecasts and offer stock recommendations) is often communicated by media. Consequently, it is reasonable to expect that analyst coverage will influence the information environment surrounding an acquisition. I explore information surrounding acquisition announcements in the U.S. stock markets with a focus on the influence of securities analysts.

Except for serial acquirers, acquisitions are rare events in a firm's life cycle that can significantly influence its performance (e.g., Moeller, Schlingemann and Stulz, 2005). Due to the lack of procedural transparency in acquisitions, outside investors lack information before deals are officially announced, or acquisition announcements present "new" information about a firm and its prospects (McWilliams and Siegel, 1997). Prior research has identified that investors resort to rumors that are most likely distorted (Ahern and Sosyura, 2015; Han and Yang, 2013) or intentionally manipulated to increase the insider's deal power (Clarkson, Joyce and Tutticci, 2006; Indjejikian, Lu and Yang, 2014; Schmidt, 2020). However, this overlooks how investors use information from analysts, who may cover acquirer or target firms (Becher, Cohn and Juergens, 2015).

Analysts serve as information intermediaries with a monitoring function. Therefore, their coverage enhances transparency, and they convey signals to investors (Crawford, Roulstone and So, 2012; Demiroglu and Ryngaert, 2010; Kelly and Ljungqvist, 2012; Mola, Rau and Khorana, 2013). Analysts tend to cover firms whose values are difficult to estimate that have a high ratio of intangible assets or insufficient evaluation records made by the preceding analysts (Barth, Kasznik and McNichols, 2001; Crawford et al., 2012). Large analyst forecast errors, perceived as earnings surprises by the market, are widely recognized as an information shock across various financial and managerial dimensions (Asquith, Mikhail and Au, 2005; Clement and Tse, 2003; Loh and Stulz, 2018). Despite rich documentation corroborating analysts as information providers, research on the analysts' role in acquisitions remains limited.

To my knowledge, only Tehranian, Zhao and Zhu (2014) predict an acquirer firm's post-acquisition performance using target firm analysts' coverage decisions after their firms are delisted. While the analysts' role in pre-acquisition dynamics is neglected (Becher et al., 2015), analyst monitoring entails both positive and negative consequences. Analyst coverage benefits financial reporting integrity, employee welfare, and corporate reputation (Bradley, Mao and Zhang, 2022; Yu, 2008). Still, negative consequences of analyst coverage relate to firms potentially catering to analysts to a firm's long-term detriment. For example, covered firms are pressured to abandon investments that are not profitable for investors, particularly those that are long-term, costly, and risky. For example, investors are known to resist R&D investments by firms (Gentry and Shen, 2013; Guo, Pérez-Castrillo and Toldrà-Simats, 2019; He and Tian, 2013). Though analyst coverage influences internal capital allocation (Busenbark et al., 2022) and corporate social performance (Luo et al., 2015; Qian, Lu and Yu, 2019), their consequences may be benign. For example, research suggests that R&D reduction pressured by analysts can encourage more efficient R&D investments, such as acquisition of an R&D firm or creation of a corporate venture capital (Guo et al., 2019).

Building on prior research, I argue that an acquirer or target firm with analyst coverage is likely to possess greater pre-acquisition market recognition and status compared to a firm lacking such coverage. Further, given the substantial impact of an acquisition on the involved firms and markets, providing investors with ready access to information becomes crucial for making informed investment decisions. Analysts serve as important intermediaries in conveying information about potential acquisition prospects and act as monitors overseeing the acquisition processes. Consequently, it is probable that analyst coverage will enhance the market value of an acquirer. Whether through information dissemination or supervision, firms with extensive analyst coverage are expected to attract more investors and generate a stronger market response (through the media, newspapers, magazines, and word of mouth) surrounding acquisition announcements.

My primary contribution involves demonstrating that investor reactions to acquisition announcements are influenced by analyst coverage. Drawing on information economics, analyst coverage can diminish information asymmetry for investors. In the specific context of acquisitions involving both the acquirer and the target, analysts play a crucial role in providing insight into the acquisition's strategy and the potential synergies that could enhance acquisition performance. Given that acquirers usually have resource surplus while the targets may face resource constraints, the success of an acquisition heavily depends on the transparency of information related to the target firms. Therefore, analyst coverage of a target firm can serve as a signal to investors regarding the quality of decision-making by top executives. Presumably, the most significant reduction in information asymmetry occurs when there is analyst coverage for both the acquirer and the target firm. However, I only find a substantial effect for analyst coverage of target firms.

Hypothesis development

Information economics links analyst coverage at acquisition announcement and information or a signal provided to investors that is incorporated into abnormal returns. In reviewing the role of analysts, the effect extends beyond coverage of acquiring firms. Specifically, there are three categories of analysts involved in an acquisition: acquirer firm analysts, target firm analysts, and analysts covering both firms. Overlapping coverage provides insights comparable to related industry classification or geographic proximity (Ali and Hirshleifer, 2020; Huang et al., 2022; Parsons, Sabbatucci and Titman, 2020). Still, each group of analysts is assumed to share two common interests: (1) enhancing information transparency for the firms they cover, and (2) advancing their own professional careers (Ali and Hirshleifer, 2020; Becher et al., 2015; Hong, Kubik and Solomon, 2000; Tehranian et al., 2014). For example, target firm analysts likely initiate coverage of an acquirer if they think it will perform well (due to career concerns), signaling an acquirer's long-term performance (Tehranian et al., 2014). When acquirer or target analysts provide a significantly more favorable assessment of the acquirer's value compared to the target's value, it often results in a successful deal completion (Becher et al., 2015). In contrast, less favorable assessment of the acquirer as compared to the target leads to deal dissolution (Becher et al., 2015). As illustrated in Figure 4.1, I anticipate that these three groups of analysts for acquirer–target pairs have incrementally significant effects on investor reactions. I also consider the moderating effect of cross-border acquisitions, as they have greater information asymmetry (Boeh, 2011).

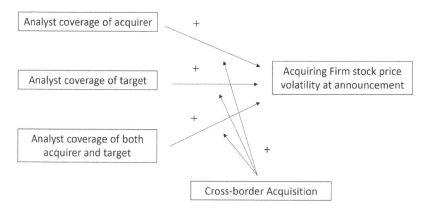

Figure 4.1   Hypothesized framework

Acquirer analyst

When they cover a firm, analysts research and report information (Bradley, Gokkaya and Liu, 2017; Crawford et al., 2012; Kelly and Ljungqvist, 2012; Mola et al., 2013). At acquisition announcement, analyst-covered firms are most likely to attract investor attention not merely for coverage premium, but also for quality information provided by the analysts. Coverage premium is not anything replaceable by firm size. Acquirer or relative firm size tends to have a negative impact on acquisition likelihood and post-acquisition performance (Heeley, King and Covin, 2006; Tehranian et al., 2014). Also, firm size has a negative influence on abnormal return volatility. These findings imply that coverage premium is related to informational superiority.

Prior research shows analysts are likely to write positive evaluations and rarely issue negative recommendations for their firms (Michaely and Womack, 1999; Morgan and Stocken, 2003). This bias is not always harmful, but often creates a "virtuous circle" in which firms strive to meet the official expectations (Guo et al., 2019; Kasznik and McNichols, 2002; McVay, Nagar and Tang, 2006). Even if analysts produce negative evaluations and recommendations, firms would typically take actions to address or mitigate concerns. As a result, attention garnered by covered firms is not solely a result of informational transparency, but also of the performance feedback provided by analysts. This heightened attention can lead to either positive or negative movements in stock prices, depending on the nature of the information. Aside from the information's quality as being positive or negative, the measure of *informativeness* (i.e., the magnitude of information), can be assessed by considering the *variance* of stock returns around pivotal information events. If analyst coverage increases information transparency and stimulates both the firm and the market through public performance feedback, it is likely to increase the magnitude of the firm's return volatility. Thus, I predict:

Hypothesis 1: Acquirer analyst coverage increases the acquirer firm's abnormal return volatility at acquisition announcements.

Target analyst

Previous research documents the importance of target firm analysts in the acquisition completions (Becher et al., 2015) and post-acquisition performance (Tehranian et al., 2014). Often, acquirer firms tend to be larger, profitable, and financially affluent, whereas target firms are smaller and may be financially constrained. In view of analysts as monitoring functionaries, target firm coverage convinces investors to think that analysts are more informed about firms receiving acquisition bids. As information intermediaries, target firm analysts will create a more transparent information environment surrounding the focal acquisition processes for investors. Considering that analyst coverage renders information around target firms more transparent, its impact can go in both directions. When the information conveys positive news, investors will tend to buy shares, or sell them when there is negative news. Regardless of whether the information content is positive or negative, analyst coverage of a target firm will increase return volatility. Further, the influence of target firm analysts on stock market reactions is expected to be more substantial than that of acquirer firm analysts, as information about a target is more salient at acquisition announcement.

Hypothesis 2: The impact of target firm coverage on the acquirer firm's abnormal return volatility at acquisition announcements will be significantly larger than the impact of acquirer firm coverage.

Shared analyst

A single analyst can also cover both an acquirer and target firm simultaneously. In such cases, overlapping coverage can offer more comprehensive information, contributing to changes in an acquirer's stock price. The overlap in coverage serves as a clear signal that the information originates from the coordinated efforts of adept analysts focusing on both the acquirer and target, instilling confidence in investors. For instance, Ali and Hirshleifer (2020) find that firms with shared coverage operate within the same industry, diminishing ambiguity for firms, analysts, and investors when one firm acquires another in the same industry.

Hypothesis 3: The impact of overlapping coverage of both acquirer and target firms on the acquirer firm's abnormal return volatility at acquisition announcements will be significantly more pronounced than the impact of target firm coverage alone.

Cross-border acquisitions

Barriers to cross-border acquisitions have been extensively documented (e.g., Dikova, Sahib and Van Witteloostuijn, 2010; Reus and Lamont, 2009). Since 2003, different countries' application of International Financial Reporting Standards and heterogeneous transition periods in accounting systems rendered a financial analysis of a foreign firm especially difficult (Daske et al., 2008). Even if many entry barriers to international markets have dropped, securities laws make strong differences between countries (Bonetti, Duro and Ormazabal, 2020; Khurana and Wang, 2019; Stulz, 2009). If the target is located outside the U.S.A., analysts will have difficulties either monitoring the firm or delivering information about it to the U.S. markets. Thus, a previously strong positive impact of shared and target firm analysts on the acquirer return volatility will be impaired by the targets being foreign.

Hypothesis 4: The impact of shared and target firm analysts on the acquirer firm's abnormal return volatility at acquisition announcements will significantly be reduced when the targets are foreign firms.

Method

Acquirer firms that are not publicly listed in the U.S.A. are excluded to enable collecting stock price information, but private and international targets are included. Raw data for U.S. stock prices, acquisitions, and firm financials are obtained from the databases CRSP, SDC Platinum, and Compustat North America, respectively. Global stock prices and firm financials are pooled from Compustat Global, and I/B/E/S was the source of U.S. and international analysts. Macroeconomic country statistics are collected from the official website of the World Bank. The sample includes 21,582 acquisitions by the U.S. acquirers over 1996-2019, and target firms are across 77 countries, including the U.S.A.

Since the research design is to test the impact of analyst coverage on market reaction to a focal U.S. acquirer firm at acquisition announcement, I construct a proxy for market reaction as abnormal return (*CAR*) volatility over the three-day window (−1,+1) around the announcement (day=0). Above all, abnormal returns are calculated as the (positive or negative) difference between actual and expected returns.

Expected returns are estimated by running the following regression of CAPM for each firm over the window (−120,−21) and obtaining the firm-specific alpha (α) and beta (β).

Return is the actual return of a firm (i) on a day (t) over the window (−120,−21). Market return is the value-weighted average return across the country on a day (t). The resulting coefficients alpha (α) and beta (β) are the intercept and sensitivity to market returns that are unique to a focal firm (i). Applying α, β, and market return from the window (−1,+1) provides the *expected* return of a focal firm on the day of interest. Thus, the actual return less (constructed) expected return serves as the abnormal return. Abnormal return *volatility* is the average of the squared abnormal returns over the window designated. While abnormal return volatility is tested as the dependent variable, some independent variables are log-transformed.

To increase validity, target firm country and year fixed effects, as well as key dyadic controls such as acquirer-target industry relatedness (King et al., 2021), are included in the analysis. Endogeneity concerns only surface as to whether statistical significance is due to other latent factors, not analyst coverage. If analysts choose to cover a focal firm only based on foreknowledge of its prospects, analyst coverage may be spurious, but the firm's prospects are real. A series of articles have done research to circumvent these concerns by using the cases of brokerage house mergers or shutdowns as an exogeneous shock to analysts' coverage decisions (Hong and Kacperczyk, 2010; Kelly and Ljungqvist, 2012; Qian et al., 2019). In unreported analysis, I mitigate this issue by performing robustness tests that eliminate recent coverage initiation around acquisition announcements.

Results

Since acquirer, target, and overlapping analysts are severely skewed in distribution, they are log-transformed. Large values such as deal amounts, acquirer, and target firm market capitalization are also log-transformed. Numerically discontinuous values are log-transformed (percentage of cash payment is either 0, 50, or 100). Because acquirer, target, and overlapping analysts are highly correlated, I test those variables of interest individually. Acquirer firm analysts' average days of focal firm coverage (*Acq_analy_exper*) and mean number of collective coverage (*Acq_firm_cover*) are highly correlated. Still, I run a regression including both variables, since they are controls of lesser interest.

Results for six regression models are reported in Table 4.1, and I first discuss significant control variables. The size of deal value (*Deal_value*), as well as acquirer and target firm's market-to-book ratios (*Acq_MBt-1*, *Targ_MBt-1*), increase abnormal return volatility at acquisition announcement (−1,+1). *Deal_value*, *Acq_MBt-1*, and *Targ_MBt-1* also provide information that increases an acquirer's stock price volatility. Investors may perceive an announcement of a larger deal between acquirer and target growth firms as high risk–high return investment opportunities. These investment opportunities will attract more speculative investors, and lead risk-averse investors to sell. In other words, there will be more volatility in stock returns surrounding the announcement days.

Acquirer and target firm's market capitalization (*Acq_mkt_capt-1*, *Targ_mkt_capt-1*) and acquirer firm's return on assets (*Acq_ROAt-1*) reduce abnormal return volatility at announcements. These values indicate the firm's financial and operational slack in current standing. Investors are likely to perceive acquisition announcements between value firms with larger *Acq_mkt_capt-1*, *Targ_mkt_capt-1*, and *Acq_ROAt-1* as low risk–low return investment opportunities associated with lower price volatility. Consistent with prior research on debt's disciplining effect on managerial opportunism

Table 4.1   Analyst influence at acquisition announcement

Dependent variable:	Abnormal return volatility (−1,+1)					
	(1)	(2)	(3)	(4)	(5)	(6)
Acq_analyst$t$-1	0.005 (1.09)			0.005 (1.21)		
Targ_analyst$t$-1		0.011** (1.99)			0.013** (2.12)	
Ovlp_analyst$t$-1			0.014* (1.91)			0.014* (1.83)
Deal_value	0.043*** (17.66)	0.043*** (17.27)	0.043*** (17.55)	0.043*** (17.65)	0.043*** (17.26)	0.043*** (17.54)
Acq_mkt_cap$t$-1	−0.069*** (−25.01)	−0.069*** (−24.92)	−0.069*** (−24.87)	−0.069*** (−25.01)	−0.069*** (−24.91)	−0.069*** (−24.86)
Targ_mkt_cap$t$-1	−0.002*** (−3.02)	−0.002*** (−3.09)	−0.002*** (−2.93)	−0.002*** (−3.03)	−0.002*** (−3.09)	−0.002*** (−2.93)
Acq_lev$t$-1	−0.035** (−2.22)	−0.035** (−2.18)	−0.035** (−2.22)	−0.035** (−2.21)	−0.035** (−2.17)	−0.035** (−2.22)
Targ_lev$t$-1	−0.010 (−0.29)	−0.015 (−0.41)	−0.015 (−0.43)	−0.011 (−0.30)	−0.016 (−0.45)	−0.015 (−0.41)
Acq_MBt-1	0.033*** (14.04)	0.033*** (14.04)	0.033*** (14.01)	0.033*** (14.04)	0.033*** (14.04)	0.033*** (14.01)
Targ_MBt-1	0.018** (2.42)	0.018** (2.33)	0.019** (2.53)	0.018** (2.42)	0.018** (2.33)	0.019** (2.53)

Dependent variable:	Abnormal return volatility (−1,+1)					
	(1)	(2)	(3)	(4)	(5)	(6)
Acq_ROAt-1	−0.438*** (−11.76)	−0.438*** (−11.75)	−0.438*** (−11.76)	−0.438*** (−11.76)	−0.438*** (−11.75)	−0.438*** (−11.76)
Targ_ROAt-1	0.022 (0.59)	0.020 (0.53)	0.020 (0.52)	0.023 (0.60)	0.021 (0.54)	0.020 (0.52)
Acq_equity_issue$t$-1	−0.019 (−0.62)	−0.019 (−0.62)	−0.019 (−0.62)	−0.019 (−0.61)	−0.019 (−0.62)	−0.019 (−0.62)
Acq_analy_exper$t$-1	−0.001 (−0.65)	−0.001 (−0.66)	−0.001 (−0.66)	−0.001 (−0.65)	−0.001 (−0.66)	−0.001 (−0.66)
Acq_revis_sig$t$-1	0.010** (2.17)	0.010** (2.16)	0.010** (2.17)	0.010** (2.17)	0.010** (2.17)	0.010** (2.17)
Acq_firm_cover$t$-1	−0.007 (−1.53)	−0.007 (−1.55)	−0.007 (−1.53)	−0.007 (−1.53)	−0.007 (−1.55)	−0.007 (−1.53)
Cross_border	0.063 (0.60)	0.064 (0.61)	0.064 (0.61)	0.064 (0.61)	0.065 (0.62)	0.063 (0.60)
Acq_mna_exper	−0.019*** (−4.96)	−0.019*** (−4.96)	−0.019*** (−4.92)	−0.019*** (−4.96)	−0.019*** (−4.96)	−0.019*** (−4.92)
Paid_cash	−0.002 (−1.45)	−0.002 (−1.45)	−0.002 (−1.38)	−0.002 (−1.43)	−0.002 (−1.42)	−0.002 (−1.38)
Ind_distance	−0.013** (−2.39)	−0.013** (−2.42)	−0.013** (−2.43)	−0.013** (−2.40)	−0.013** (−2.44)	−0.013** (−2.43)
Friendly_deal	0.045** (2.40)	0.048** (2.52)	0.046** (2.45)	0.044** (2.35)	0.047** (2.45)	0.046** (2.46)

Dependent variable:	Abnormal return volatility $(-1,+1)$					
	(1)	(2)	(3)	(4)	(5)	(6)
Targ_GDP_pc	0.002 (0.08)	0.003 (0.09)	0.003 (0.10)	0.003 (0.09)	0.003 (0.10)	0.003 (0.09)
Acq_analyst$t$-1 × Cross-border				-0.005 (-0.72)		
Targ_analyst$t$-1 × Cross-border					-0.010 (-0.92)	
Ovlp_analyst$t$-1 × Cross-border						0.015 (0.51)
Target country FE	Yes	Yes	Yes	Yes	Yes	Yes
Year FE	Yes	Yes	Yes	Yes	Yes	Yes
Adj. R-Sq.	0.1359	0.1360	0.1359	0.1359	0.1360	0.1359
Observations	23043	23043	23043	23043	23043	23043

Note: * p < .05; ** p < .01; ** p < .001.

(Hitt et al., 1991; Bergh, 1997; King et al., 2021), the acquirer firm's high leverage reduces abnormal return volatility at acquisition announcements. Target firm's leverage is irrelevant to the acquirer's return volatility.

Independent variables of interest include the number of analysts (i.e., coverage) by acquirer, target, and the overlap between them. Before discussing their results, I address analyst characteristics as controls. The natural logarithm of the rolling average number of coverage days across analysts covering an acquirer firm at a focal announcement (*Acq_analy_expert-1*) mitigates abnormal return volatility. A reasonable interpretation is that investors perceive the analysts' amount of experience covering a focal firm as a criterion to (dis) trust their reports about it. In addition, a longer history of coverage alludes to stability and prominence of the firm for investors. Investors will perceive investment in it as a low risk–low return opportunity. The mean value of dramatic forecast revisions among analysts (*Acq_revis_sigt-1*) increases abnormal return volatility around acquisition announcements, as inaccurate earnings forecasts imply high risk–high return opportunities from a firm (Malloy, 2005). In creating the sample, I defined firm coverage as the number of firms an analyst covers in a given year. On the firm level, an acquirer can have analysts with various firm coverages. The firm-year mean value of firm coverage across analysts (*Acq_firm_covert-1*) reduces abnormal return volatility. This implies that an acquirer firm covered by analysts who, in turn, cover multiple other firms simultaneously—presumably analysts who are hired by large brokerage houses—provides investors with a signal of stability and renown among others. Again, investors will consider the investment as safe but not rewarding in high returns.

Next, I share results for acquiring firm controls. Acquirer acquisition experience from the past three years (*Acq_mna_exper*) and larger cash payments in deals (*Paid_cash*) report a negative impact on abnormal return volatility (*Paid_cash* at 10% sig. levels). These results are consistent with prior research documenting that an acquirer's past acquisition experiences, as well as higher ratios of cash payments in deals, increase performance on announcements and in post-acquisitions (Franks, Harris and Titman, 1991; Haleblian and Finkelstein, 1999; King et al., 2021). Results imply that acquisition experiences and cash payments provide a signal of a smooth and successful deal, which is unattractive for speculative investors but, for risk-averse investors, creates no motives to cash out. Thus, they reduce abnormal return volatility.

Finally, I report the results on three different kinds of analyst coverage associated to test the hypotheses. Control variables proxy the information content related to firm size, status, and financial and operational slack that may influence stock returns. Analyst coverage implies both human-generated quality information and channels to disseminate it. If analyst coverage increases abnormal return volatility, I interpret it as coverage enhancing information efficiency around the announcements.

In Models (1) and (2) of Table 4.1, acquirer firm coverage (*Acq_analystt-1*) is not significant and Hypothesis 1 does not receive support. However, target firm analysts (*Targ_analystt-1*) significantly increase abnormal return volatility, supporting Hypothesis 2. Consistent with Tehranian et al. (2014), target firm analysts are the more agile players at information exchange because, when an acquisition fails, the damage will be greater on target firms and the reputation of target firm analysts (Mikhail, Walther and Willis, 1999; Renneboog and Vansteenkiste, 2019). In Model (3), the overlapping coverage between acquirer and target firms (*Ovlp_analystt-1*) is statistically significant and positive, but it has a slightly smaller t-statistic ($t=1.96$) than that of *Targ_analystt-1* ($t=2.04$), but the slope for *Ovlp_analystt-1* is larger. Models 2 and 3 also do not display significant differences in R-squared, leading us to conclude Hypothesis 3 is not supported.

In all six models of Table 4.1, cross-border acquisitions (*Cross_border*) do not impact abnormal return volatility significantly. Nor do the interactions between analyst coverage and cross-border acquisitions deliver any significant coefficients. Thus, Hypothesis 4 is not supported. Nevertheless, with the interaction terms included, *Ovlp_analystt-1* has a reduced slope and t-statistic, whereas *Targ_analystt-1* has them increased. This corroborates target firm analysts play a role in disseminating information on acquisitions.

Discussion

I develop and test information economic expectations for analysts reducing information asymmetry for investors at acquisition announcement. Controls are consistent with information economic expectations of acquiring and target firm characteristics signaling decision quality of acquiring firm managers and levels of risk. While analyst coverage of an acquiring firm whether alone or combined with target analyst coverage is not a significant predictor of stock price volatility at acquisition announcement, target firm analyst coverage is significantly associated with stock price volatility. This suggests that investors in an acquiring firm are more sensitive to information about targets, as target firm information tends to be less available (e.g., private firms). Next, additional implications for research and practice are summarized.

Research implications

The overarching implication of my research is that analysts play a vital role in enhancing the efficiency of stock market pricing. Uncertainty associated with acquisitions tends to dampen acquirer stock price volatility, as investors deal with the ambiguity of a deal's success. However, as analysts furnish information on the acquiring and target firms they cover, investors can reassess their investment decisions faster, making acquiring firm stock prices more volatile due to increased buying and selling activity. The most significant impact on stock price volatility occurs when a target firm is covered because it provides greater information for evaluating the performance implications of acquiring a target. This underscores the importance of the target firm in resolving uncertainties surrounding acquisitions. Still, an unresolved issue persists regarding the potential conflict of interest and systematic bias in analysts' research and forecasts, warranting additional research on analysts and their impact on firms. Another fruitful avenue for research is examining the textual content of analyst recommendations and earnings conference calls to examine information conveyed to investors.

I also confirm that cross-border acquisitions remain challenging due to geographic distance, legal, and cultural differences between countries. Future research focused on overcoming cross-border barriers in acquisitions within the context of information technology represents a promising avenue for both academic scholarship and practical insights. Beyond analyst coverage, acquirers with more internationally diverse corporate boards may have advantages in identifying, completing, and integrating target firms.

Manager implications

A clear implication to managers of firms is that analyst coverage decreases information asymmetry with investors. For managers of acquiring firms, stronger investor reactions proxied by price volatility results when there is less uncertainty about a target firm. This implies that analyst coverage of target firms signals that acquiring firm managers have better information about a target firm, and it enables investors to better assess implications from acquiring a target.

Limitations and future research

All research has limitations, and I discuss some research design trade-offs. First, the U.S.A. is arguably among the most efficient stock markets in the world. As a result, it is a conservative test of the effect of analysts on investor reactions to acquisition announcements. Still, analyst coverage involves small numbers, and it may be hard to observe the impact of analysts even if they exist. Further, my focus on the U.S.A. continues a trend of most acquisition research focusing on locations where information is available. While this is mitigated by including private and cross-border targets, research continues to focus on the minority of acquisitions where information is observable. It is like only studying the visible portion of an iceberg. Still, we limit endogeneity concerns, as (generally) only public firms have analyst coverage. Additionally, analysts may impact more than acquirer stock price volatility, and research needs to consider additional effects including trading volume. Overall, the application of information economics to acquisition research shows that analysts provide information on covered firms to reduce information asymmetry, and the impact is greatest when target firms are covered by analysts.

References

Ahern, K., & Sosyura, D. (2015). Rumor has it: sensationalism in financial media. *Review of Financial Studies*, 28(7), 2050–2093.

Akerlof, G. (1978). The market for "lemons": quality uncertainty and the market mechanism. In *Uncertainty in Economics* (pp. 235–251). Academic Press.

Ali, U., & Hirshleifer, D. (2020). Shared analyst coverage: unifying momentum spillover effects. *Journal of Financial Economics*, 136(3), 649–675.

Asquith, P., Mikhail, M., & Au, A. (2005). Information content of equity analyst reports. *Journal of Financial Economics*, 75(2), 245–282.

Barkema, H., & Schijven, M. (2008). How do firms learn to make acquisitions? A review of past research and an agenda for the future. *Journal of Management*, 34(3), 594–634.

Barth, M., Kasznik, R., & McNichols, M. (2001). Analyst coverage and intangible assets. *Journal of Accounting Research*, 39(1), 1–34.

Becher, D., Cohn, J., & Juergens, J. (2015). Do stock analysts influence merger completion? An examination of postmerger announcement recommendations. *Management Science*, 61(10), 2430–2448.

Bergh, D. (1997). Predicting divestiture of unrelated acquisitions: an integrative model of ex ante conditions. *Strategic Management Journal*, 18(9), 715–731.

Boeh, K. (2011). Contracting costs and information asymmetry reduction in cross-border M&A. *Journal of Management Studies*, 48(3), 567–590.

Bonetti, P., Duro, M., & Ormazabal, G. (2020). Disclosure regulation and corporate acquisitions. *Journal of Accounting Research*, 58(1), 55–103.

Bradley, D., Gokkaya, S., & Liu, X. (2017). Before an analyst becomes an analyst: does industry experience matter? *Journal of Finance*, 72(2), 751–792.

Bradley, D., Mao, C., & Zhang, C. (2022). Does analyst coverage affect workplace safety? *Management Science*, 68(5), 3464–3487.

Busenbark, J., Semadeni, M., Arrfelt, M., & Withers, M. (2022). Corporate-level influences on internal capital allocation: the role of financial analyst performance projections. *Strategic Management Journal*, 43(1), 180–209.

Clarkson, P., Joyce, D., & Tutticci, I. (2006). Market reaction to takeover rumour in internet discussion sites. *Accounting & Finance*, 46(1), 31–52.

Clement, M., & Tse, S. (2003). Do investors respond to analysts' forecast revisions as if forecast accuracy is all that matters? *Accounting Review*, 78(1), 227–249.

Crawford, S., Roulstone, D., & So, E. (2012). Analyst initiations of coverage and stock return synchronicity. *Accounting Review*, 87(5), 1527–1553.

Daske, H., Hail, L., Leuz, C., & Verdi, R. (2008). Mandatory IFRS reporting around the world: early evidence on the economic consequences. *Journal of Accounting Research*, 46(5), 1085–1142.

Demiroglu, C., & Ryngaert, M. (2010). The first analyst coverage of neglected stocks. *Financial Management*, 39(2), 555–584.

Dikova, D., Sahib, P., & Van Witteloostuijn, A. (2010). Cross-border acquisition abandonment and completion: the effect of institutional differences and organizational learning in the international business service industry, 1981–2001. *Journal of International Business Studies*, 41, 223–245.

Franks, J., Harris, R., & Titman, S. (1991). The postmerger share-price performance of acquiring firms. *Journal of Financial Economics*, 29(1), 81–96.

Gentry, R., & Shen, W. (2013). The impacts of performance relative to analyst forecasts and analyst coverage on firm R&D intensity. *Strategic Management Journal*, 34(1), 121–130.

Graebner, M., Heimeriks, K., Huy, Q., & Vaara, E. (2017). The process of postmerger integration: a review and agenda for future research. *Academy of Management Annals*, 11(1), 1–32.

Guo, B., Pérez-Castrillo, D., & Toldrà-Simats, A. (2019). Firms' innovation strategy under the shadow of analyst coverage. *Journal of Financial Economics*, 131(2), 456–483.

Haleblian, J., & Finkelstein, S. (1999). The influence of organizational acquisition experience on acquisition performance: a behavioral learning perspective. *Administrative Science Quarterly*, 44(1), 29–56.

Haleblian, J., Devers, C. E., McNamara, G., Carpenter, M., & Davison, R. (2009). Taking stock of what we know about mergers and acquisitions: a review and research agenda. *Journal of Management*, 35(3), 469–502.

Han, B., & Yang, L. (2013). Social networks, information acquisition, and asset prices. *Management Science*, 59(6), 1444–1457.

He, J., & Tian, X. (2013). The dark side of analyst coverage: the case of innovation. *Journal of Financial Economics*, 109(3), 856–878.

Heeley, M., King, D., & Covin, J. (2006). Effects of firm R&D investment and environment on acquisition likelihood. *Journal of Management Studies*, 43(7), 1513–1535.

Hitt, M., Hoskisson, R., Ireland, R., & Harrison, J. (1991). Effects of acquisitions on R&D inputs and outputs. *Academy of Management Journal*, 34(3), 693–706.

Hong, H., & Kacperczyk, M. (2010). Competition and bias. *Quarterly Journal of Economics*, 125(4), 1683–1725.

Hong, H., Kubik, J., & Solomon, A. (2000). Security analysts' career concerns and herding of earnings forecasts. *Rand Journal of Economics*, 31(1), 121–144.

Huang, S., Lee, C., Song, Y., & Xiang, H. (2022). A frog in every pan: information discreteness and the lead-lag returns puzzle. *Journal of Financial Economics*, 145(2), 83–102.

Indjejikian, R., Lu, H., & Yang, L. (2014). Rational information leakage. *Management Science*, 60(11), 2762–2775.

Kasznik, R., & McNichols, M. (2002). Does meeting earnings expectations matter? Evidence from analyst forecast revisions and share prices. *Journal of Accounting Research*, 40(3), 727–759.

Kelly, B., & Ljungqvist, A. (2012). Testing asymmetric-information asset pricing models. *Review of Financial Studies*, 25(5), 1366–1413.

Khurana, I., & Wang, W. (2019). International mergers and acquisitions laws, the market for corporate control, and accounting conservatism. *Journal of Accounting Research*, 57(1), 241–290.

King, D., Wang, G., Samimi, M., & Cortes, A. (2021). A meta-analytic integration of acquisition performance prediction. *Journal of Management Studies*, 58(5), 1198–1236.

Loh, R., & Stulz, R. (2018). Is sell-side research more valuable in bad times? *Journal of Finance*, 73(3), 959–1013.

Luo, X., Wang, H., Raithel, S., & Zheng, Q. (2015). Corporate social performance, analyst stock recommendations, and firm future returns. *Strategic Management Journal*, 36(1), 123–136.

Malloy, C. (2005). The geography of equity analysis. *Journal of Finance*, 60(2), 719–755.

McVay, S., Nagar, V., & Tang, V. (2006). Trading incentives to meet the analyst forecast. *Review of Accounting Studies*, 11, 575–598.

McWilliams, A., & Siegel, D. (1997). Event studies in management research: theoretical and empirical issues. *Academy of Management Journal*, 40(3), 626–657.

Michaely, R., & Womack, K. (1999). Conflict of interest and the credibility of underwriter analyst recommendations. *Review of Financial Studies*, 12(4), 653–686.

Mikhail, M., Walther, B., & Willis, R. (1999). Does forecast accuracy matter to security analysts? *Accounting Review*, 74(2), 185–200.

Moeller, S., Schlingemann, F., & Stulz, R. (2005). Wealth destruction on a massive scale? A study of acquiring-firm returns in the recent merger wave. *Journal of Finance*, 60(2), 757–782.

Mola, S., Rau, P., & Khorana, A. (2013). Is there life after the complete loss of analyst coverage? *Accounting Review*, 88(2), 667–705.

Morgan, J., & Stocken, P. (2003). An analysis of stock recommendations. *RAND Journal of Economics*, 34(1), 183–203.

Parsons, C., Sabbatucci, R., & Titman, S. (2020). Geographic lead-lag effects. *Review of Financial Studies*, 33(10), 4721–4770.

Qian, C., Lu, L., & Yu, Y. (2019). Financial analyst coverage and corporate social performance: evidence from natural experiments. *Strategic Management Journal*, 40(13), 2271–2286.

Renneboog, L., & Vansteenkiste, C. (2019). Failure and success in mergers and acquisitions. *Journal of Corporate Finance*, 58, 650–699.

Reus, T., & Lamont, B. (2009). The double-edged sword of cultural distance in international acquisitionss. *Journal of International Business Studies*, 40, 1298–1316.

Schijven, M., & Hitt, M. (2012). The vicarious wisdom of crowds: toward a behavioral perspective on investor reactions to acquisition announcement. *Strategic Management Journal*, 33(11), 1247–1268.

Schmidt, D. (2020). Stock market rumors and credibility. *Review of Financial Studies*, 33(8), 3804–3853.

Stulz, R. (2009). Securities laws, disclosure, and national capital markets in the age of financial globalization. *Journal of Accounting Research*, 47(2), 349–390.

Tehranian, H., Zhao, M., & Zhu, J. (2014). Can analysts analyze mergers? *Management Science*, 60(4), 959–979.

Welch, X., Pavićević, S., Keil, T., & Laamanen, T. (2020). The pre-deal phase of mergers and acquisitions: a review and research agenda. *Journal of Management*, 46(6), 843–878.

Yu, F. (2008). Analyst coverage and earnings management. *Journal of Financial Economics*, 88(2), 245–271.

5   Social media and firm performance: a review

Paige Costanzo and Christine Kirkland

Introduction

Information asymmetry is a major challenge in acquisition research (Dalton et al., 2007; Zaheer, Hernandez and Banerjee, 2010), as it can lead to negative outcomes such as employee turnover and negative investor reactions (Dierkens, 1991; Rafferty and Restubog, 2010; Schweiger and Denisi, 1991). Information asymmetry in acquisitions is often caused by a lack of communication, so greater and better communication is often submitted as a solution (Ellis et al., 2012; Graebner et al., 2017). Advances in technology have also increased the number of communication channels, but communication in acquisitions remains infrequently examined (Angwin et al., 2016; Bansal and King, 2022).

Social media is an underexplored area of communication that has the potential to impact acquisition and overall firm performance. However, there is a lack of systematic study on the antecedents, mechanisms, and outcomes of the use of social media for firms. To our knowledge, there are only three studies that have examined the relationship between social media use and firm performance in acquisitions. First, social media popularity at the country-level positively affects the intensity of bidding competition and the proportion of cash paid in the merger and acquisition (M&A) market (Jayasuriya and O'Neill, 2021). Second, the use of social media reduces information asymmetry surrounding acquisitions and mitigates negative reactions (Mazboudi and Khalil, 2017). Third, senior executives' social media use increases both the likelihood of firms engaging in M&As and the positive perception of these transactions (Wang, Lau and Xie, 2021). These studies suggest that social media can be a valuable tool for communication in acquisitions.

Research on social media and acquisition performance is limited, so we examine the topic of social media and firm performance more broadly. In defining firm performance as the outcome, we used financial or market returns, innovation, and survival. We conduct a systematic and interdisciplinary review of research to summarize knowledge and offer avenues for future research (Kunisch et al., 2023). On balance, the results of our review suggest that the adoption of social media along with a larger social media presence positively influences firm performance. This is consistent with anecdotal observations of how Elon Musk turned stock options from his 2018 compensation package at Tesla into billions of dollars due in part to his social media posts. However, it is important to note that these posts attracted Securities and Exchange Commission attention and led to a settlement (Chase, 2022; Krisher, 2022). In addition, controversy surrounding a transgender influencer promoting Bud Light has corresponded to Anheuser-Busch losing several billion dollars in stock market valuation (Norton, 2023). Simply, conflicting perceptions justify an examination of research.

Reviewing a link between social media and firm performance offers multiple contributions and avenues for acquisition research. First, we capture as many studies as possible that discuss the impacts of social media use on firm performance. Although there seems to be an overall positive relationship, there is a need to look more closely at methodology, antecedents, mechanisms, and outcomes of social media use. Second, beyond the three studies mentioned above, social media is largely overlooked in acquisition research. There is a paucity of research on communication in acquisitions let alone what suitable channels are for different stakeholders. Finally, we uncover an overlooked research gap on social media use and its relationship with firm performance. Practically, it is useful for executives and managers to know how communication can differentially impact the various measurements of firm performance. Specifically, there is a need for research on social media's impact in acquisitions.

Method

Elsbach and van Knippenberg (2020) recommend a broad review of emerging areas of research to help frame a topic and shape future research, and we performed a multi-pronged and staged approach to identify articles (Figure 5.1). We searched Google Scholar and JSTOR using the FT50 journal list to identify relevant, empirical articles using the terms "social media" and "firm performance" in a broad cross-section of research. We did not restrict the use of social media to key events, such as acquisitions, and the initial search resulted in approximately 1,800 potential articles. However, using the titles we identified significant duplicate, irrelevant, and non-peer-reviewed articles from the search results. For example, articles focused on brands and marketing were excluded, reducing the number to 55 focal articles.

From these 55 articles, we examined their references cited for potentially relevant articles, and included an additional 33 articles from this search. This process resulted in 88 articles screened at the second stage by reviewing abstracts and coding. Coding of articles was pilot tested with a research supervisor to provide increased validity of coding and article screening (Amiri, King and Duesing, 2022). A second researcher repeated the coding and screening process. The initial screen was largely successful, and 45 articles were eliminated following closer review with two articles included from a reviewer's suggestion. The final sample included 45 articles from 41 journals indicated by asterisks in the References section.

The coding process for the final sample included reading the full article and using the communication of process (Berlo, 1977). We first coded the methods of each paper regarding if the social media sources studied were internal or external to the firm, and if they were employees, customers, activists, or investors. We then coded the social media messages studied, and if the article examined the tone, content, or volume of the messages as well as the channel, or platform(s) studied. The final coded sample also included the research setting, sample, location, theoretical perspective, method, level of analysis, variables, outcomes, statistical analysis, and key findings. The coding process was iterative, as we continuously refined the categories.

Literature review

Acquisitions are disruptive events for a variety of stakeholders, including employees, investors, suppliers, and customers, driving a need for communication (Bansal and King, 2022; Kato and Schoenberg, 2014). Viewing social media offers a way for firms to communicate with stakeholders, we organize our review around the communication of process, involving a source, message, channel, and receiver (Berlo, 1977). A potential advantage of social media is that it broadcasts messages to various stakeholders. As a result, we do not specifically identify a "receiver" of social media posts, and we consider receivers as any stakeholder to a firm (e.g., employee, customer, investor).

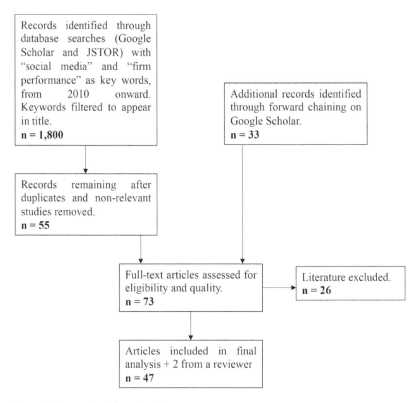

Figure 5.1   Article selection process

Source

Communication begins with a sender, or the source of the information presented to others. Research has examined the differential effects of various sources of social media on firm performance. We organize the discussion of the source of social media messages into internal, external, and mixed senders (Table 5.1). Overall, the research suggests that the source of social media messages can have a significant impact on firm performance. Firms should carefully consider the sources of social media messages when developing their social media strategy.

Eighteen articles examined the firm as the source of social media messages, while only four looked at employee content. Two of these latter articles examined upper-level executives' use of social media. Grant, Hodge and Sinha (2018) found that CEO social media use can affect firm performance differ-

Table 5.1   Social media source

Origin	Source
Internal	*Employee Account*: Grant et al., 2018; Heavey et al., 2020; Kamboj et al., 2017; Wang et al., 2021
	Firm Account: Ahmad et al., 2018; Ahmad et al., 2019; Ainin et al., 2015; Alarcón-del-Amo et al., 2018; Etim et al., 2018; Fan et al., 2021; Fischer & Reuber, 2014; Gavino et al., 2019; Mazboudi & Khalil, 2017; Papa et al., 2018; Parveen et al., 2016; Ravaonorohanta & Sayumwe, 2020; Saridakis et al., 2018; Saxton & Waters, 2014; Schniederjans et al., 2013; Tajvidi & Karami, 2021; Thakur & Arora, 2021; Yasa et al., 2020
External	*Activists*: Dinh et al., 2017; Kim & Youm, 2017; McAlister et al., 2012
	Customers: Candi et al., 2018; Datta et al., 2019; Kim & Youm, 2017; Luo & Zhang, 2013; McAlister et al., 2012; Nguyen et al., 2020
	Investors: Datta et al., 2019; Dinh et al., 2017; Kim & Youm, 2017; McAlister et al., 2012; Vrontis et al., 2021
Mix	*Internal and External*: Bai & Yan, 2023; Bocconcelli et al., 2017; Cheng & Shiu, 2019; Jayasuriya & O'Neill, 2021; Jones et al., 2015; Lee et al., 2018; Odoom et al., 2017; Pérez-González et al., 2017; Pratono, 2018; Quinton & Wilson, 2016; Scuotto et al., 2017; Wang et al., 2016

entially by impacting investors' willingness to invest. However, Wang and colleagues (2021) found that "social" CEOs engaging on social media increases the likelihood of firms engaging in M&A and ultimately increases firm performance. Further bolstering the argument that internal use of social media increases firm performance is that it allows for greater information processing which leads to a better reputation and access to resources through the building of trust by strategic leaders (Heavey et al., 2020).

Nine studies examined messages from external accounts. These external messages are from customers and investors. Customer involvement on social media can lead to greater innovation (Candi et al., 2018; Datta, Sahaym and Brooks, 2019), growth opportunities (Kim and Youm, 2017), increased performance (Luo and Zhang, 2013; McAlister, Sonnir and Shively, 2012), and stock holdings (Nguyen, Calantone and Krishan, 2020). Investor social media use can increase firm performance through innovation (Datta et al., 2019), stock returns (Dinh, Kopf and Seitz, 2017; McAlister et al., 2012), analyst stock recommendations (Kim and Youm, 2017), and successful equity crowdfunding campaigns (Vrontis et al., 2021). Overall, the research suggests that the use of social media by external stakeholders can have a positive impact on firm performance. However, it is important to note the impact of social media on firm performance may depend on the specific context and its use.

There is mixed evidence on the relationship between small and medium-sized enterprise (SME) social media use and firm performance. Some studies have found that external stakeholders increase innovation through contributions on social media (Candi et al., 2018) and increase crowdfunding success (Datta et al., 2019; Vrontis et al., 2021), others argued that social media has a negative impact on small businesses (Grimmer, Grimmer and Mortimer, 2018). However, there is more consistent evidence that external social media messages have a positive relationship with firm performance. Notably, the SME studies relied on surveys while the public firm studies relied more heavily on archival data so firm size, legal structure, perceptions, or public listing of the firm may play a role on the relationship between social media and firm performance. For example, public firms may be more likely to benefit from social media use than private firms as they are subject to more scrutiny from investors and the media.

Twelve articles included both internal and external sources of social media messages. CEO social media capability positively moderates the relationship between the firms' social media capability and firm performance (Bai and Yan, 2023). Also, social media strategy represents an overall strategic resource used for effective networking (Bocconcelli, Cioppi and Pagano, 2017; Pratono, 2018; Wang, Pauleen and Zhang, 2016) and interdependencies exist between social media use and its motivations (Odoom, Anning-Dorson and Achcampong, 2017). There are positive effects for SME innovation (Cheng and Shiu, 2019; Pérez-González, Trigueros-Preciado and Popa, 2017; Scuotto, Del Giudice and Carayannis, 2017), enhanced business image (Jones, Borgman and Ulusoy, 2015), higher consumer engagement when using humor and emotion (Lee, Hosanagar and Nair, 2018), and enhanced credibility along with new contracts (Quinton and Wilson, 2016). Therefore, there is ample evidence that the source of social media messages can differentially impact firm performance.

Message

The message is the information that is relayed on social media. It can have different aspects or subtext that convey additional meaning. We organized social media messages around the tone (positive or negative), type of content, and volume (implied or explicit) (Table 5.2). Negative social media messages are only studied with positive social media messages. Not considering negative

Table 5.2   Social media message

Aspects	Message
Tone	*Positive*: Fischer & Reuber, 2014; Grant et al., 2018
	Negative:
	Mixed Positive and Negative: Kim & Youm, 2017; McAlister et al., 2012; Nguyen et al., 2020; Schniederjans et al., 2013
Content	*Informational*: Bai & Yan, 2023; Bocconcelli et al., 2017; Cheng & Shiu, 2019; Dinh et al., 2017; Grimmer et al., 2018; Heavey et al., 2020; Jones et al., 2015; Kamboj et al., 2017; Mazboudi & Khalil, 2017; Pérez-González et al., 2017; Pratono, 2018; Saridakis et al., 2018; Scuotto et al., 2017; Yasa et al., 2020
	Mixed Informational and Branding: Ahmad et al., 2018; Alarcón-del-Amo et al., 2018; Lee et al., 2018; Parveen et al., 2016; Saxton & Waters, 2014; Schniederjans et al., 2013; Thakur & Arora, 2021
Volume (implied or explicit)	Ahmad et al., 2019; Ainin et al., 2015; Alarcón-del-Amo et al., 2018; Candi et al., 2018; Datta et al., 2019; Etim et al., 2018; Fischer & Reuber, 2014; Gavino et al., 2019; Jayasuriya & O'Neill, 2021; Jones et al., 2015; Luo & Zhang, 2013; McAlister et al., 2012; Nguyen et al., 2020; Odoom et al., 2017; Papa et al., 2018; Quinton & Wilson, 2016; Ravaonorohanta & Sayumwe, 2020; Saridakis et al., 2018; Vrontis et al., 2021; Wang et al., 2016; Wang et al., 2021

messages may bias expectations for a positive association between social media use and firm performance.

Our review shows that, while tone, content, and volume are studied, tone has the least consideration, and no research considers only negative content. A wide array of manual and statistical methods was used to study the social media messages and 26 of the studies include a combination of tone and content analysis. The difficulty in obtaining the tone and content of messages is clear, and there are far fewer studies using qualitative methods. Both Heavey and colleagues (2020) and Kim and Youm (2017) state that data collection and coding used a manual process.

Message content in studies is either informational, or mixed informational and branding. Since we excluded articles solely focused on brands and marketing, the largest category was informational or firms discussing their products and services. Seven of the studies considered both the informational and branding messages sent from companies, but only one study distinguished the impacts of information from branding. Lee and colleagues (2018) found that mentioning deals and prices alone lowers consumer engagement, but, including humor and emotion, increases consumer engagement and firm performance. Meanwhile, others found that social media use more generally has a positive impact on stock returns (Schniederjans, Cao and Schniederjans, 2013), perceived firm performance (Alarcón-del-Amo, Rialp-Criado and Rialp-Criado, 2018), customer relations (Parveen, Jaafar and Ainin, 2016; Thakur and Arora, 2021), and stakeholder response to messages (Ahmad, Ahmad and Bakar, 2018; Saxton and Waters, 2014).

Fourteen studies focused on informational messages' impact on firm performance. Findings suggest CEO social media capability moderates the relationship between the firm's social media capability and firm performance (Bai and Yan, 2023), social media helps access new markets (Bocconcelli et al., 2017), strengthens reputation (Heavey et al., 2020) and client relationships (Jones et al., 2015), and increases market performance (Mazboudi and Khalil, 2017; Dinh et al., 2017) and innovation (Pérez-González et al., 2017; Scuotto et al., 2017). Additionally, studies use multiple measures of firm performance to increase the robustness of these positive results (e.g., Cheng and Shiu, 2019) used market share, sales, and return on investment; Kamboj, Kumar and Rahman, 2017; Yasa, Adnyani and Rahmayanti, 2020).

Finally, we summarize findings on volume or number of social media messages (e.g., tweets, retweets, posts). The 21 studies considering volume and firm performance show a lack of consensus. While Jayasuriya and O'Neill (2021) find that social media popularity at the country level positively impacts firm performance, Ahmad, Abu Bakar and Ahmad (2019) find no relationship between social media adoption of SMEs and firm performance. Additionally, Gavino and colleagues (2019) find that neither personal nor business use of social media impacts revenue for entrepreneurs. However, other studies find a positive impact on both financial and non-financial firm performance (Ainin et al., 2015; Emmanuel et al., 2022; Luo and Zhang, 2013; Odoom et al., 2017; Ravaonorohanta and Sayumwe, 2020), perceptual firm performance (Alarcón-del-Amo et al., 2018), innovation (Candi et al., 2018; Papa et al., 2018), crowdfunding success (Datta et al., 2019), and quality (Fischer and Reuber, 2014). An important contextual difference appears to exist for SMEs and between large companies and SMEs.

Table 5.3   Social media channel

Channel	
Twitter	Dinh et al., 2017; Fischer & Reuber, 2014; Grant et al., 2018; Heavey et al., 2020; Kim & Youm, 2017; Mazboudi & Khalil, 2017; Ravaonorohanta & Sayumwe, 2020; Vrontis et al., 2021; Wang et al., 2021
Facebook	Ainin et al., 2015; Lee et al., 2018; Saxton & Waters, 2014
Other	Bai & Yan, 2023; Luo & Zhang, 2013; Quinton & Wilson, 2016; Schniederjans et al., 2013
Multiple	Ahmad et al., 2018; Ahmad et al., 2019; Bocconcelli et al., 2017; Gavino et al., 2019; Jones et al., 2015; McAlister et al., 2012; Nguyen et al., 2020; Odoom et al., 2017; Tajvidi & Karami, 2021; Wang et al., 2016; Yasa et al., 2020
Not specified	Alarcón-del-Amo et al., 2018; Candi et al., 2018; Cheng & Shiu, 2019; Datta et al., 2019; Etim et al., 2018; Fan et al., 2021; Grimmer et al., 2018; Jayasuriya & O'Neill, 2021; Kamboj et al., 2017; Papa et al., 2018; Parveen et al., 2016; Pérez-González et al., 2017; Pratono, 2018; Saridakis et al., 2018; Scuotto et al., 2017; Thakur & Arora, 2021

Channel

The channel used to transmit a message reflects the variety of social media platforms. We summarize social media platforms examined by existing research (Table 5.3). Overall, Twitter and Facebook receive the most research attention. However, additional platforms, such as Reddit, Twitch, and Discord, may be significant. Additionally, regional differences in the preferred social media platforms depend on government regulation, privatization, and accessibility.

For research examining the impact of Twitter, eight studies considered developed nations, and one an unspecified region (Fischer and Reuber, 2014). Regardless of the type of performance measured, all studies indicate positive relationships between Twitter and firm performance. Four studies used market-based measures, including abnormal returns (Dinh et al., 2017; Mazboudi and Khalil, 2017), accounting-based measures (Vrontis et al., 2021), or mixed market- and accounting-based measures (Ravaonorohanta and Sayumwe, 2020). The remaining five studies examine outcomes associated with reputation (Heavey et al., 2020), firm quality (Fischer and Reuber, 2014), change in analyst stock recommendations (Kim and Youm, 2017), and likelihood of engaging in M&As (Wang et al., 2021).

Research focused on Facebook finds a positive relationship between the various measures of firm performance, though they each used different methods and samples. The first study used surveys on SMEs (Ainin et al., 2015), the second used Amazon Turk with natural language processing (NLP; Lee et al., 2018), and the third used content analysis of nonprofits (Saxton and Waters, 2014). Only one of three studies uses typical forms of financial (e.g., sales) and non-financial (e.g., number of employees) performance (Ainin et al., 2015). The other two studies use consumer engagement (Lee et al., 2018) and public response (Saxton and Waters, 2014) as their outcome variables.

Beyond Twitter or Facebook, we group four studies into "other" channels with one study each using Sina Weibo (Bai and Yan, 2023), Webnet reviews (Luo and Zhang, 2013), LinkedIn (Quinton and Wilson, 2016), and a mix of websites (Schniederjans et al., 2013). Again, all the studies find a positive relationship with performance, but they use different measures, including resource endowments (Bai and Yan, 2023), sales and brand equity (Luo and Zhang, 2013), new contracts and problem-solving (Quinton and Wilson, 2016), and stock returns (Schniederjans et al., 2013).

Next, 11 studies use multiple channels, including, but not limited to: Instagram, YouTube, WhatsApp, company websites, TripAdvisor, LINE, WeChat, Snapchat, and Pinterest. Performance outcomes observed include new customers (Ahmad et al., 2018; Jones et al., 2015), sales and revenue (Ahmad et al., 2019; Gavino et al., 2019), new markets (Bocconcelli et al., 2017), stock returns (McAlister et al., 2012), profitability (Tajvidi and Karami, 2021), collaboration (Wang et al., 2016), and the use of multiple performance metrics (Nguyen et al., 2020; Odoom et al., 2017; Yasa et al., 2020). Interestingly, two studies found no link between social media adoption and firm performance (Ahmad et al., 2019; Gavino et al., 2019). The former studied the properties of SMEs while the latter focused on the revenue of entrepreneurs. A third study revealed that different channels can have different outcomes on firm performance (Grant et al., 2018). Again, studies show conflicting outcomes for SMEs and entrepreneurs, or large, public firms.

The remaining 16 studies fell into the category of unspecified channels and find positive relationships with their measurements of firm performance and the adoption, popularity, or use of social media. Two studies use archival data (Jayasuriya and O'Neill, 2021; Saridakis et al., 2018) and others use surveys. While most study SMEs or entrepreneurs, there is greater diversity in samples with studies on the IT sector in emerging markets (Kamboj et al., 2017; Thakur and Arora, 2021), the Nigerian telecommunication sector (Etim, Uzonna and

Worgu, 2018), or exporters in Spain (Alarcón-del-Amo et al., 2018) and firms in Malaysia (Parveen et al., 2016).

Discussion

A review of 45 papers on the effects of social media on firm performance reveals a largely positive relationship between the two. Still, this only scratches the surface of potential effects, as there are other factors to consider. Social media impacts firm performance through a variety of mechanisms which we have broken down into source, message, and channel. We review research to assess social media's relevance to the acquisition process and mitigating information asymmetry (Dalton et al., 2007; Zaheer et al., 2010). Social media can provide two-way communication between the firm and all stakeholder groups, but existing research rarely considers internal and external sources simultaneously.

Before discussing implications for management research, it is important to note the limitations of our review. First, the number of articles in our sample is too small for thematic analysis. Second, studies often lack consistent information, or fully defined measures, making comparison difficult. For example, one-third of the articles were atheoretical, and studies used different conceptualizations of similar variables. Third, due to missing information and a small sample size, we were not able to examine social media's impact on M&A processes or when communication happens.

Research implications

The ability to connect with different and multiple stakeholder groups simultaneously offers a potentially optimal solution to communication challenges. However, one communication strategy is ambiguity (Eisenberg, 1984). Ambiguity allows firms to pursue multiple goals that may or may not be unanimously agreed upon by different stakeholder groups. Better communication through these platforms may allow for fewer interpretations of the information available, hindering strategic options and even firm performance. The extent ambiguity is desirable may explain observed differences on the impacts of social media for SMEs and large firms. Further, it underscores the importance of using multiple dimensions of firm performance, both market and non-market, to study the effects of social media.

Communication can help create successful acquisitions as it can help to ward off the negative externalities of information asymmetry (Ellis et al., 2012; Graebner et al., 2017), but not every stage of the acquisition process allows for public communication. When CEOs engage in strategic communication by announcing acquisitions with offsetting information, it can positively impact firm performance by reducing negative investor reactions (Graffin, Haleblian and Kiley, 2016). Our results support that social media can positively impact firm performance, but the relationship is more pronounced for public companies, studied through archival data, than for SMEs and entrepreneurs, studied through surveys and interviews.

In considering communication and firm performance, direct effects of social media may be less important than indirect effects. For instance, open innovation and customer engagement may indirectly influence firm performance (Candi et al., 2018), collaborative problem-solving (Quinton and Wilson, 2016), or gaining access to new markets (Bocconcelli et al., 2017). By facilitating open innovation, social media can help firms to develop successful new products and services to help firms expand and grow their profits. For example, communicating via social media can help firms to build trust with stakeholders.

For acquisition research, social media has the potential to remedy informational asymmetry across the M&A process of target selection to integration. For example, integration is critical to acquisition success (Graebner et al., 2017), so the use of social media platforms internal or external to the firm may more efficiently disseminate information. By sharing information and collaborating on tasks, teams can potentially experience a smooth and efficient acquisition process. In considering future research directions, our review identifies research gaps or conflicting findings for outcomes in emerging versus more developed markets, SMEs and large firms, phases of the acquisition process, and using advanced analytical methods. Below, we summarize the future research directions for source, message, and channel.

Source. Research often fails to account for both internal and external sources of information from social media. This gap is important because information asymmetry affects organizational communication both internally (Bansal and King, 2022) and externally (Rogan and Sorenson, 2014). Internal communication can have a positive effect on dispersion of ideas, and external communication increases organizational innovation from environmental scanning (Damanpour, 1991). For instance, Slack has become a vital tool for organizations to facilitate the transfer of internal information (Johnson, 2023), but internal social media platforms that help coordination following an acquisition remain unstudied.

There is also less attention on outspoken individuals, either internal or external to the firm. Although in the case of Elon Musk (Krisher, 2022) his outspokenness led to the intervention of the Securities and Exchange Commission, we do not know how CEOs impact firm performance through their use of social media. Further, how are external social media users changing the landscape for individual firms or industries? For example, Carl Icahn, an activist investor, and his tweets on Apple led to significant positive cumulative abnormal returns (Dinh et al., 2017). Additionally, the collapse of Silicon Valley Bank was accelerated by social media (Yerushalmy, 2023) and it has contributed to losses by Anheuser-Busch (Norton, 2023). This reflects a need to consider additional stakeholders in the study of acquisitions (see Chapter 10).

Message. Research in our review does not individually examine negative messages. Given the collapse of Silicon Valley Bank and experience of Anheuser-Busch, negative messages clearly impact firm performance, alluding to an important research gap. Both tone and content from our review are relevant to firm performance, and NLP is a useful future direction of research for the tone, content, and volume of messages (Lee et al., 2018). Using these more advanced applications allows for the use of more extensive data from a variety of sources which could uncover differences across platforms or message content. For example, three studies looked at "buzz" or emotional content (Luo and Zhang, 2013; McAlister et al., 2012; Nguyen et al., 2020) that could influence acquisition decisions.

Given that firms can use ambiguity to their advantage and that providing information can improve investor reactions, it is imperative to look at how social media is used. Is it purely to signal that firms are open to communication and in that way reduce information asymmetry (Connelly et al., 2011) or does the quality of the information communicated play a role in firm performance? For example, rival firms may use disclosed information to make competitive attacks following an acquisition (King and Schriber, 2016).

Channel. Unfortunately, the largest category of channels included studies that did not specify the channels used. As Grant and colleagues (2018) found, there was a difference in firm performance by disclosure medium between conference calls and Twitter. We can therefore infer that social media platforms may affect firm performance differentially. Fortunately, the second largest category examined multiple channels. This is likely a positive direction for social media research in organizational studies as different platforms may serve as conduits for different signals and types of information. Future research can build on this foundation to differentiate how and when certain types of information impact firms, and more specifically, acquisition performance.

Further, technology dynamism has increased the number of platforms, and there is an absence of research studying Reddit and Discord. Reddit is a notable absence given its role in "blowing up" GameStop's and AMC's stock via online trading (Morrow, 2021), and Discord facilitated the leak of classified documents (Looft and Steakin, 2023). The latter is relevant to acquisitions, as social media could facilitate insider trading.

Conclusion

Overall, before offering consistent advice or implications for managers, more research is needed. Our review of research at the intersection of social media and firm performance suggests social media affects firm performance differentially, and considering this context is increasingly relevant as platforms proliferate. We outline future directions for acquisition research that take advantage of more advanced technologies and methodologies. Social media has the potential to be a valuable tool for improving the success of acquisitions, but research needs to explore how social media influences the M&A process and informational asymmetry.

References (reviewed studies are indicated with an asterisk)

*Ahmad, S., Abu Bakar, A., & Ahmad, N. (2019). Social media adoption and its impact on firm performance: the case of the UAE. *International Journal of Entrepreneurial Behavior & Research*, 25(1), 84–111.
*Ahmad, S., Ahmad, N., & Bakar, A. (2018). Reflections of entrepreneurs of small and medium-sized enterprises concerning the adoption of social media and its impact on performance outcomes: evidence from the UAE. *Telematics and Informatics*, 35(1), 6–17.
*Ainin, S., Parveen, F., Moghavvemi, S., Jaafar, N., & Mohd Shuib, N. (2015). Factors influencing the use of social media by SMEs and its performance outcomes. *Industrial Management & Data Systems*, 115(3), 570–588.
*Alarcón-del-Amo, M., Rialp-Criado, A., & Rialp-Criado, J. (2018). Examining the impact of managerial involvement with social media on exporting firm performance. *International Business Review*, 27(2), 355–366.

Amiri, S., King, D., & Duesing, R. (2022). Managing divestments as projects: benefits of stakeholder orientation. *International Journal of Project Management*, 40, 385–397.

Angwin, D., Mellahi, K., Gomes, E., & Peter, E. (2016). How communication approaches impact mergers and acquisitions outcomes. *International Journal of Human Resource Management*, 27(20), 2370–2397.

*Bai, L., & Yan, X. (2023). Impact of social media capability on firm performance: new evidence from China. *Asian Business & Management*, 22(1), 118–136.

Bansal, A., & King, D. (2022). Communicating change following an acquisition. *International Journal of Human Resource Management*, 33(9), 1886–1915.

Berlo, D. (1977). Communication as process: review and commentary. *Annals of the International Communication Association*, 1(1), 11–27.

*Bocconcelli, R., Cioppi, M., & Pagano, A. (2017). Social media as a resource in SMEs' sales process. *Journal of Business & Industrial Marketing*, 32(5), 693–709.

*Candi, M., Roberts, D., Marion, T., & Barczak, G. (2018). Social strategy to gain knowledge for innovation. *British Journal of Management*, 29(4), 731–749.

Chase, R. (2022). Elon Musk pay package at Tesla challenged in court. *USA Today*, November 15. https://www.usatoday.com/story/tech/2022/11/15/elon-musks-salary -and-perks-questioned-tesla-lawsuit/10706772002/.

*Cheng, C., & Shiu, E. (2019). How to enhance SMEs customer involvement using social media: the role of social CRM. *International Small Business Journal*, 37(1), 22–42.

Connelly, B., Certo, T., Ireland, R., & Reutzel, C. (2011). Signaling theory: a review and assessment. *Journal of Management*, 37(1), 39–67.

Dalton, D., Hitt, M., Certo, S., & Dalton, C. (2007). The fundamental agency problem and its mitigation. *Academy of Management Annals*, 1(1), 1–64.

Damanpour, F. (1991). Organizational innovation: a meta-analysis of effect of determinants and moderators. *Academy of Management Journal*, 34, 555–590.

*Datta, A., Sahaym, A., & Brooks, S. (2019). Unpacking the antecedents of crowdfunding campaign's success: the effects of social media and innovation orientation. *Journal of Small Business Management*, 57, 462–488.

Dierkens, N. (1991). Information asymmetry and equity issues. *Journal of Financial and Quantitative Analysis*, 26, 181–199.

*Dinh, T., Kopf, K., & Seitz, B. (2017). The power of social media–shareholder activism via Twitter and a firm's market value. *Die Unternehmung: Swiss Journal of Business Research and Practice*, 71(1), 50–73.

Eisenberg, E. (1984). Ambiguity as strategy in organizational communication. *Communication Monographs*, 51(3), 227–242.

Ellis, K., Weber, Y., Raveh, A., & Tarba, S. (2012). Integration in large, related M&As: linkages between contextual factors, integration approaches and process dimensions. *European Journal of International Management*, 6, 368–394.

Elsbach, K., & van Knippenberg, D. (2020). Creating high-impact literature reviews: an argument for "integrative reviews." *Journal of Management Studies*, 57(6), 1277–1289.

*Emmanuel, B., Zhao, S., Egala, S., Mammet, Y., & Godson, K. (2022). Social media and its connection to business performance: a literature review. *American Journal of Industrial and Business Management*, 12(5), 877–893.

*Etim, A., Uzonna, I., & Worgu S. (2018). Social media usage and firm performance: reflections from the Nigerian telecommunication sector. *International Journal of Management Science and Business Administration*, 4(6), 7–16.

*Fan, M., Qalati, S., Khan, M., Shah, S., Ramzan, M., & Khan, R. (2021). Effects of entrepreneurial orientation on social media adoption and SME performance: the moderating role of innovation capabilities. *PLoS ONE*, 16(4), e0247320.

*Fischer, E., & Reuber, A. (2014). Online entrepreneurial communication: mitigating uncertainty and increasing differentiation via Twitter. *Journal of Business Venturing*, 29(4), 565–583.

*Gavino, M., Williams, D., Jacobson, D., & Smith, I. (2019). Latino entrepreneurs and social media adoption: personal and business social network platforms. *Management Research Review*, 42(4), 469–494.

Graebner, M., Heimeriks, K., Huy, Q., & Vaara, E. (2017). The process of postmerger integration: a review and agenda for future research. *Academy of Management Annals*, 11(1), 1–32.

Graffin, S., Haleblian, J., & Kiley, J. (2016). Ready, AIM, acquire: impression offsetting and acquisitions. *Academy of Management Journal*, 59(1), 232–252.

*Grant, S., Hodge, F., & Sinha, R. (2018). How disclosure medium affects investor reactions to CEO bragging, modesty, and humblebragging. *Accounting, Organizations and Society*, 68, 118–134.

*Grimmer, L., Grimmer, M., & Mortimer, G. (2018). The more things change the more they stay the same: a replicated study of small retail firm resources. *Journal of Retailing and Consumer Services*, 44, 54–63.

*Heavey, C., Simsek, Z., Kyprianou, C., & Risius, M. (2020). How do strategic leaders engage with social media? A theoretical framework for research and practice. *Strategic Management Journal*, 41(8), 1490–1527.

*Jayasuriya, D., & O'Neill, B. (2021). Social media's impact on the global mergers and acquisitions market. *Journal of Risk and Financial Management*, 14(4), 157.

Johnson, J. (2023). How to use slack for workplace communication. *Business.com*, March 22. https:// www .business .com/ articles/ how -slack -is -changing -workplace -communication/.

*Jones, N., Borgman, R., & Ulusoy, E. (2015). Impact of social media on small businesses. *Journal of Small Business and Enterprise Development*, 22(4), 611–632.

*Kamboj, S., Kumar, V., & Rahman, Z. (2017). Social media usage and firm performance: the mediating role of social capital. *Social Network Analysis and Mining*, 7, 1–14.

Kato, J., & Schoenberg, R. (2014). The impact of post-merger integration on the customer–supplier relationship. *Industrial Marketing Management*, 43(2), 335–345.

*Kim, E., & Youm, Y. (2017). How do social media affect analyst stock recommendations? Evidence from S&P 500 electric power companies' Twitter accounts. *Strategic Management Journal*, 38(13), 2599–2622.

King, D., & Schriber, S. (2016). Addressing competitive responses to acquisitions. *California Management Review*, 58(3), 109–124.

Krisher, T. (2022). Is the SEC muzzling Elon Musk's right to free speech when Twitter CEO's tweeting about Tesla? *USA Today*, December 23. https://www.usatoday.com/story/tech/2022/12/23/musk-sec-twitter-tesla-free-speech/10949072002/.

Kunisch, S., Denyer, D., Bartunek, J., Menz, M., & Cardinal, L. (2023). Review research as scientific inquiry. *Organizational Research Methods*, 26(1), 3–45.

*Lee, D., Hosanagar, K., & Nair, H. (2018). Advertising content and consumer engagement on social media: evidence from Facebook. *Management Science*, 64(11), 5105–5131.

Looft, C., & Steakin, W. (2023). Discord user in group where secret documents surfaced details how members admired alleged leaker. *ABC News*. https://abcnews.go

.com/US/discord-user-group-secret-documents-surfaced-details-members/story?id=98661438.

*Luo, X., & Zhang, J. (2013). How do consumer buzz and traffic in social media marketing predict the value of the firm? *Journal of Management Information Systems*, 30(2), 213–238.

*Mazboudi, M., & Khalil, S. (2017). The attenuation effect of social media: evidence from acquisitions by large firms. *Journal of Financial Stability*, 28, 115–124.

*McAlister, L., Sonnier, G., & Shively, T. (2012). The relationship between online chatter and firm value. *Marketing Letters*, 23, 1–12.

Morrow, A. (2021). Everything you need to know about how a Reddit group blew up GameStop's stock. *CNN Business*, January 28. https://www.cnn.com/2021/01/27/investing/gamestop-reddit-stock/index.html.

*Nguyen, H., Calantone, R., & Krishnan, R. (2020). Influence of social media emotional word of mouth on institutional investors' decisions and firm value. *Management Science*, 66(2), 887–910.

Norton, T. (2023). Fact check: did Anheuser-Busch lose $4bn value amid Dylan Mulvaney issue? *Newsweek*. https://www.newsweek.com/fact-check-did-anheuser-busch-lose-4bn-value-amid-dylan-mulvaney-issue-1793996.

*Odoom, R., Anning-Dorson, T., & Acheampong, G. (2017). Antecedents of social media usage and performance benefits in small-and medium-sized enterprises (SMEs). *Journal of Enterprise Information Management*, 30(3), 383–399.

*Papa, A., Santoro, G., Tirabeni, L., & Monge, F. (2018). Social media as tool for facilitating knowledge creation and innovation in small and medium enterprises. *Baltic Journal of Management*, 13(3), 329–344.

*Parveen, F., Jaafar, N., & Ainin, S. (2016). Social media's impact on organizational performance and entrepreneurial orientation in organizations. *Management Decision*, 54(9), 2208–2234.

*Pérez-González, D., Trigueros-Preciado, S., & Popa, S. (2017). Social media technologies' use for the competitive information and knowledge sharing, and its effects on industrial SMEs' innovation. *Information Systems Management*, 34(3), 291–301.

*Pratono, A. (2018). From social network to firm performance: the mediating effect of trust, selling capability and pricing capability. *Management Research Review*, 41(6), 680–700.

*Quinton, S., & Wilson, D. (2016). Tensions and ties in social media networks: towards a model of understanding business relationship development and business performance enhancement through the use of LinkedIn. *Industrial Marketing Management*, 54, 15–24.

Rafferty, A., & Restubog, S. (2010). The impact of change process and context on change reactions and turnover during a merger. *Journal of Management*, 36(5), 1309–1338.

*Ravaonorohanta, N., & Sayumwe, M. (2020). Social media presence and organizational performance: an empirical study on companies' presence on Twitter. *Contemporary Management Research*, 16(2), 123–144.

Rogan, M., & Sorenson, O. (2014). Picking a (poor) partner: a relational perspective on acquisitions. *Administrative Science Quarterly*, 59(2), 301–329.

*Saridakis, G., Lai, Y., Mohammed, A., & Hansen, J. (2018). Industry characteristics, stages of e-commerce communications, and entrepreneurs and SMEs revenue growth. *Technological Forecasting and Social Change*, 128, 56–66.

*Saxton, G., & Waters, R. (2014). What do stakeholders like on Facebook? Examining public reactions to nonprofit organizations' informational, promotional, and community-building messages. *Journal of Public Relations Research*, 26(3), 280–299.

*Schniederjans, D., Cao, E., & Schniederjans, M. (2013). Enhancing financial perfor-mance with social media: an impression management perspective. *Decision Support Systems*, 55(4), 911–918.

Schweiger, D., & Denisi, A. (1991). Communication with employees following a merger: a longitudinal field experiment. *Academy of Management Journal*, 34(1), 110–135.

*Scuotto, V., Del Giudice, M., & Carayannis, E. (2017). The effect of social networking sites and absorptive capacity on SMES' innovation performance. *The Journal of Technology Transfer*, 42, 409–424.

*Tajvidi, R., & Karami, A. (2021). The effect of social media on firm performance. *Computers in Human Behavior*, 115, 105174.

*Thakur, P., & Arora, R. (2021). Role of social media in improving organizational performance: a study in the Indian IT sector. *Journal of Asia-Pacific Business*, 22(4), 247–259.

*Vrontis, D., Christofi, M., Battisti, E., & Graziano, E. (2021). Intellectual capital, knowledge sharing and equity crowdfunding. *Journal of Intellectual Capital*, 22(1), 95–121.

*Wang, Q., Lau, R., & Xie, H. (2021). The impact of social executives on firms' mergers and acquisitions strategies: a difference-in-differences analysis. *Journal of Business Research*, 123, 343–354.

*Wang, W., Pauleen, D., & Zhang, T. (2016). How social media applications affect B2B communication and improve business performance in SMEs. *Industrial Marketing Management*, 54, 4–14.

*Yasa, N., Adnyani, I., & Rahmayanti, P. (2020). The influence of social media usage on the perceived business value and its impact on business performance of Silver Craft SMEs in Celuk Village, Gianyar-Bali. *Academy of Strategic Management Journal*, 19(1), 1–10.

Yerushalmy, J. (2023). "The first Twitter-fuelled bank run": how social media com-pounded SVB's collapse. *The Guardian*. March 16. https:// www .theguardian .com/ business/ 2023/ mar/ 16/ the -first -twitter -fuelled -bank -run -how -social -media -compounded-svbs-collapse.

Zaheer, A., Hernandez, E., & Banerjee, S. (2010). Prior alliances with targets and acqui-sition performance in knowledge-intensive industries. *Organization Science*, 21(5), 1072–1091.

6   The importance of network studies on mergers and acquisitions

Christina Öberg

Introduction

The phenomenon of networks and mergers and acquisitions (M&As) increasingly intersects, and relevant research has lagged business practice. Elon Musk's acquisition of Twitter (now X) exemplifies how different types of networks overlap, including social network of users; rumors surrounding Musk and his business engagements on a business network level; increased influencer dependence; expected supplier contribution to technical development by open-sourcing code; and user and advertiser reactions with networks among individuals and companies thereby being present. The example also reflects a connection between Musk and Twitter past network dynamics influencing the acquisition and subsequent network effects. The Twitter acquisition serves as a prominent example of how M&As have profound network implications, and what happened is briefly summarized.

Elon Musk acquired Twitter and subsequently merged it with X Corp, in 2022, sparking strong reactions among Twitter users who expressed a diminished level of trust in the platform. Musk, on the other hand, justified the acquisition by emphasizing the importance of freedom of speech, suggesting that he purchased Twitter based on the company's previous treatment of content and advocating against censorship of users' posts. Prior to the acquisition, Musk utilized Twitter to spread negative rumors about the company, leading to a debate on whether he had manipulated the firm's value before acquiring it (see also Chapter 8). He later turned to Twitter to seek public input on various decisions, including whether he should step down as CEO. Following the acquisition, the stock price of Tesla, a company co-founded by Musk, declined by 12 percent. Ideas emerged regarding making Twitter's feed code open source and encouraging influencers to create subscription-based models linked to Twitter, resulting in staff reductions at the company. Those who had previously felt neglected by Twitter found a renewed platform to express their viewpoints, leading to feelings of harassment and caused some societal groups to leave Twitter. The overall impact of Musk's acquisition of Twitter is still evolving, but it clearly has network effects while deliberately trying to influence various types of networks. But what, then, is a "network"?

The term network encompasses various meanings, all characterized by a minimum of three interconnected actors (Cook and Emerson, 1978). As in the Twitter acquisition, these actors can be individuals, organizations, or a combination of both (Anderson, Håkansson and Johanson, 1994; Uzzi, 1997). Research often employs the term "ecosystems" as synonymous to networks (Aarikka-Stenroos and Ritala, 2017; Järvi, Almpanopoulou and Ritala, 2018). Networks may exhibit a central node orchestrating operations or consist of a dense network of interdependent actors (Dhanarag and Parkhe, 2006). They can be constructed and potentially temporal, with customers situated externally to the network, or they can represent the entire business landscape, encompassing interconnected and interdependent suppliers, collaborators, and customers (Håkansson and Snehota, 1995) and thereby be an analytical lens to understand business strategies. Social networks, interconnected individuals, serve as the foundation for enduring connections among organizations and act as facilitators for the transfer of knowledge both within and between firms. Simultaneously, the process of digitalization has paved the way for business interactions to take place among individuals rather than solely between companies. The emergence of social media as new platforms has profoundly altered the essence of social networks. Networks can be analyzed from a holistic perspective, focusing on structures as normally the case in network theory, or from the standpoint of individual actors (Öberg, 2022b). We can thus conceive networks as composed of individuals, organizations, or a combination of both, constructed and possibly temporal or unlimited in space. Further, we can explore how digitalization introduces novel network forms. When comparing networks as tools for comprehending the business landscape to constructed networks, it becomes evident that networks can serve as conceptual lenses for researchers or as substantial structures based on contractual agreements, for instance.

One common thread among all types of networks is the interconnectivity of actors, potential interdependencies among them, and the persistence of connections among these actors. In our increasingly interconnected society, as highlighted by Castells (2000), the importance of gaining a deeper understanding of networks becomes ever more pronounced.

M&As revolve around a change in majority ownership of a company (acquisition) or the consolidation of two previously independent entities (merger). Motives, integrations, and performance are the core themes of M&A research (Haleblian et al., 2009). Empirically, M&As have been researched from strategy, finance, human resource management, and marketing perspectives. However, the examination of networks has been relatively limited, primarily focusing on interpersonal social networks (Öberg, 2022a) and how they can inspire M&A activities (Haunschild, 1993). Yet, through discussing networks in the context of M&As, it is possible to envision how firms may acquire other organizations based on their past social and business connections, to reach the other party's business network or even as reactions to changes within the network. Integration needs to take into consideration effects on business networks of acquirer and targets, include their possible integration, or take place as integrations of network-based business models. Performance includes measurements related to gains, losses, and reactions from network parties, and changes in negotiation power and strategies for engaging with them. These examples merely scratch the surface, and Elon Musk's acquisition of Twitter offers additional contemporary insights into the evolving dynamics of networks and transactions that span the realms of both social and business networks.

I present a broad overview of different conceptualizations of networks and offer insights into previous research on M&A–network relationships, including dimensions of networks relevant to M&A and M&A research. To explore the added value of networks as analytical units in M&A research, their significance, and their potential impact on future research agendas, I first discuss the background on network research and exemplify the multitude of conceptualizations of networks. Then I develop (1) network motives, (2) network integration, (3) network reactions, and (4) M&A performance. By outlining network implications for M&As, the goal is to inspire future research (cf., Meglio, 2022).

Networks: background

The importance of networks is not only emphasized in how we currently experience a boom of social media, network-based organizations, business models, and innovation efforts. The importance also comes forth in how networks as a conceptual lens help us to understand how various individuals, businesses, business deals, and societal changes are interconnected and interdependent, thereby affecting each other. A too narrow lens on individual actors fails to recognize how, for instance, M&A motives, integration, and performance follow from other actors, their connections, and reactions. Meanwhile, the presence of substantive networks – such as alliances, networked organizations, communities – often means that M&As target only a portion of the knowledge and resources enabling the delivery of a product.

In the past, networks have been separated between social and business networks, based on individuals or firms constructing the nodes in the networks. Recent development blurs this separation and partly redefines social networks as well as how business is organized. Table 6.1 exemplifies different types of conceptual and substantive networks and their characteristics, which are discussed below related to business life and organizations.

Social networks

Social networks refer to connections among individuals. These networks can transcend corporate boundaries, diluting the impact of such boundaries in favor of person-to-person connections (Tsai and Ghoshal, 1998). We can think about the social network as individuals that support and care for each other. Social networks play a pivotal role in facilitating knowledge transfer within and between firms, cultivating what is commonly known as social capital. This encompasses the inherent value embedded within the connections among individuals within the firm, encompassing shared norms and fostering collaborative efforts that contribute to the creation of intellectual capital (Nahapiet and Ghoshal, 1998). In research, the social dimension of business exchange is discussed in terms of over- and under-socialized perspectives. As argued by Granovetter (1985), business exchanges are embedded in social connections, where business decisions are influenced by these connections. This helps in grasping why decisions are not taken on pure economic conditions but include components of trust and commitment (Morgan and Hunt, 1994).

Social network research provides a vocabulary that encompasses the structural, relational, and cognitive aspects of networks (Nahapiet and Ghoshal, 1998) and which can also help to understand also other types of networks. The structural dimension examines an actor's position in the network, with centrality and periphery used to gauge its importance. From a structural perspective, this entails assessing the number of direct connections an actor has, where platforms or orchestrators serve as examples of central actors at the business level. Complexity refers to the number of actors in the network, while density refers to the number of connections in relation to the total possible connections if all actors were interconnected (Tsai and Ghoshal, 1998). The relational dimension focuses on the nature of connections among parties, including the

Table 6.1   Network differences and dimensions

Type	Dimension	Explanation	Examples	Sample references
Social network	Social network	Network based on connections among individuals. In literature explained in structural, relational, and cognitive dimensions. May be within a firm or across firm borders, there embedding business connections socially	Friends or colleagues, board elite	Burt (1992); Tsai & Ghoshal (1998)
Business network	Markets-as-networks (conceptual lens)	Firms' interconnectivity and interdependence based on repeated business transactions	Firms redundantly being part of business networks. Networks include suppliers, customers, collaboration partners, etc. Through each firm being connected to someone else business networks are indefinite	Håkansson & Snehota (1989)
	Net/Alliance/Service ecosystem	Network constructed for a specific purpose, with customers normally external to the network	Air flight alliance, firms collaborating for a housing project, firms together delivering a service to a customer	Das (2006)
Contemporary hybrid networks	Platform-based network	Network of firms or individuals with a central node providing bridging and brokering services	Network to enhance production in a region. Platform-based network with an intermediary	Dhanarag & Parkhe (2006); Nambisan & Sawhney (2011)
	Networked organization	Network of self-employed individuals together deliver a solution to customers external to the networked organization	Freelancers in the freelance economy working for a shared output, importantly based on un-predefined specs	Öberg (2018)

presence of trust. Finally, the cognitive dimension pertains to goal alignment or misalignment among actors.

As we have entered the digital age, social networks have received a new meaning: describing various platforms – Facebook, X, Instagram, etc. – where individuals interact digitally. Business models and networked organizations are progressively shifting towards an individual-centric paradigm, where economic transactions partially or entirely substitute for social connections grounded in commitment and trust.

Business networks

A business network reflects how firms are interconnected. Research orients in different ways to these networks and emphasizes the social components of them to different degrees. Networks among firms are often described in ways that make them synonymous to *nets, alliances,* and *service ecosystems.* These networks refer to constructed multi-party collaborations that are spatially delimited and potentially time bound (Möller and Halinen, 2017), characterized by parties working together towards a shared output. They include control and contracts regarding how to operate and what responsibilities each party carries, which downplays the social component of these networks. Examples include the Star Alliance, a network of airlines that cover routes for each other to be able to offer worldwide traveling for passengers. Service ecosystems describe how multiple parties jointly create offerings to customers and these types of networks also appear for large-scale development projects and production, then often orchestrated by a central party.

Markets-as-networks (also referred to as the Industrial Marketing and Purchasing Group tradition) has problematized business networks as how "no business is an island" (Håkansson and Snehota, 1989). This refers to an ontological approach, or conceptual lens, where firms are described as connected directly and indirectly in endless webs of interconnections and interdependencies through their business partners (Anderson et al., 1994). Compared to the nets, alliances, and service ecosystems, these networks are thus more of an analytical tool to understand the business landscape. To explain these networks, social connections among firm representatives play a part as these form lasting connections among the firms based on trust. Meanwhile, firms adopt each other which creates lastingness also in terms of resources and activities provided and shared. To exemplify, a firm may develop a specific machinery for or together with a customer. These networks thereby present a complex tapestry of intertwined social and business connections. Multiple parties exist on social and business levels, and their decisions reverberate through the network, impacting others across social and economic dimensions.

This means that this type of business networks is in a constant flux between stability of lastingness of connections between firms and change as these connections are constantly evolving and challenged by others in the network. In these networks, one party's activity (e.g., M&A) affects others. Firms strategize in parallel making any outcome the combined result of network considerations, reactions, and combined activities by others (Öberg, Shih and Chou, 2016). When a party is influenced by others' exchanges, they will respond to the change either amplifying (in positive cases) or diminishing (in negative cases) the impact of that change. While this reflects a firm-centric perspective, additional complexity results from other parties in a firm's network strategizing, buying, and selling. Consequently, a firm cannot automatically perceive itself as central to its network. Instead, it becomes influenced by others and their actions, resulting in a firm's strategy potentially being a reactive consequence of others' activities.

To understand how firm managers perceive their networks and how networks influence strategies, the concept of "network pictures" has gained prominence (Henneberg, Mouzas and Naudé, 2006; Öberg, Henneberg and Mouzas, 2007). Network pictures capture the portion of the vast business network that a manager perceives, the desired changes within the network, as well as any misconceptions or underestimations regarding the network and the effects of pursued strategies (Öberg, 2022b). Misconceptions can include failing to acknowledge reactions to a strategic activity and neglecting to include actors and activities beyond the network horizon (the part of the network included in the picture, recognizing the limitations of managers in comprehending limitless networks and their focus on specific actors).

Contemporary, hybrid networks

Moving into what I refer to as contemporary hybrid forms of networks where individuals and businesses may coincide or where recently developments have caused individuals to overtake positions previously held by firms, many networks operate with an orchestrator or *intermediating platform* (Dhanarag and Parkhe, 2006; Laamanen et al., 2018). This means that there is a central party filtering supply and demand, evaluating and incentivizing ideas, or managing revenue (Dahlander and Magnusson, 2008). Such networks have traditionally been constructed based on, for example, initiatives to foster developments in a region, often as public initiatives in remote areas. More recently, they have reached popularity as platform-based operations, whereby the platform creates the node through which all exchanges are filtered and monitored, such as Uber, Airbnb, and other sharing economy operations (Geissinger, Laurell and Öberg, 2021), but also for instance Alibaba and Amazon, intermediation of open-source software and other community-based operations (von Krogh and von Hippel, 2006). Social media, such as Facebook, X, and Instagram, offer other examples where business transactions among users and providers are limited. These new types of networks indicate how firms create the orchestrators or platforms while individuals increasingly take positions as users and providers. The network of providers and users is one in which resources are transferred or shared, while the platform simply becomes the orchestrator, matching users and providers, and potentially intermediating payments and evaluations. Compared to alliances, nets, and service ecosystems, contracts rarely underpin these provisions and uses.

Networked organizations (e.g., Romero and Molina, 2011) as another contemporary form of networks, lastly, describe how individual firms collaborate as producing units, or how actors collectively contribute to a shared output. The networked organization also underscores how individuals are part of social networks that both influence and are influenced by economic exchanges (Öberg, 2018). For the networked organizations, dissimilar to the alliance, a target offering is not in place, but rather: individuals work together as self-employed to bring new offerings to the market and jointly develop ideas. The freelance economy focusing on various creative outputs exemplifies this type of network.

Along these various conceptualizations of networks, we can start to understand how M&As affect individuals and firms beyond parties involved, as interconnectivity, interdependence, and lastingness of connections have implications. Below, various types of networks are discussed in regard to M&A motives, integration, and performance, to summarize what has currently been done and what possibilities present themselves once we approach M&As from a network point of view.

Network motives

M&A research considers strategic motives and managers' self-driven interests, while also examining contextual factors such as acquisition risks, deregulation, and economic booms to explain M&A frequencies (Trautwein, 1990). *Social networks* have been utilized to explain how M&As become replicated modes of expansion across firms. These networks have a particular form: board interlocks (Lamb and Roundy, 2016), where individuals serve as both nodes and ties connecting firms through their representation on multiple boards. Some studies have attempted to describe how firms acquire others to balance business connections or enhance their attractiveness as suppliers related to *business networks*. This involves providing added offerings through acquisitions, while balancing includes customers and suppliers acquiring others to gain or maintain negotiation power with counterparts. This pattern becomes cyclical and increasingly concentric with counterparts continuously engaging in M&A (Öberg and Holtström, 2006). Further, viewing networks as *alliances*, prior alliance partners merge, and past alliancing can decrease M&A risks (Porrini, 2004). However, it should be noted that positive results are not guaranteed (Frankort, 2016).

Beyond this, and not extensively explored in past M&A research, M&As can be conceptualized as ongoing strategic and interdependent business network activities (see markets-as-networks, above). Network pictures as an analytical tool for capturing sense-making for M&A network leads to recognition that M&As are contextually driven by change or adaptation. This emphasizes how other actors, their activities, and their assumed potentials influence M&A decisions, highlighting motives that differ from the strategic ideas of resources, economies of scale and scope, and market expansions (Calipha, Tarba and Brock, 2010).

A highly competitive approach, prevalent in the social network literature and vastly applicable to business networks, is the notion of structural holes (Burt, 1992). Structural holes refer to specific gatekeeping positions in a network that allow a party to access numerous new actors. Acquiring a party to bridge such a hole becomes a strategic move, repositioning the acquirer to gain access to connections and competences previously unavailable. This could be for accessing resources or competencies that are currently lacking in the acquirer's industry or for establishing pioneering positions in the digitalization of the acquirer's sector. In this context, the vocabulary associated with social networks and their comprehension of structural dimensions offers alternative perspectives for elucidating M&A motives, while also highlighting how managers can see networks as reasons for M&As.

A recent trend related to substantive networks, involves the acquisition of networked organizations and platform-based firms (Miric, Pagani and Sawy, 2021). In the sharing economy, firms such as Sailogy, a rent service for boats, acquired the sharing economy operation Antlos, focused on intermediating boat owners and tourists. In such an acquisition, M&As typically target the intermediary platform only. As these platforms usually do not possess many tangible resources beyond their brand name and knowledge of operating in the gig or sharing economies (Acquier, Daudigeos and Pinkse, 2017), questions arise on motives for what is actually acquired. Possibly, as in the Sailogy–Antlos case, it leans towards obtaining a business model (Öberg, 2021) or repositioning the acquirer as part of these new economies. The consequences of these acquisitions can be substantial and warrant further exploration. Presumably, acquiring an actor within a networked organization (excluding the central platform or orchestrator) would have even more significant consequences, as the competencies of such an actor might be random. Yet, we know very little about these M&As.

Network integration

Research on M&A integration primarily focuses on an acquirer and target, adopting a strategic management firm-to-firm or human-resource management perspective (Haspeslagh and Jemison, 1991; Risberg, 2001). Integration has been discussed in terms of task and human integration (Bauer, King and Matzler, 2016), emphasizing tangible and intangible resources, often pertaining to culture and knowledge. Integration with customers has been explored, encompassing interfaces such as brands, sales staff, and general marketing expertise (Capron and Hulland, 1999; Homburg and Bucerius, 2005). Insights suggest that customers may not be as easily transferable as often assumed in M&A decisions (Rogan, 2014), where the markets-as-networks lens help to provide answers.

Turning to how integration research can be extended to include networks, *social networks* are rarely explored in M&A integration research. Social networks can facilitate integration, but they can also make it more challenging as individuals gang up to resist integration. To expand on possibilities, we can understand social networks as possibly overlapping between the acquirer and the acquired party. Individuals in the organizations may already be friends or part of similar social circles (Palmer and Barber, 2001). Instead of solely considering similarities in cultural values and ways of operating between the acquirer and acquired party, positive social connections can help overcome resistance and align individuals towards shared value foundations (or even embed them into shared values beforehand). Social networks may furthermore extend beyond the acquirer and acquired party, increasing the likelihood of successful integration, as long as these connections remain undisturbed. Consequently, integration and integration research should address social networks between the acquirer and acquired party, the social capital in terms of the value of these connections, as well as to other network actors, such as customers and partners of acquirers and targets. The social network perspective furthermore helps us understand the intertwining of the human and business dimensions in conducting M&As (cf., Granovetter, 1985), as well as the role of culture and individual values.

Expanding on *business networks*, research predominantly within the markets-as-networks tradition has pointed to the difficulties of maintaining customers, suppliers, and collaboration partners following M&A, while integration generally means ambitions to retain a target firm's business connections. Öberg (2008) specifically links customer reactions to integration. The concept of "value carriers" was introduced to recognize products, services, and personnel important to customers. For a consultancy firm, this would be the consultant as the direct customer interface; for manufacturing firms, the maintenance staff and products. These value carriers should not be integrated as their integrations risk destroying network connections, while they span social and business networks.

Research has also pointed to how acquirers can learn through studying the target's network. To exemplify, Öberg (2013) examined network imitation as a strategy to address socio-cultural challenges in M&As, bridging the social and business networks in integration. The central argument was how a firm can learn from the interactions of the acquired party with its network counterparts. The study focused on the acquisition of innovative firms, where the acquirer needed to embrace an entrepreneurial culture to preserve the acquired party's innovativeness (cf., Ranft and Lord, 2002). This involved internalizing the acquired party's ways of interaction and values pertaining to their connections with other parties. While there currently is some research done on integration using business networks as a conceptual lens, much remains unanswered.

The integration of networks is also not least relevant for networked organizations and initiatives based on sharing, openness, communities, and crowds, that is, the contemporary forms of networks, yet not extensively explored there. Here a firm acquiring one party, as pointed out above, risks either not getting all competences or resources expected, or not being able to uphold networks of the target, or both. Overall, considering network connections for M&A integration goes beyond traditional human and task integration issues.

Network reactions

Research has indicated how M&As drive new M&As (cf., Öberg and Holtström, 2006), highlighting a contextual interdependence of M&As. However, this interdependence goes further. Interdependencies between M&As and among business network parties play a crucial role in shaping the realization of integration. When examining strategic actions related to the markets-as-networks tradition, three dimensions need to be taken into account: (1) deliberate or unintentional actions taken by a firm to modify existing networks (e.g., an M&A and integration aimed at repositioning the firm); (2) reactions of others to these actions; and (3) parallel strategic actions undertaken by other parties within the network (cf., Öberg et al., 2016). Attempts to exert control over a network would expectedly be met with network reactions that weaken such effects, including when network parties, who possess valuable resources necessary for the acquirer to adapt to the new situation, turn away from the acquirer or the acquired party.

Network impedance to change recognizes that individuals and firms tend to resist it when it is imposed. No one wants to be compelled to switch to a different product, supplier, price level, or contact person unless they have made that decision themselves. The larger the changes introduced by the M&A, the more they are weakened by reactions that spread throughout a network. This reflects that the actors benefiting the most from an M&A are often competitors that do not engage in M&As. This can be understood as a type of network effect. When a customer reacts to a supplier's integration, they choose a different supplier or a competitor to an acquirer. For example, Öberg (2008) demonstrates that integration sparks customer reactions who were initially hesitant to an M&A, confirming change begets more change, or reactions to dilute integration efforts. Moreover, business network firms responded by attempting to alter the situation, advocating for their interests, aligning with their former business partners (the acquired party if it was to be integrated with the acquirer), or aligning among customers.

Network effects thereby resemble ripples on the water. Further, Thilenius, Havila, Dahlin and Öberg (2016) illustrate how reactions can appear in parts of the network unrelated to the immediate parties involved. Much of these thoughts appear in research on *business networks* based on the markets-as-networks tradition yet are not extensively researched in relation to M&As and where networks as a conceptual lens and substantive form opens the area of studying reactions in M&A research beyond possible employee and management reactions. With new forms of networks arising, in alliances, nets, service ecosystems, and social networks, similar notions could well be explored.

M&A performance

As outlined above, networks provide new M&A motives, introduce new dimensions of integration, and offer contextualization in terms of how network parties react and strategize on their behalf. The reactions and parallel activities (Öberg et al., 2016) impact M&A performance. Prior M&A research on performance largely focuses on short-term stock market effects or highlights failures that blame an acquirer (King et al., 2004). For example, managers did not fulfill the promises of a formulated M&A plan, making integration a scapegoat.

Research emphasizes the connection between M&A performance and M&A motives. When dealing with networks in the context of M&As, repositioning may be undertaken with network reactions in mind. However, it is more likely that the acquirer is overly confident or overlooks the significance of the network when planning an M&A. Managers fail to recognize different facets of the networks and their reactions, the influence of social connections, parallel activities occurring within the network, and even the possibility that the current network or the network of the acquired party is experiencing disruptions. These aspects are embedded within networks – social, business, and contemporary – raising new questions and providing additional perspectives to research on performance.

Network implications for M&A research

In closing, the example of Elon Musk and the acquisition of Twitter demonstrates how different types of networks, such as social networks, constructed networks, business networks, and networked organizations, play a role and interact in the acquisition process. In a networked society, where trust-based relationships and digital connections are intertwined, firms operate as networks and networks function as firms. Additionally, resources are increasingly distributed among parties through coordinating platforms or ledgers. Given these dynamics, there are numerous compelling reasons to delve deeper into the significance of networks for M&As.

The depiction of M&A motives, integration, reactions, and performance in this chapter highlights numerous potential avenues for future research at the intersection of M&As and networks. These research opportunities encompass both substantive network themes and perspectives that consider networks as a conceptual lens. Furthermore, aligning with network theory, we can also view networks as methodologies. In summary, to build upon and broaden the preceding discussion, Table 6.2 presents a range of ideas for future research across the realms of motives, integration, performance, and the various types of networks.

As Table 6.2 indicates, there are several gaps to fill that foster new understandings for M&As and how these target networks or embed in them. In essence, the overarching concept of interconnectivity, interdependencies, and enduring connections that transcend the acquirer and the target company inspires various novel perspectives and inquiries within M&A research. Specifically, our knowledge remains limited when it comes to M&A transactions involving networked organizations and platforms, despite the increasing prevalence of these organizational structures. Social networks provide a lens through which we can explore alternatives to culture's influence on human interactions task integration. This shift allows us to move beyond psychological reactions and delve into sociological understandings of integration.

We also need research on M&A interdependent activities of firm (markets-as-networks) and how integration and performance dynamics unfold within this context. Structural network analyses on M&A within business networks can help us adopt a complexity perspective. By studying large samples, we can understand industry reconstructions, dynamics that extend beyond regular business operations, and how firm strategies, reactions, and parallel activities manifest at the network level. With a plethora of research opportunities along M&A motives, integration and performance discussions, I hope to have sparked interest for future studies at the M&A–network intersection.

Table 6.2   M&As and networks

	Motives	Integration	Performance
Social networks	The role of social ties for M&A beyond board interlocks: How do connections between firms affect likelihood for M&A?	Sociological understandings of integration: How is social capital considered in integration? How can social networks between individuals of acquirer and target foster integration? How do they link to culture and human integration? How do they link to successes in keeping customers, suppliers, and collaboration partners? By exploring social networks, we can furthermore complement cultural notions by examining connections at both intra- and inter-organizational levels. This lens allows us to map these connections, providing a tangible tool for uncovering aspects previously concealed within the concept of culture	How are social connections affected by M&A – between acquirer and target and beyond them? How can social capital and changes therein be captured following M&A?

	Motives	Integration	Performance
Markets-as-networks	Explore structures of M&A leading to new M&A and other strategic activities among network parties leading to M&A as responsive activities. How can we understand M&As as a reactive strategic activity of firms? Considerations on network parties when acquiring: How are they accounted for by firms? What aspects are considered? Structural holes as reasons for M&A	Beyond present focus on reactions and beyond past research predominantly in the B2B marketing domain: How is integration considered and affected by network parties' parallel strategizing and reactions? What parties are considered when planning integrations? How do considered and neglected parties react? What roles do social ties play for business partners' reactions? How can firms minimize negative responses beyond resisting integration?	How do different types of motives related to network (aligning with present network, repositioning firm) fall out in terms of performance? What critical performances follow from others strategizing in parallel? How can network pictures be associated with performance and how do they change as a consequence? How can customer and other business partner consequences be captured following M&A?
Nets/alliances/service ecosystems	Beyond research on alliances affecting likelihood for M&A (acquiring your alliance partner), inclusion of alliance partners in acquisitions: How can an alliance be acquired? What party is selected and why in acquisitions within nets, alliances, and service ecosystems?	What happens when alliance partners integrate, with the alliance and its other parties? How are service ecosystems affected by integration? How can an external acquirer integrate with an alliance?	How does the performance of an alliance change when acquired? (i.e., how does the organizational form affect financial and other performances?)

	Motives	Integration	Performance
Platform-based networks	Explore what is acquired and motives: business models, actual operations or what is the target in the acquisition of a platform operator? Why do platforms acquire and whom? What role do M&A play in developments of one-sided platform operations?	How is the network of platforms affected by integration with an acquirer? How is a business model transferred to an acquirer? What aspects need to be considered?	How does an acquired business model affect performances and connections to networks? How do M&A of platforms unfold in relation to these motivations? How should their performance be captured?
Networked organizations	Issues related to acquiring self-employed individuals and acquisitions within networked organizations: Why are they performed? How common are they?	What happens when a networked organization becomes a company through integration?	How does the performance of a networked organization change when acquired? (i.e., how does the organizational form affect financial and other performances?)

References

Aarikka-Stenroos, L., & Ritala, R. (2017). Network management in the era of eco-systems: systematic review and management framework. *Industrial Marketing Management*, 67, 23–36.

Acquier, A., Daudigeos, T., & Pinkse, J. (2017). Promises and paradoxes of the sharing economy: an organizing framework. *Technological Forecasting & Social Change*, 125(1), 1–10.

Anderson, J., Håkansson, H., & Johanson, J. (1994). Dyadic business relationships within a business network context. *Journal of Marketing*, 58, 1–15.

Bauer, F., King, D., & Matzler, K. (2016). Speed of acquisition integration: separating the role of human and task integration. *Scandinavian Journal of Management*, 32(3), 150–165.

Burt, R. (1992). *Structural Holes: The Social Structure of Competition*. Cambridge, MA: Harvard University Press.

Calipha, R., Tarba, S., & Brock, D. (2010). Mergers and acquisitions: a review of phases, motives, and success factors. *Advances in Mergers and Acquisitions*, 9, 1–24.

Capron, L., & Hulland, J. (1999). Redeployment of brands, sales forces, and general marketing management expertise following horizontal acquisitions: a resource-based view. *Journal of Marketing*, 63(2), 41–54.

Castells, M. (2000). *The Rise of the Network Society* (2nd edn.). Malden, MA: Blackwell.

Cook, K., & Emerson, R. (1978). Power equity and commitment in exchange networks. *American Sociological Review*, 43, 721–739.

Dahlander, L., & Magnusson, M. (2008). How do firms make use of open source communities? *Long Range Planning*, 41(6), 629–649.

Das, T. (2006). Strategic alliance temporalities and partner opportunism. *British Journal of Management*, 17(1), 1–21.

Dhanarag, C., & Parkhe, A. (2006). Orchestrating innovation networks. *Academy of Management Review*, 31(3), 659–669.

Frankort, H. (2016). When does knowledge acquisition in R&D alliances increase new product development? The moderating roles of technological relatedness and product market competition. *Research Policy*, 45(1), 291–302.

Geissinger, A., Laurell, C., & Öberg, C. (2021). Copycats among underdogs: echoing the sharing economy business model. *Industrial Marketing Management*, 96, 287–299.

Granovetter, M. (1985). Economic action and social structure: the problem of embeddedness. *American Journal of Sociology*, 91(3), 481–510.

Håkansson, H., & Snehota, I. (1989). No business is an island: the network concept of business strategy. *Scandinavian Journal of Management*, 5(3), 187–200.

Håkansson, H., & Snehota, I. (1995). *Developing Relationships in Business Networks*. London: Routledge.

Haleblian, J., Devers, C., McNamara, G., Carpenter, M., & Davison, R. (2009). Taking stock of what we know about mergers and acquisitions: a review and research agenda. *Journal of Management*, 35(3), 469–502.

Haspeslagh, P., & Jemison, D. (1991). *Managing Acquisitions: Creating Value through Corporate Renewal*. New York: The Free Press.

Haunschild, P. (1993). Interorganizational imitation: the impact of interlocks on corporate acquisition activity. *Administrative Science Quarterly*, 38(4), 564–592.

Henneberg, S., Mouzas, S., & Naudé, P. (2006). Network pictures: concepts and representation. *European Journal of Marketing*, 40(3–4), 408–429.

Homburg, C., & Bucerius, M. (2005). A marketing perspective on mergers and acquisitions: how marketing integration affects postmerger performance. *Journal of Marketing*, 69(1), 95–113.

Järvi, K., Almpanopoulou, A., & Ritala, P. (2018). Organization of knowledge ecosystems: prefigurative and partial forms. *Research Policy*, 47(8), 1523–1537.

King, D., Dalton, D., Daily, C., & Covin, J. (2004). Meta-analyses of post-acquisition performance: indications of unidentified moderators. *Strategic Management Journal*, 25(2), 187–200.

Laamanen, T., Pfeffer, J., Rong, K., & Van de Ven, A. (2018). Editors' introduction: business models, ecosystem, and society in the sharing economy. *Academy of Management Discoveries*, 4(3), 213–219.

Lamb, N., & Roundy, P. (2016). The "ties that bind" board interlocks research: a systematic review. *Management Research Review*, 39(11), 1516–1542.

Meglio, O. (2022). Reshaping M&A research: strategies and tactics for a new research agenda. *European Management Journal*, 40(6), 823–831.

Miric, M., Pagani, M., & Sawy, O. (2021). When and who do platform companies acquire? Understanding the role of acquisitions in the growth of platform companies. *MIS Quarterly*, 45(4), 2159–2174.

Möller, K., & Halinen, A. (2017). Managing business and innovation networks: from strategic nets to business fields and ecosystems. *Industrial Marketing Management*, 67, 5–22.

Morgan, R., & Hunt, S. (1994). The commitment-trust theory of relationship marketing. *Journal of Marketing*, 58, 20–38.

Nahapiet, J., & Ghoshal, S. (1998). Social capital, intellectual capital, and the organizational advantage. *Academy of Management Review*, 23(2), 242–266.

Nambisan, S., & Sawhney, M. (2011). Orchestration processes in network-centric innovation: evidence from the field. *Academy of Management Perspectives*, 25(3), 40–57.

Öberg, C. (2008). The importance of customers in mergers and acquisitions. Doctoral thesis, Linköping University, Linköping.

Öberg, C. (2013). Network imitation to deal with socio-cultural dilemmas in acquisitions of young, innovative firms. *Thunderbird International Business Review*, 55(4), 387–403.

Öberg, C. (2018). Social and economic ties in the freelance and sharing economies. *Journal of Small Business and Entrepreneurship*, 30(1), 77–96.

Öberg, C. (2021). Acquisitions for new business models. In S. Finkelstein and C. L. Cooper (eds.), *Advances in Mergers and Acquisitions* (Volume 19, pp. 79–99). Bingley: Emerald Publishing.

Öberg, C. (2022a). How do we comprehend networks in mergers and acquisitions? A co-citation analysis. Paper presented at the IMP, Florence.

Öberg, C. (2022b). Network pictures: cognition in a networked context. In R. J. Galavan & K. J. Sund (eds.), *Thinking about Cognition: New Horizons in Managerial and Organizational Cognition* (pp. 89–102). Bingley: Emerald Publishing Group.

Öberg, C., Henneberg, S., & Mouzas, S. (2007). Changing network pictures: the evidence from mergers and acquisitions. *Industrial Marketing Management*, 36(7), 926–940.

Öberg, C., & Holtström, J. (2006). Are mergers and acquisitions contagious? *Journal of Business Research*, 59(12), 1267–1275.

Öberg, C., Shih, T., & Chou, H. (2016). Network strategies and effects in an interactive context. *Industrial Marketing Management*, 52, 117–127.

Palmer, D., & Barber, B. (2001). Challengers, elites and owning families: a social class theory of corporate acquisitions in the 1960s. *Administrative Science Quarterly*, 46(1), 87–120.

Porrini, P. (2004). Can a previous alliance between an acquirer and a target affect acquisition performance? *Journal of Management*, 30(4), 545–562.

Ranft, A., & Lord, M. (2002). Acquiring new technologies and capabilities: a grounded model of acquisition implementation. *Organizational Science*, 13(4), 420–441.

Risberg, A. (2001). Employee experiences of acquisition processes. *Journal of World Business*, 36(1), 58–84.

Rogan, M. (2014). Too close for comfort? The effect of embeddedness and competitive overlap on client relationship retention following an acquisition. *Organization Science*, 25(1), 185–203.

Romero, D., & Molina, A. (2011). Collaborative networked organisations and customer communities: value co-creation and co-innovation in the networking era. *Production Planning & Control*, 22(5–6), 447–472.

Thilenius, P., Havila, V., Dahlin, P., & Öberg, C. (2016). Business netquakes: analysing relatedness of events in dynamic business networks. In P. Thilenius, C. Pahlberg, & V. Havila (eds.), *Extending the Business Network Approach* (pp. 315–331). Basingstoke: Palgrave Macmillan.

Trautwein, F. (1990). Merger motives and merger prescriptions. *Strategic Management Journal*, 11(4), 283–295.

Tsai, W., & Ghoshal, S. (1998). Social capital and value creation: the role of intrafirm networks. *Academy of Management Journal*, 41(4), 464–476.

Uzzi, B. (1997). Social structure and competition in interfirm networks: the paradox of embeddedness. *Administrative Science Quarterly*, 42(1), 35–67.

von Krogh, G., & von Hippel, E. (2006). The promise of research on open source software. *Management Science*, 52(7), 975–983.

7 Reimagining M&A integration: a project-based view on M&As

Joana Geraldi and Satu Teerikangas

Introduction

Despite ongoing corporate interest in conducting mergers and acquisitions (M&As), research reports lamenting results (King et al., 2021; Thanos and Papadakis, 2012). One of the fundamental factors contributing to poor outcomes lies in the management of the acquisition process, in particular the post-acquisition integration phase (Graebner et al., 2017; Teerikangas and Thanos, 2018). Since the 1960s, studies have advanced our understanding of M&A management significantly (Steigenberger, 2017; Larsson and Finkelstein, 1999). Despite developments, most of this research has remained embedded in the self-sustained context of literature on M&As (Mirc, Rouzies and Teerikangas, 2017; Thanos et al., 2022).

We advance our understanding of M&A management by offering a research agenda at the intersection between M&A and project studies, that is, the research field dedicated to research in, on, and around projects (Geraldi and Söderlund, 2018). Our work demonstrates that the connection between these two fields is particularly intriguing and rich because M&A and project phenomena bear similarities. Both projects and M&As occur frequently, yet they are plagued by failures and surrounded by heated academic discussions on their outcomes and performance (Geraldi, Teerikangas and Birollo, 2022; Ika and Pinto, 2022; Vaara, 2002). The management of M&As and that of projects are connected in practice; practitioners refer to M&A projects as "integration projects." Moreover, "integration managers" used by serial acquirers (Ashkenas and Francis, 2000) bear striking similarities to the role of "project managers" (e.g., Crawford, 2000; Müller and Turner, 2007). Further, M&As have the essential project characteristics of uniqueness and temporality (Very and Gates, 2007), and they are considered a *type of project* of utmost complex-

ity (Geraldi, Maylor and Williams, 2011; Vester, 2002). Finally, project termi-
nology is used in the M&A literature without explicit connections to project
studies. For example, integration following "the deal" is considered temporary,
only existing until the integration project is "completed" (Angwin, 2004).

Until recently, neither M&A practice nor research turned to the project literature to enhance understanding and the success of M&A projects (Meglio,
2022). M&A scholars' skepticism towards the project literature is partly under-
standable. The literature has traditionally been perceived as practice-oriented,
marked by a technocratic view on management, while lacking academic
sophistication and theorizing. However, in recent years, the literature on
projects, also referred to as project studies (Geraldi and Söderlund, 2018), has
evolved significantly. Today, it counts with a strong theoretical base and the
attention of well-known management and organizational scholars, while publications in the field can be found both in specialized journals with high impact
and in highly ranked, leading mainstream management and organizational
journals (Locatelli et al., 2023; Söderlund, 2011). From this perspective, there
is much to learn, also theoretically, from project studies.

The first steps in bridging M&A and project studies have been taken (Very
and Gates, 2007; Birollo and Teerikangas, 2019; Geraldi et al., 2022; Bansal,
King and Meglio, 2022; Martinsuo et al., 2022; Meglio, 2022). Previous
M&A research has underscored the challenge and significance of integration
projects in achieving acquisition success. For example, Birollo and Teerikangas
(2019) confirm a role of projects as facilitators of integration by establishing relational spaces and fostering connections among the managers from
acquired and acquiring organizations. However, M&As carried out via projects can manifest in different forms. Birollo and Teerikangas (2019) identify
a combination of change projects, transition projects, or integration projects.
Similarly, Bansal et al. (2022) and Nogeste (2010) view acquisitions not as
individual projects, but as programs comprising multiple integration projects.

The question of how projects organize pre- and post-acquisition warrants
additional examination. We draw on the conceptual idea of projects, programs, and portfolios as modes of organizing M&As (Geraldi et al., 2022) to
develop a rich research agenda to advance M&A research both empirically and
conceptually. The next sections provide a short description of project studies
and projects, programs, and portfolios as modes of organizing, first in general
and then applied to M&As. We conclude with initial conceptual thoughts on
the development of a project-based theory of the firm and a research agenda
to conceptualize and develop the work further. This chapter builds upon our
earlier work on the subject, specifically the research conducted by Geraldi et al.

(2022). In this extension, we aim to contribute to the M&A literature by presenting a comprehensive research agenda, diverging from the focus on project studies emphasized in our previous publication.

Project studies: a brief introduction

Project Studies explores the organizing of projects, for and by projects (Geraldi and Söderlund, 2018), from a wide variety of scholarly backgrounds, empirical settings, and theoretical angles. This diversity has led to a long list of terms and concepts revealing different features and forms of organizing projects, including project organizing, project-led organizations, project-based organizing, project networks, program management, project portfolio management, project society, project landscapes, projectification, programmification, project lineage, project ecologies, and project networks, agile, among other things. While there may be differing opinions on its specific nature, there is consensus that the organizational phenomenon in question (referred to as "projects" at times, and not at other times) exhibits the following common characteristics:

- *Temporary*: projects are organizing forms that have an institutionalized termination, that is, they start with an intention to be discontinued (Lundin and Söderholm, 1995);
- *Deliberate vehicle of change*: projects relate to *a purposeful action* that is *managed* and aims to transform existing systems, the organization, and/or the physical environment; the intention is that while the organizing vehicle ceases to exist, its legacy should endure; and
- *Team*: projects usually require the orchestration of a variety of skills and knowledge bases, sometimes crossing organizational boundaries to meet their objectives (Sydow, Lindkvist and DeFillippi, 2004).

Moreover, the field of study has two broad, stereotypical, alternative perspectives towards the organizing of projects (Andersen, 2014; Geraldi et al., 2008; Lenfle and Loch, 2010), namely: (1) a technocratic perspective focusing on the application of project, program, and portfolio management tools and techniques, which is the dominant practice and understanding of projects in M&A contexts, and (2) an organizational perspective exploring the management of temporary forms of organizing, emphasizing value creation, people and their contributions, without pre-setting specific management styles or tools. The second perspective is broader and encompasses the first, as the technocratic view is one of the many forms of organizing temporary endeavors.

We adopt the second perspective to open a space to contrast different modes of organizing M&As. What we will in the following section characterize as "projects" embodies the first perspective.

Reconceptualizing M&A management

Building on Geraldi et al. (2022), we pursue a co-constitutive approach to organizing (Cunha and Putnam, 2017; Putnam, Fairhurst and Banghart, 2016) and have chosen to view projects, programs, and portfolios as modes of organizing, that is, considering that management processes shape, and are shaped by, what is to be managed. For example, Geraldi et al. (2022, p. 441) make the distinction:

> … an acquisition is not a project, program, or portfolio *a priori*, but instead, it becomes one, as managers choose to manage it as such. This means that any merger or acquisition can be managed as a project, a program, or a portfolio, and thereby be transformed into a project, program, or portfolio. Each choice involves different management foci, consequently determining what gets managed, how the strategic organisational change unfolds, and ultimately, the kind of organisation that is being created through the change.

Accordingly, we focus on three modes of organizing: projects, programs, and portfolios, as described in Table 7.1. First, we suggest examining M&As as projects using technocratic project management principles and practice. Second, we advocate a shift from viewing M&As as individual projects to adopting a broader program perspective. By doing so, we can explore the interconnectedness and interdependencies among multiple integration projects within an M&A program and how this holistic view influences the overall outcomes, processes, and timelines of the integration efforts. Third, we reevaluate M&As with a portfolio perspective that invites us to reconsider the firm as a bundle of M&As at different levels of integration. This can paint a more complex and realistic view of contemporary firms, particularly large (often multinational) enterprises that have been growing through M&As. By delving into these areas, we aim to expand and enrich our existing understanding of M&As through the lens of project studies.

Projects and M&A

When managers treat M&As according to the traditional and technocratic view on projects, they focus on rationality, predictability, and control. They carefully calculate the financial prospects and set strategic objectives during

Table 7.1   Overview of project-based modes for organizing M&A social media source

	M&A as projects	M&A as programs	M&A as portfolios
Purpose	Meet pre-defined scope within time and to budget, preferably smoothly, resuming operations as soon as possible	Yield strategic intended and emergent benefits related to the acquisition/merger	Continuous integration of a stream of mergers/ acquisitions, transforming gain in ownership into strategic value
Management process	Linear, goal-oriented process, driven by an ethos of rationality, predictability, and control	Linear, strategic, and goal-oriented, but with an ethos of learning, adapting, and developing as work progresses	Cyclical effort, focusing energy on competing goals and interests. A portfolio displays strategic direction through actions and commitments as opposed to words
Timeframe	M&A finished when the project is completed. While delays happen, a date is usually pre-defined, and delays are seen as unexpected disruptions	M&A converges towards integration without fully achieving it. Therefore, directing the program's attention and ending it is a strategic choice	M&A is an ongoing activity orchestrating a conglomerate integrated at various degrees

the pre-deal phase. In the post-deal phase, they emphasize specific actions to integrate administrative, physical, and operational systems (Shrivastava, 1986). Technocratic approaches using tools, such as Gantt charts and resource plans, dominate the management of M&As in practice. The project mode of organizing M&As involves a clear project scope, avoiding changes to plans, and adhering to fixed timelines. As projects start with a pre-defined end date, managers consider the acquisition completed when the project is finished, assuming the desired levels of integration have been reached. The technocratic view of projects has been widely explored in project studies and its findings offer M&A integration managerial best practices, such as project controls and monitoring techniques, project risk and opportunity management practices (Very and Gates, 2007) and governance practices within and across projects (Winch, 2014).

M&A practice and research tend to treat integration as a project and hence as having been completed once integration is over. It has become an established practice to expect practical results from post-deal integration action within the first 30, 60, 100, and 300 days following a deal (Angwin, 2004). In other words, it is generally expected that, on average, one year is sufficient for the post-acquisition integration to be completed. This relatively short and pre-defined timeframe has been found not to match the experienced duration of ensuring structural integration, social integration, human integration, cultural integration, or the formation of a new identity following a merger or acquisition (Birkinshaw, Bresman and Håkansson, 2000; Quah and Young, 2005; Teerikangas and Laamanen, 2015).

While providing a sense of security and predictability, a project mode of organizing can have disadvantages, mostly masking long-term issues, such as (1) managerial integration challenges; (2) impacts on participating organizations' structural, cultural, identity, political and emotional make-ups; and (3) performance improvement. For example, the early post-deal years tend to be spent dealing with unanticipated rises in integration costs and change efforts, and result in a negative human toll (Teerikangas and Thanos, 2018). This can create turnover in managerial and expert talent (Bilgili et al., 2017), limiting the sought performance gains (Graebner, 2004). Next, we turn to program and portfolio modes of organizing that are less present in M&A practices.

M&A as programs

We define a program as "a framework to host and manage a set of related projects in a coordinated way to obtain benefits that could not be obtained by managing projects individually" (Pellegrinelli, 2008). The distinction between projects and programs remains contested (Pellegrinelli, Partington and Geraldi, 2011). For projects, the output of each sub-project is meaningless, unless coordinated and delivered with other projects. Yet in programs, each project has its own "business case" for creating value (e.g., strategic benefits) when integrated with other, related, projects.

A program can also be considered as an approach to management that shapes activities around different projects, each with its own business case. An important implication of such an approach is that the learning gained by the implementation of the first project(s) can be applied to the next project(s) within the program, as we can better understand their effectiveness in realizing the sought benefits. This also means that the program does not need to be finished for it to achieve benefits (e.g., a return on investment). Consequently, while programs are temporary, they do not have a pre-defined timeframe, as projects do. Similarly, the scope of programs is open to change as programs develop and the teams learn from their experience.

Accordingly, organizing an acquisition as a program involves managing various parallel projects in the pre- and post-acquisition phases. The pre- and post-acquisition phases are temporally and legally consecutive, thus divided into complex legal processes of handing over ownership and responsibilities. Taking a closer look, the process perspective to M&As (Haspeslagh and Jemison, 1991; Jemison and Sitkin, 1986) suggests rethinking the separation between the pre- and post-deal phases. A program approach can provide an organizational vehicle to smooth this divide, as managers can organize each phase (both pre- and post-) as independent projects within the acquisition's overall program. As independent projects within a common program, bridges between specific projects of pre- and post-acquisition can be made. Another possibility afforded by this mode of organizing is to extend integration into the pre-acquisition phase to start the integration planning projects then (i.e., the planning of organizational integration, human resources, and cultural integration; Haspeslagh and Jemison, 1991; Teerikangas, Very and Pisano, 2011).

A more extreme option would be to use a program approach to dilute the divide significantly by reconsidering the activities around an M&A as different interdependent projects that lead to the strategic integration between the firms. As such, not entire companies are bought at once, but consecutively, in a way that makes the most strategic sense. The first "mini" acquisitions are framed deliberately as trials that the subsequent ones can learn from. Such an approach will smooth the transition between pre- and post-acquisition phases and enhance the learning between the phases. An acquirer will therefore benefit with the lessons learned from ongoing projects informing and influencing other projects within the program.

What these options have in common is the organizing of the M&A as a collective of projects that are designed to be adaptable and learn from one another. In so doing, the program approach accommodates uncertainty, contextual changes, and the evolving integration process. It allows for the addition of new projects to capture emerging synergies or address challenges. Defining the end of the M&A process in a program is flexible, with termination being a deliberate choice based on the realization of benefits or resource allocation decisions. Unlike projects, programs are strategic in nature. When applied to M&As, the goal is strengthening a parent firm with the addition of an acquired firm. Therefore, the level of integration achieved is a matter of judgment, and new (e.g., integration) projects can be launched until desired synergies are reached. While most M&A research favors a project-based approach, selected empirical studies highlight the benefits and complexities of the program mode of organizing M&As (Bansal et al., 2022; Geraldi et al., 2022; Martinsuo et al., 2022).

M&A as a portfolio of projects and programs

A portfolio can be defined as a framework of projects and programs, but these projects and programs are not necessarily inter-related or aimed at a common purpose; they only compete for the same scarce resources. Portfolios, unlike projects and programs, are not temporary. While projects and programs within portfolios can themselves be completed or terminated, the portfolio remains "alive."

Organizing an acquisition as a portfolio involves creating an ongoing platform to design, coordinate, and control multiple projects and programs associated with the acquisition. It recognizes M&A as complex processes requiring deliberate management and allows for the allocation of attention and resources. Therefore, unlike projects and programs, time is cyclical and, as such, always evolving but never-ending. The portfolio mode of organizing can have several strategic objectives that might be conflicting. It therefore organizes to maximize value creation by prioritizing, allocating resources and enabling learning and flexibility between projects and programs. It addresses practical challenges as they emerge and supports the long-term convergence of acquired firms into acquiring firms provided, if it yields expected and emerging benefits. Instead of aiming for attending pre-defined scope or integration, it holds the firm together as it blends semi-integrated firms within the overall organizational framework. This mode of organizing is particularly relevant for serial acquirers and conglomerates with multiple acquisitions at different levels of integration. The portfolio approach ensures that attention and resources are managed across a series of acquisitions, promoting both short- and long-term integration goals.

Discussion: advancing M&A with project studies

We now turn to outline a research agenda inspired by our journey across the lands of project studies. We focus on three research directions inspired by current and classic debates in project studies—organizing processes, temporality, and purpose. We anticipate that these themes (see Table 7.1) can advance M&A research in ways that can be both enlightening and impactful.

Organizing processes

As current research suggests, there are multiple modes of organizing M&A. We propose three ideal-typical modes, with distinguishable, conceptual boundaries. Future studies could build, extend, and provide nuance for our three modes of organizing by empirically exploring how M&A projects are managed. We assume a traditional and technocratic project study perspective dominates M&A-espoused practice. However, the challenges of M&A integration require a greater focus on people and probably would incorporate other organizing practices while keeping a veneer of technocratic rationality and predictability afforded by the project mode of organizing. Future research exploring how these different modes of organizing co-exist in management practices and the myriad tensions and paradoxes they create would be a fruitful avenue for future studies.

Further, future research could explore new innovative modes of organizing M&A in practice. Are there any organizations brave enough to abandon classic recipes for M&A management and attempt novel approaches? Could contemporary project study perspectives inspire M&A management, such as agile (a widely adopted method still needing conceptual development, e.g., Stjerne, Geraldi and Wenzel, 2022; Whiteley, Pollack and Matous, 2021; Leybourne, 2009), or vanguard/exploratory projects (e.g., Lenfle, Midler and Hällgren, 2019; Gasparro et al., 2022)?

Temporality

Engagement with project studies and its modes of organizing can challenge M&A scholars to consider time and temporality, as these modes of organizing make time horizons and rhythms salient. Critically speaking, M&A integration has mainly been studied from the perspective of the immediate post-deal aftermath, omitting the long-term integration of the target into the buying firm. We argue that this can lead to a mis-assessment of the inherent challenges in making M&A work. M&A research begs for a greater effort to look at M&A integration from a long-term perspective by studying what happens in the first months and years (Birollo, Rouleau and Teerikangas, 2023), as well as the first ten years, following a deal (Quah and Young, 2005).

An important theme inspired by a temporal view of M&A relates to the tension between temporary and permanent organizations. Project studies have extensively researched the interface between temporary and permanent organizations, giving rise to various organizational tensions, including attachment versus detachment (Sahlin-Andersson and Söderholm, 2002), long-term versus short-term orientations (Prencipe and Tell, 2001), and learning within and from projects (e.g., Bakker et al., 2016; Lampel, Scarbrough and Macmillan, 2008).

M&As present an incarnation of such organizational tensions. The M&A project/program/portfolio will not only have tensions with existing permanent structures but also exist to form such structures in the long term. Yet, due to their temporary nature, time in these organizations is constantly "running out" (Lundin and Söderholm, 1995). This temporal boundary creates incentives for prioritizing quick delivery over fulfilling long-term commitments. As a result, temporary organizations often embody Bauman's concept of "liquid modernity," where "long-term thinking and planning will be increasingly surrendered to the moment" (Clegg and Baumeler, 2010, p. 1728). Paradoxically, the very temporality of temporary organizations contains both the ambition for long-term vision and the potential for short-term thinking, posing challenges to realizing the strategic change they were intended to achieve (Geraldi, Stjerne and Oehmen, 2020). Tensions are amplified in the M&A and deserve attention, as there are not only one permanent and one temporary organization, but two permanent organizations merging through a temporary one. For instance, the position of an M&A's project manager sandwiched between two permanent organizations and connected to a temporary mission to combine them (Birollo et al., 2023). Project studies can be supplemented here with institutional logics or role conflicts providing a rich theoretical foundation for further exploration (Gautier, Pache and Santos, 2023). Temporality offers another potential theoretical avenue to extend temporal horizons and explore identity formation processes through connections to distant pasts and projections into a new future (Hernes and Schultz, 2020) and how projects act, in the moment, to create and recreate such connections.

Another possibility is to build on the research on projects and inter-organizational projects, on the one hand (Sydow and Braun, 2018; Dille, Hernes and Vaagaasar, 2023; Stjerne, Söderlund and Minbaeva, 2019), and M&A research, on the other (Granqvist and Gustafsson, 2016). This calls for future research on the temporal work, structure, and entrainment involved in the integration process, pursuing lines of inquiry such as: (1) How do deadlines impact the unfolding of the project, (2) How do M&A managers create momentum, and (3) How do acquired and acquiring firms differ in terms of their temporal structures, for example, rhythm, and how these different structures become entrained?

Purpose

M&A integration processes exist to shape acquired and acquiring firms or merged firms into a functioning whole. Treating M&A integration as a short-term one-year project misleads us into thinking that integration is "a state that can be achieved." Given the difficulty that most established firms experience in integrating newly acquired firms and the conceptual hiccup involved in positing that two formerly distinct organizations could be fully integrated, we argue that M&A integration is a myth that can never be fully achieved. In so doing, we call for more caution in the study and practice of M&As concerning what are the sought vs. attainable goals when engaging in M&A integration. Instead, we propose seeing M&A integration as a never-finishing process that converges into integration without ever becoming 100 percent integrated (e.g., logarithmic curve).

As argued by Geraldi et al. (2022), this observation leads to important theoretical implications referring to the nature of contemporary conglomerates formed by M&As. Future research could benefit from revising and extending theories of the firm to explain such an emerging notion of the firm. Theories of the firm seek to explain the nature of firms, including their existence, boundaries, and internal organization. Prominent theories include transaction cost theory, behavioral theory, knowledge-based theory, and attention-based theory.

Particularly relevant to M&A is transaction cost economics (TCE) which explains why transactions are organized through firms rather than solely by market mechanisms. TCE posits that if the costs of organizing activities in the market exceed those of organizing them internally, firms will emerge. M&A are central to TCE as they redefine the boundaries between firms and markets. By combining previously separate entities, M&As alter ownership structures, which in turn affect the nature and modes of operation of the involved organizations.

Projects, programs, and portfolios serve as organizational modes that hold acquiring and acquired firms together, creating a firm that is constantly evolving. These modes of organizing influence the level of integration within the firm and shape its overall nature. Opting for different modes of organizing M&A can lead to varying degrees of integration, with portfolios offering the advantage of easily integrating multiple acquisitions. Consequently, firms that grow through M&A may have different parts operating at different levels of integration and maturity. Accordingly, we argue that integration, rather than just ownership, defines the boundaries of a firm. By exploring the role of projects, programs, and portfolios in M&A, we bridge the gap between project studies and the core questions of the theory of the firm.

Conclusion

By applying project studies to the context of M&A, we contribute to the extant literature by reassessing: (1) what M&As are, (2) how they are managed, and (3) the timeframe in which they are managed. Moreover, our approach offers at least two additional contributions.

It reminds us of the generic lack of mutual learning and cross-fertilization that has come to characterize academic research. Applying how project studies and M&A research can benefit each other suggests that academic research in general would benefit from extending research beyond artificial boundaries and disciplinary silos. Thus, we regret the current fragmentation of scientific knowledge and call for its integration. We are not against a paradigmatic development of knowledge, as defended by Pfeffer (1993), because we agree that there is a need for specialized knowledge and middle-range theories that would allow us to understand management within various contexts. However, with Knudsen (2003), we argue that paradigms alone are not enough to enhance our understanding of management.

We probably have all come across the fable of the blind men and the elephant. In a similar way, it may be that we need to connect the dots to get back to the elephant—"management." Indeed, it seems that we have come to over-fragment the study of management into disciplines, and it is for this reason that initiatives to integrate insights from different "disciplines" and "contexts" of management should be encouraged. Future theory development needs to go beyond individual fields of research to consider their intersections. By doing so, our understanding of a single context or phenomenon will improve, but also we will gain an enhanced understanding of management overall.

References

Andersen, E. (2014). Two perspectives on project management. In R. A. Lundin & M. Hällgren (eds.), *Advancing Research on Projects and Temporary Organizations* (pp. 140–149). Copenhagen Business School Press & Liber.

Angwin, D. (2004). Speed in M&A integration: the first 100 days. *European Management Journal*, 22(4), 418–430.

Ashkenas, R., & Francis, S. (2000). Integration managers: special leaders for special times. *Harvard Business Review*, 78(6), 108–116.

Bakker, R., DeFillippi, R., Schwab, A., & Sydow, J. (2016). Temporary organizing: promises, processes, problems. *Organization Studies*, 37(12), 1703–1719.

Bansal, A., King, D., & Meglio, O. (2022). Acquisitions as programs: the role of sensemaking and sensegiving. *International Journal of Project Management*, 40(3), 278–289.

Bilgili, T., Calderon, C., Allen, D., & Kedia, B. (2017). Gone with the wind: a meta-analytic review of executive turnover, its antecedents, and postacquisition performance. *Journal of Management*, 43, 1966–1997.

Birkinshaw, J., Bresman, H., & Håkansson, L. (2000). Managing the post-acquisition integration process: how the human integration and task integration processes interact to foster value creation. *Journal of Management Studies*, 37(3), 395–425.

Birollo, G., Rouleau, L., & Teerikangas, S. (2023). In the "crossfire" of the acquisition process: exploring middle managers' unfolding mediation dynamics. *European Management Journal*. https://doi.org/10.1016/j.emj.2023.06.003.

Birollo, G., & Teerikangas, S. (2019). Integration projects as relational spaces enabling post-acquisition integration. *International Journal of Project Management*, 37, 1003–1016.

Clegg, S., & Baumeler, C. (2010). Essai: from iron cages to liquid modernity in organization analysis. *Organization Studies*, 31(12), 1713–1733.

Crawford, L. (2000). Project management competence: the value of standards. Henley University, Henley.

Cunha, M., & Putnam, L. (2017). Paradox theory and the paradox of success. *Strategic Organization*, 17(1), 95–106.

Dille, T., Hernes, T., & Vaagaasar, A. (2023). Stuck in temporal translation? Challenges of discrepant temporal structures in interorganizational project collaboration. *Organization Studies*, 44(6), 867–888.

Gasparro, K., Zerjav, V., Konstantinou, E., & Casady, C. (2022). Vanguard projects as intermediation spaces in sustainability transitions. *Project Management Journal*, 53(2), 196–210.

Gautier, A., Pache, A., & Santos, F. (2023). Making sense of hybrid practices: the role of individual adherence to institutional logics in impact investing. *Organization Studies*, 44(9). https://doi.org/10.1177/01708406231181693.

Geraldi, J., Maylor, H., & Williams, T. (2011). Now, let's make it really complex (complicated): a systematic review of the complexities of projects. *International Journal of Operations & Production Management*, 31(9), 966–990.

Geraldi, J., & Söderlund, J. (2018). Project studies: what it is, where it is going. *International Journal of Project Management*, 36(1), 55–70.

Geraldi, J., Stjerne, I., & Oehmen, J. (2020). Acting in time: temporal work enacting tensions at the interface between temporary and permanent organisations. In T. Braun & J. Lampel (eds.), *Tensions and Paradoxes in Temporary Organizing* (Research on Sociology of Organizations, vol. 67) (pp. 81–103). Bingley: Emerald Group Publishing.

Geraldi, J., Teerikangas, S., & Birollo, G. (2022). Project, program and portfolio management as modes of organizing: theorising at the intersection between mergers and acquisitions and project studies. *International Journal of Project Management*, 40(4), 439–453.

Geraldi, J., Turner, J., Maylor, H., Söderholm, A., Hobday, M., & Brady, T. (2008). Innovation in project management: voices of researchers. *International Journal of Project Management*, 26(5), 586–589.

Graebner, M. (2004). Momentum and serendipity: how acquired firm leaders create value in the integration of technology firms. *Strategic Management Journal*, 25(8–9), 751–777.

Graebner, M., Heimeriks, K., Huy, Q., & Vaara, E. (2017). The process of post-merger integration: a review and agenda for future research. *Academy of Management Annals*, 11(1), 1–32. https://doi.org/10.5465/annals.2014.0078.

Granqvist, N., & Gustafsson, R. (2016). Temporal institutional work. *Academy of Management Journal*, 59(3), 1009–1035.

Haspeslagh, P., & Jemison, D. (1991). The challenge of renewal through acquisitions. *Planning Review*, 19, 27–30.

Hernes, T., & Schultz, M. (2020). Translating the distant into the present: how actors address distant past and future events through situated activity. *Organization Theory*, 1(1). https://doi.org/10.1177/2631787719900999.

Ika, L., & Pinto, J. (2022). The "re-meaning" of project success: updating and recalibrating for a modern project management. *International Journal of Project Management*, 40(7), 835–848.

Jemison, D., & Sitkin, S. (1986). Corporate acquisitions: a process perspective. *Academy of Management Review*, 11(1), 145–163.

King, D., Wang, G., Samimi, M., & Cortes, F. (2021). A meta-analytic integration of acquisition performance prediction. *Journal of Management Studies*, 58(5), 1198–1236.

Knudsen, C. (2003). Pluralism, scientific progress, and the structure of organization theory. In H. Tsoukas & C. Knudsen (eds.), *The Oxford Handbook of Organizationl Theory: Meta-Theoretical Perspectives* (pp 262–288). Oxford: Oxford University Press.

Lampel, J., Scarbrough, H., & Macmillan, S. (2008). Managing through projects in knowledge-based environments: special issue introduction by the guest editors. *Long Range Planning*, 41(1), 7–16.

Larsson, R., & Finkelstein, S. (1999). Integrating strategic, organisational, and human resource perspectives on mergers and acquisitions: a case survey of synergy realisation. *Organisation Science*, 10(1), 1–26.

Lenfle, S., & Loch, C. (2010). Lost roots: how project management came to emphasize control over flexibility and novelty. *California Management Review*, 53(1), 32–55.

Lenfle, S., Midler, C., & Hällgren, M. (2019). Exploratory projects: from strangeness to theory. *Project Management Journal*, 50(5), 519–523.

Leybourne, S. (2009). Improvisation and agile project management: a comparative consideration. *International Journal of Managing Projects in Business*, 2(4), 519–535.

Locatelli, G., Ika, L., Drouin, N., Müller, R., Huemann, M., Söderlund, J., Geraldi, J., & Clegg, S. (2023). A manifesto for project management research. *European Management Review*, 20(1), 3–17.

Lundin, R., & Söderholm, A. (1995). A theory of the temporary organization. *Scandinavian Journal of Management*, 11(4), 437–455.

Martinsuo, M., Teerikangas, S., Stensaker, I., & Meredith, J. (2022). Managing strategic projects and programs in and between organizations: special issue editorial. *International Journal of Project Management*, 40(5), 499–504.

Meglio, O. (2022). Reshaping M&A research: strategies and tactics for a new research agenda. *European Management Journal*, 40(6), 823–831.

Mirc, N., Rouzies, A., & Teerikangas, S. (2017). Do academics actually collaborate in the study of interdisciplinary phenomena? A look at half a century of research on mergers & acquisitions. *European Management Review*, 14(3), 333–357.

Müller, R., & Turner, J. (2007). Matching the project manager's leadership style to project type. *International Journal of Project Management*, 25(1), 21–32.

Nogeste, K. (2010). Understanding mergers and acquisitions (M&As) from a program management perspective. *International Journal of Managing Projects in Business*, 3(1), 111–138.

Pellegrinelli, S. (2008). Program management. In *Thinking and Acting as a Great Programme Manager* (pp. 3–16). London: Palgrave Macmillan.

Pellegrinelli, S., Partington, D., & Geraldi, J. (2011). Program management: an emerging opportunity for research and scholarship. In P.W.G Morris, J. Pinto, & J. Söderlund (eds.), *The Oxford Handbook of Project Management* (pp. 252–272). Oxford: Oxford University Press.

Pfeffer, J. (1993). Barrier to the advance of organizational science: paradigm development as a dependable variable. *Academy of Management Review*, 18(4), 599–620.

Prencipe, A., & Tell, F. (2001). Inter-project learning: processes and outcomes of knowledge codification in project-based firms. *Research Policy*, 30(9), 1373–1394.

Putnam, L., Fairhurst, G., & Banghart, S. (2016). Contradictions, dialectics, and paradoxes in organizations: a constitutive approach. *Academy of Management Annals*, 10(1), 65–171.

Quah, P., & Young, S. (2005). Post-acquisition management: a phases approach for cross-border M&A. *European Management Journal*, 23(1), 65–75.

Sahlin-Andersson, K., & Söderholm, A. (2002). *Beyond Project Management: New Perspectives on the Temporary-Permanent Dilemma*. Liber Ekonomie.

Shrivastava, P. (1986). Postmerger integration. *Journal of Business Strategy*, 7(1), 65–76.

Söderlund, J. (2011). Pluralism in project management: navigating the crossroads of specialization and fragmentation. *International Journal of Management Reviews*, 13(2), 153–176.

Steigenberger, N. (2017). The challenge of integration: a review of the M&A integration literature. *International Journal of Management Reviews*, 19(4), 408–431.

Stjerne, I., Geraldi, J., & Wenzel, M. (2022). Strategic practice drift: how open strategy infiltrates the strategy process. *Journal of Management Studies*. https://doi.org/10.1111/joms.12895.

Stjerne, I., Söderlund, J., & Minbaeva, D. (2019). Crossing times: temporal boundary-spanning practices in interorganizational projects. *International Journal of Project Management*, 37(2), 347–365.

Sydow, J., & Braun, T. (2018). Projects as temporary organizations: an agenda for further theorizing the interorganizational dimension. *International Journal of Project Management*, 36(1), 4–11.

Sydow, J., Lindkvist, L., & DeFillippi, R. (2004). Project-based organizations, embeddedness and repositories of knowledge: editorial. *Organization Studies*, 25(9), 1475–1489.

Teerikangas, S., & Laamanen, T. (2015). Structure first! Temporal dynamics of structural & cultural integration in cross-border acquisitions. In C. Cooper & S. Finkelstein (eds.), *Advances in Mergers and Acquisitions*, vol. 12 (pp. 109–152). Amsterdam: JAI Press.

Teerikangas, S. & Thanos, I. (2018). Looking into the "black box": unlocking the effect of integration on acquisition performance. *European Management Journal*, 36(3), 366–380.

Teerikangas, S., & Very, P., & Pisano, V. (2011). Integration managers' value-capturing roles and acquisition performance. *Human Resource Management*, 50(5), 651–683.

Thanos, I., Angwin, D., Bauer, F., & Teerikangas, S. (2022). Editorial: boundary spanning and boundary breaking research in M&A: taking stock and moving forward to reinvent the field. Introduction to the special issue on Reshaping M&A scholarship:

broadening the boundaries of M&A research. *European Management Journal*, 40(6). https://doi.org/10.1016/j.emj.2022.11.002.

Thanos, I., & Papadakis, V. (2012). The use of accounting-based measures in measuring M&A performance: a review of five decades of research. In C.L. Cooper and S. Finkelstein (eds.), *Advances in Mergers and Acquisitions*, (Volume 10, pp.103–120). Bingley: Emerald Group Publishing.

Vaara, E. (2002). On the discursive construction of success/failure in narratives of post-merger integration. *Organization Studies*, 23(2), 211–248.

Very, P., & Gates, S. (2007). M&A as project. In D. Angwin (ed.), *Mergers and Acquisitions* (pp. 181–203). Hoboken, NJ: Wiley Blackwell.

Vester, J. (2002). Lessons learned about integrating acquisitions. *Research-Technology Management*, 45(3), 33–41.

Whiteley, A., Pollack, J., & Matous, P. (2021). The origins of agile and iterative methods. *The Journal of Modern Project Management*, 8(3). https://journalmodernpm.com/index.php/jmpm/article/view/JMPM02502.

Winch, G. (2014). Three domains of project organising. *International Journal of Project Management*, 32(5), 721–731.

8 Blending causation and effectuation in acquisitions: a research agenda

Olimpia Meglio

Introduction

Acquisitions represent a popular corporate restructuring strategy firms rely on to achieve multiple goals, including renewing business models, accessing resources, and capabilities that would be too costly or time-consuming to develop internally, or increasing market share (Capron and Mitchell, 1998; Trautwein, 1990; Walter and Barney, 1990). Acquisitions have also proven effective as a substitute for R&D (see Hitt et al., 1991; King, Slotegraaf and Kesner, 2008) or to support internationalization processes from both developed or emerging countries (Madhok and Kehyani, 2012; Park et al., 2018; Park and Meglio, 2019). By combining exploitation with exploration, acquisitions enable firms to pursue entrepreneurial opportunities (cf., Dimov, 2011; King et al., 2018).

Despite their popularity, acquisitions typically display mixed success (King et al., 2004, 2021) due to the complexity, uncertainty, and ambiguity surrounding acquisitions (Jemison and Sitkin, 1986; Meglio and Risberg, 2010). Overall, acquisition scholars have produced a significant body of studies to identify antecedent, moderating, or mediating variables that influence value creation across different stages of the process (King et al., 2021). Existing research highlights that acquisitions may destroy value (Meyer, 2008; Seth, Song and Pettit, 2002) or offer the opportunity for serendipity value (Colman and Lunnan, 2011; Graebner, 2004). Another important insight is that post-acquisition integration is crucial to creating value from acquisitions (Haspeslagh and Jemison, 1991), resulting in an extensive body of research on integration models, mechanisms, or leadership (cf., Angwin and Meadows, 2015; Meglio, King and Risberg, 2015; Teerikangas, Véry and Pisano, 2011). Taken together, research findings and their managerial implications outline that to be successful acquiring firms should carefully pre-plan how to integrate the merging companies

(De Noble, Gustafson and Hergert, 1988). While useful, this perspective remains narrow and incomplete for several reasons.

First, the effectiveness of an integration plan is contingent upon a comprehensive assessment of resources and capabilities of the target firm, as it is fraught with information asymmetries spanning the acquisition process (Cuypers, Cuypers and Martin, 2017). Information asymmetry refers to difficulties in identifying targets and assessing potential value from the combination during the pre-acquisition stage (Welch et al., 2020), and extending available information to planning how to create value during integration (Graebner et al., 2017; Haspleslagh and Jemison, 1991).

Second, acquisition decisions are influenced by different types of biases that may lead to sub-optimal choices in both pre- and post-acquisition stages (Aschbacher and Kroon, 2023). While rational heuristics may offer guidance, they do not eliminate and can even accentuate biases related to the interactive and social nature of acquisition decision-making processes where rational, political, and emotional aspects intertwine (Osmani, 2017). Further, acquisition decision biases are compounded by information asymmetry (Rogan and Sorenson, 2014).

Third, existing research has increasingly shown that more nuanced solutions to integration priorities are needed to balance competing demands, in terms of resources, and time horizons (Meglio et al., 2015). This is also in line with studies highlighting that integration requires continuous adaptation of initial plans based on feedback from the field, through a combination of sense-making and sense-giving activities (Bansal, King and Meglio, 2022). For example, emphasis on planning downplays serendipity, or unexpected benefits from the acquisition that provide renewal (Colman and Lunnan, 2011; Graebner, 2004). If information during integration can offer unanticipated benefits, it becomes relevant to understand how such benefits can be achieved.

In sum, acquisitions processes are more complex than traditionally depicted (see Angwin and Meadows, 2015; Risberg, King and Meglio, 2015) reinforcing the need for novel perspectives on acquisitions (Thanos et al., 2022). I follow recent calls to reshape acquisition research (Meglio, 2022) to advance the idea that effectuation may shed new light on acquisitions and help better frame the acquisition process, especially in knowledge-intensive (Coff, 1999) or entrepreneurial contexts (Ragozzino and Reuer, 2010).

Theoretically, effectuation is about the unfolding process of entrepreneurial action in radically uncertain situations, that is, situations wherein the consequences of one's actions and the conditions and/or factors of success are difficult, if not impossible, to accurately predict (Grégoire and Cherchem, 2020). Effectuation has garnered considerable attention since the early 2000s (Sarasvathy, 2001), starting from the entrepreneurship field and venturing into creativity, innovation, marketing (Grégoire and Cherchem, 2020), and project management, a perspective recently applied also to the investigation of acquisitions (cf., Birollo and Teerikangas, 2019; Geraldi, Teerikangas and Birollo, 2022).

Since effectuation appears to support decision-making in entrepreneurial and other management contexts, I suggest it may work equally well in acquisition decision environments. For example, acquisitions are consistently described as uncertain, ambiguous, complex, and risky, as they combine goal-driven and non-goal-driven logic to increase adaptation and flexibility (Öberg, 2015; Schriber, Bauer and King, 2019). More specifically, an effectuation perspective may prove particularly useful for a better understanding of actual integration processes and how value is imaginatively co-created in acquisitions, especially those involving small entrepreneurial firms (Graebner, 2004).

The considerations above suggest it is worthwhile exploring the intersection of effectuation and acquisition research and suggesting future research directions. To achieve this aim, I focus on both meso- and micro-levels of analysis. Specifically, after discussing how causation and effectuation logics may complement one another, I adapt Arend, Sarooghi and Burkemper's (2015) framework to an acquisition context. Next, I will discuss the micro level of analysis and how the four effectual principles may apply to acquisitions. I then conclude by developing a research agenda.

Contrasting effectuation and causation in acquisitions

Existing studies depict acquisitions as complex and heterogeneous events (Larsson and Finkelstein, 1999) surrounded by ambiguity and uncertainty (Jemison and Sitkin, 1986). Handling the challenges inherent in acquisitions poses acquiring companies' managers several dilemmas across the acquisition process (Graebner, 2004; Teerikangas et al., 2011). What to buy, how much pay for a target, how, and to what extent, and when to integrate represent major areas of concern that typically result in multiple, intertwined decisions acquiring firms' managers need to take.

Traditionally, acquisition research acknowledges that decisions are affected by information asymmetries, are inherently biased, and typically taken under considerable time pressure, leading to potential problems and cognitive pitfalls affecting the quality of decisions (Graebner et al., 2017). Aschbacher and Kroon (2023) highlight potential errors in the pre-acquisition phase, arising from misleading due diligence, improperly negotiating terms or premium price, or simply forcing a deal that should not be done. Moving to the post-acquisition phase, potential errors generally involve what, how, and when to integrate the merging companies. Each decision requires in turn multiple decisions, and complications can also be attributed to the interdependencies among different decisions that imply re-iterations and continuous adjustments of assumptions that further magnify pitfalls and biases (Aschbacher and Kroon, 2023). Executives and advisors typically rely on heuristics (cf., Bingham and Eisenhardt, 2011; Vuori, Laamanen and Zollo, 2023) that represent simple rules to make acquisitions more manageable. While useful, they do not offset the risk of errors or sub-optimal decisions.

Against this background, acquisition research is predominantly informed by a focus on causation. According to Sarasvathy (2001), causation logic builds upon desired effects and identifies means to achieve them. While it recognizes that the future is to a certain extent unpredictable, a causation logic provides a repertoire of means to achieve the intended outcome. In other words, causation represents the logic underlying the managerial work based on planning goals and controlling results based on identified milestones.

From this foundation, acquisition scholars have initially compared different acquisition typologies (related/unrelated; friendly/hostile; domestic/cross-border) to see what type performs better. However, research has failed to provide conclusive results (Homberg, Rost and Osterloh, 2009; Kusewitt, 1985; Tuch and O'Sullivan, 2007). Over time, more emphasis has been placed on the integration phase (Graebner et al., 2017; Jemison and Sitkin, 1986), reflecting the idea that a good integration starts before the deal is closed, again emphasizing the importance of planning. Acquisition scholars have developed integration models and mechanisms to provide an *ex ante* repertoire of solutions to solve integration dilemmas (Haspleslagh and Jemison, 1991; Zaheer, Castañer and Souder, 2013). The underlying logic is to anticipate integrative demands based on deals' characteristics, such as the degree of relatedness (Bauer and Matzler, 2014), geographical (Chakrabarti and Mitchell, 2013), or cultural (Reus and Lamont, 2009) or technological distance (Patel and King, 2016). Identified factors are then used to predict what post-merger integration will require in terms of coordination and autonomy (Puranam, Singh and

Zollo, 2006; Zaheer et al., 2013) or task and human integration (Birkinshaw, Bresman and Håkanson, 2000).

While initially conceived as orthogonal and mutually exclusive, integrative models have been increasingly regarded as coexisting (Zaheer et al., 2013). Scholars recommend going beyond either/or integrative models and highlight the importance of more nuanced solutions to integration priorities (Angwin and Meadows, 2015) where integration and autonomy are blended into hybrid approaches (Schweizer, 2005). Moreover, sense-making and sense-giving help integration leaders to progressively refine integration plans during the post-acquisition stage and adapt integration mechanisms based on evolving responses from the target company (Bansal et al., 2022). Overall, these findings call for additional inquiry into how to balance competing demands (between task and human integration or exploitation and exploration) especially in entrepreneurial acquisitions (Brueller and Capron, 2021). These considerations pave the way to examining acquisitions from an effectual lens.

Effectuation addresses uncertainty in human decisions and choices (Sarasvathy, 2001). More specifically, it offers an alternative description of entrepreneurial processes where resource-poor entrepreneurs act to create a new market artifact (Arend et al., 2015). Instead of trying to predict the future in ambiguous and uncertain contexts, effectuation focuses on means, resources, and capabilities one can mobilize, which in turn determine the goals and courses of action one might choose to pursue (Grégoire and Cherchem, 2020). In other words, effectuation reverses the means–end chain and emphasizes the importance of an adaptive approach (Wiltbank et al., 2006).

Effectuation logic is reported to flourish in an unstable operating environment that is difficult to predict, as it allows swift reactions to environmental change (Sarasvathy and Dew, 2005). Effectuation research has been primarily employed to investigate entrepreneurial efforts, such as introducing new disruptive offerings that radically change the market, or when it is difficult to obtain accurate and reliable information about customers, channels, or price. Radical changes typically bring actors to venture into unknown territories where it is no longer possible to rely upon extrapolation from prior cases (McMullen and Dimov, 2013) due to high uncertainty and volatility. Uncertainty provides an ideal setting for co-creation with all actors and stakeholders being potentially involved. An effectuation perspective does not rule out a general sense of what is to be accomplished; rather, it provides room for serendipity and imagination in entrepreneurial action (Sarasvathy, 2001).

I argue that an effectuation perspective renders the complexity and ambiguity of the interactions between the merging parties towards the co-creation value from the deal (Jemison and Sitkin, 1986). Acquisitions resemble the conditions of uncertainty and radical changes that effectuation scholars refer to. Acquisitions pose significant challenges before and after the deal is signed, which are essentially related to information asymmetries (Meglio, King and Shijaku, 2023). These issues appear especially salient in acquisitions involving small entrepreneurial firms (Graebner, 2009). The acquisition of technology startups by incumbents typically aims to obtain technological know-how, product extension, or internationalization to respond to shorter life cycles (Madhok and Keyhani, 2012). They pose peculiar challenges to acquiring firms regarding how to balance multiple demands, in highly volatile contexts (Brueller and Capron, 2021). One challenge is the tacit and sticky knowledge embedded in people and organizational processes and it extends to the post-acquisition stage due to uncertainty about how to transfer/share resources or capabilities (cf., Ranft and Lord, 2002) and how to create planned synergies (Coff, 1999).

Extant research identifies two mechanisms to cope with information asymmetries between potential merging parties. First, firms use an alliance as a precursor of an acquisition (King, Shijaku and Urtasun, 2023). Second, firms use corporate venture capital as a window into emerging technology that can facilitate integration after the acquisitions (Brueller and Capron, 2021). Still, these remedies do not offer guidance on how to integrate the merging companies and create value, including serendipitous value. In these circumstances, an effectual approach, based on continuous learning and adaptation to changes in the operating environment can offer an alternative, although complementary, perspective to the integration process.

Blending effectuation and causation in acquisitions

I propose an integrative model of acquisition processes that combines effectuation and causation. Figure 8.1 displays an overarching model of acquisitions that builds upon Arend and colleagues (2015) and is particularly useful to focus on the inter-organizational level of analysis. Figure 8.2 zooms into micro-processes, and it builds on Sarasvathy (2001) to examine how effectual principles may foster value creation in an acquisition context.

An integrative model

Figure 8.1 represents an adaptation of Arend and colleagues' (2015) framework to the acquisition context, using both acquiring and acquired firms. The framework displays the following pillars: context, individual criteria, individual means, co-creators, contingencies.

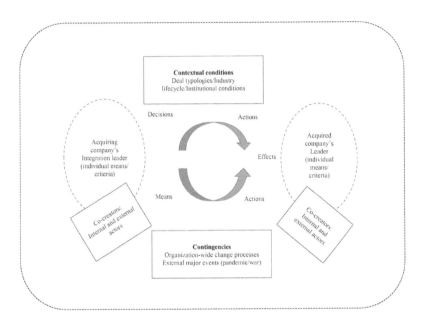

Figure 8.1   An integrative model of acquisitions

Context

Acquisition research highlights that acquisitions are complex events, surrounded by uncertainty and ambiguity that arise from contextual conditions. Contextual conditions may denote environmental conditions (economic landscape, institutional conditions, industry life cycle) or deals' characteristics. There is already a significant body of research on environmental conditions. For instance, scholars have investigated how consolidation processes in mature industries or technological convergence across seemingly distant industries eventually result in different acquisition waves (Auster and Sirower, 2002) and typologies (Napier, 1989). Different scenarios prompt different acquisition typologies and in turn integrative priorities and solutions (Bower, 2001).

Contextual conditions also relate to how the merging companies are inter-twined. For instance, acquisitions may be related or unrelated, friendly or hostile, domestic or cross-border (Meglio and Risberg, 2012). Like external conditions, acquisition typologies offer an initial glimpse into integration priorities and solutions. However, adopting an intertemporal perspective, contextual conditions also influence the post-acquisition process through sense-making processes of actors involved (Bansal et al., 2022). Actors may have convergent/divergent sense-making of how the acquisition will unfold and this contributes to decreasing/increasing (respectively) the ambiguity surrounding the deal. The combination of different conditions influences the sources of synergies from the deal (assessed *ex ante*) and extend to the way such synergies will be achieved during the post-acquisition phase (assessed *ex post*).

Individual means

Acquisition research has primarily focused on integration mechanisms that integration leaders or teams rely upon to pursue task and human integration (Birkinshaw et al., 2000). An effectuation perspective innovates acquisition research by broadening the repertoire of means (see below).

Individual criteria

Acquisitions involve multiple actors and stakeholders (Meglio, 2015). Each individual or group may have her/his own aspirations and goals to achieve through the acquisition. However, acquisition research does not openly describe them as criteria, rather as goals or stakes. Some of these goals are purely financial; some are a combination of economic and non-economic goals. Some goals are instantaneous; some goals require time to be attained (Meglio, 2015). More importantly, attaining goals takes time and resources; therefore, goals may converge or conflict with one another, and the way different goals interact with one another will shape the acquisition process. Integrating the merging companies is a matter of balancing competing goals (Meglio et al., 2015). Effectuation emphasizes strategic alliances and pre-commitments from stakeholders to mitigate or eliminate uncertainty and create value (Sarasvathy, 2001). Again, this is echoed by acquisition research emphasizing stakeholders' engagement (Bettinazzi and Zollo, 2017) and using alliances as precursors of acquisitions (King et al., 2023).

Co-creators

Acquisition literature is extensively focused on value creation processes. While they are inter-organizational arrangements, the idea of co-creation is almost missing in existing acquisition research. An effectuation perspective represents a step towards embracing a value co-creation perspective, by emphasizing the interactions among planners and executers or acquiring and target employees or unions (Stensaker, Colman and Grøgaard, 2023).

The acquisition process involves different hierarchical levels across the boundaries of the merging companies. The more extensive the integration is, the higher the number of individuals involved. Traditionally, the integration process is depicted as an interaction between planners and executers (Graebner et al., 2017). However, the extensive reliance on integration mechanisms that favor employees' engagement, including transition teams or socialization (Meglio et al., 2015), signals a shift towards considering all employees from the merging parties as co-creators of the integration. The same considerations apply equally well to all actors involved in the deal, including consultants (Parvinen and Tikkanen, 2007), customers, or suppliers (Anderson, Havila and Salmi, 2001).

The idea of co-creation should be extended to external actors playing a role in acquisitions, from investment bankers to consultancy firms, from regulatory bodies to suppliers and customers. In other words, the idea of co-creation does justice to the inter- and intra-organizational dynamics and provides a more complete picture of acquisition processes.

Contingencies

Contingencies do shape post-acquisition processes. Contingency represents a broad term to refer, for instance, to other organization-wide change processes under way in the acquiring or the target company (Rouzies, Colman and Angwin, 2019). Contingencies may also refer to external and unpredictable events, such as pandemics or war (Bauer, Friesl and Dao, 2022). Contingencies are double-edge situations, meaning that they can either present opportunities to catch or threats to mitigate.

Effectual principles

Zooming into micro-level processes, an effectuation perspective may guide acquisition research by examining value co-creation processes. The contribution of effectual principles towards co-creation is visualized in Figure 8.2 that starts with means at hand (also known as bird in hand principle). Indeed, an important connotation of an effectuation logic is the reversal of means–ends chain. As a result, an effectuation perspective takes means as a starting point. Means at hand are related three fundamental questions: who I am, what I know, whom I know. Let's analyze how they could work in an acquisition context.

Who I am

Who I am is essentially related to the resource and capabilities endowment of both the acquiring and the target firm that together shape the value co-creation process. The primary means is making sense of the situation (through documents and people). Based on ongoing assessment of the current situation as it unfolds, you develop/refine your integration plan (see Bansal et al., 2022).

What I know

What I know deals with previous experience in handling acquisitions that the acquiring company may have and the repertoire of heuristics the management team may rely upon (Vuori et al., 2023). An important caveat is the conditions of ambiguity, uncertainty, and information asymmetries that typically surround acquisitions that in turn make it difficult to codify experience into meaningful and effective tools. Existing studies highlight that there is a U-shaped relationship between the number of previous deals and the focal acquisition performance (Haleblian and Finkelstein, 1999).

Whom I know

Whom I know emphasizes the importance of leveraging existing ties, and forming new ones (Spedale, Van Den Bosch and Volberda, 2007), as well as considering the institutional context (Maas, Heugens and Reus, 2019). These topics have been only sparsely touched upon in existing studies and have the potential to offer important insights into the value co-creation process. Institutional context may even refer to informal rules or practices in use in the market for corporate control industry and significantly shape whether and how the value creation takes place in an acquisition. Overall, the consideration of institutional context brings to the fore important actors who actively contribute to either create value or destroy it. For instance, Fani, Kalanoski and Bertrand (2023) underline the advantages associated with arbitrage opportunities that lead rivals to increase their corporate development initiatives.

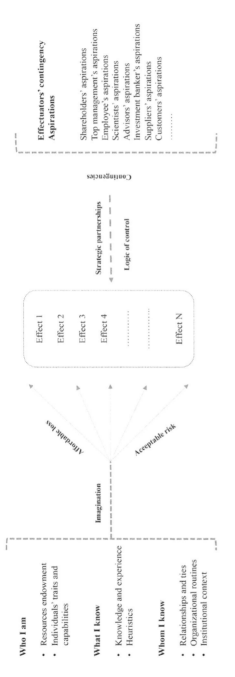

Figure 8.2   Effectual principles in an acquisition context

The combination of these factors is leveraged by imagination, that extends the aspects related to the three key questions of who I am, what I know, and whom I know. Relying on imagination at this stage reflects an attempt to identify innovative solutions to integration issues, such as novel coordination mechanisms or models. Imagination is almost absent in acquisition research, due to its predominant emphasis on ready to use models and mechanisms.

Imagination is not free from constraints; selection criteria—affordable loss and acceptable risk—are equally important principles inspiring an effectuation approach. In other words, actors leverage the means at their disposal by constantly contrasting the expected loss and the affordable risk. They both serve as selection filters that lead to the pursued effect (in Figure 8.2 there is a set of alternative effects).

The right side of Figure 8.2 displays the influence of contingencies that set the ground for strategic partnerships, as discussed above. Here, emphasis is placed on stakeholders' aspirations and their impact upon acquisitions. In other words, an effectuation lens goes beyond a strict focus on shareholders to consider the goals and stakes of different individuals and organizations within the merging companies or in the external environment.

In sum, an effectual perspective innovates traditional models of acquisitions in that it advances the idea of co-creation of value and visualizes how different actors iteratively contribute to distinct patterns through processes of self-organization (Goldstein, 1999). Self-organization implies that actors in a situation react to the pattern they together create, and as a result that pattern alters itself, causing the actors to react anew.

Conclusion

Acquisition research is predominantly inspired by causation logic. This chapter advances an effectuation perspective to provide an alternative, complementary perspective to acquisition research that can inform both the inter-organizational and the micro levels of analysis.

At the inter-organizational level of analysis, an effectuation lens highlights the role of co-creators of value by highlighting how different actors iteratively contribute to distinct patterns through processes of self-organization (Goldstein, 1999). In doing so, an effectuation perspective provides a more holistic and dynamic picture of how different actors contribute to either co-create or destroy value across the acquisition process. For instance, by highlighting self-organization processes it suggests that actors in a situation react to the pattern they together create, and as a result that pattern alters itself, causing the actors to react anew. The idea of co-creation is almost missing in acquisition research and appears particularly promising to achieve a better grasp of acquisitions and value.

At the micro level of analysis, it emphasizes individual principles towards value co-creation that include the role of imagination that has been neglected by acquisition research. An *effectual design*, conceptually interpreted as a creative synthesis of planning and openness to novelty, may lead to a better understanding of how serendipitous value is co-created across the acquisition process and what is the contribution of different actors involved. The role of creativity and imagination in designing novel integrative solutions could represent an important addition to existing research.

In closing, effectuation may offer a novel complementary perspective to further our understanding of post-acquisition processes. Existing frameworks and tools are inspired by a causation logic that assumes that acquisition leaders know what they have bought and how to integrate the target within the acquiring organization. Unfortunately, acquisitions are fraught with information asymmetries crossing the entire process and make the dynamics of the integration process difficult to predict and plan. Effectuation logic can augment the causation logic, providing a complementary route towards value creation when the environment is less predictable, and a more nuanced and adaptive approach is required.

References

Anderson, H., Havila, V., & Salmi, A. (2001). Can you buy a business relationship? On the importance of customer and supplier relationships in acquisitions. *Industrial Marketing Management*, 30(7), 575–586.

Angwin, D., & Meadows, M. (2015). New integration strategies for post-acquisition management. *Long Range Planning*, 48(4), 235–251.

Arend, R., Sarooghi, H., & Burkemper, A. (2015). Effectuation as ineffectual? Applying the 3E theory-assessment framework to a proposed new theory of entrepreneurship. *Academy of Management Review*, 40(4), 630–651.

Aschbacher, J., & Kroon, D. (2023). Falling prey to bias? The influence of advisors on the manifestation of cognitive biases in the pre-M&A phase of organizations. *Group & Organization Management*. https://doi.org/10596011231171455.

Auster, E., & Sirower, M. (2002). The dynamics of merger and acquisition waves: a three-stage conceptual framework with implications for practice. *The Journal of Applied Behavioral Science*, 38(2), 216–244.

Bansal, A., King, D., & Meglio, O. (2022). Acquisitions as programs: the role of sensemaking and sensegiving. *International Journal of Project Management*, 40(3), 278–289.

Bauer, F., Friesl, M., & Dao, M. (2022). Run or hide: changes in acquisition behaviour during the COVID-19 pandemic. *Journal of Strategy and Management*, 15(1), 38–53.

Bauer, F., & Matzler, K. (2014). Antecedents of M&A success: the role of strategic complementarity, cultural fit, and degree and speed of integration. *Strategic Management Journal*, 35(2), 269–291.

Bettinazzi, E. L., & Zollo, M. (2017). Stakeholder orientation and acquisition performance. *Strategic Management Journal*, 38(12), 2465–2485.

Bingham, C., & Eisenhardt, K. (2011). Rational heuristics: the "simple rules" that strategists learn from process experience. *Strategic Management Journal*, 32(13), 1437–1464.

Birkinshaw, J., Bresman, H., & Håkanson, L. (2000). Managing the post-acquisition integration process: how the human integration and task integration processes interact to foster value creation. *Journal of Management Studies*, 37(3), 395–425.

Birollo, G., & Teerikangas, S. (2019). Integration projects as relational spaces: a closer look at acquired managers' strategic role recovery in cross-border acquisitions. *International Journal of Project Management*, 37(8), 1003–1016.

Bower, J. (2001). Not all M&As are alike: and that matters. *Harvard Business Review*. https://hbr.org/2001/03/not-all-mas-are-alike-and-that-matters.

Brueller, N., & Capron, L. (2021). Acquisitions of startups by incumbents: the 3 Cs of co-specialization from startup inception to post-merger integration. *California Management Review*, 63(3), 70–93.

Capron, L., & Mitchell, W. (1998). Bilateral resource redeployment and capabilities improvement following horizontal acquisitions. *Industrial and Corporate Change*, 7(3), 453–484.

Chakrabarti, A., & Mitchell, W. (2013). The persistent effect of geographic distance in acquisition target selection. *Organization Science*, 24(6), 1805–1826.

Coff, R. (1999). How buyers cope with uncertainty when acquiring firms in knowledge-intensive industries: caveat emptor. *Organization Science*, 10(2), 144–161.

Colman, H., & Lunnan, R. (2011). Organizational identification and serendipitous value creation in post-acquisition integration. *Journal of Management*, 37(3), 839–860.

Cuypers, I., Cuypers, Y., & Martin, X. (2017). When the target may know better: effects of experience and information asymmetries on value from mergers and acquisitions. *Strategic Management Journal*, 38(3), 609–625.

De Noble, A., Gustafson, L., & Hergert, M. (1988). Planning for post-merger integration: eight lessons for merger success. *Long Range Planning*, 21(4), 82–85.

Dimov, D. (2011). Grappling with the unbearable elusiveness of entrepreneurial opportunities. *Entrepreneurship Theory and Practice*, 35(1), 57–81.

Fani, V., Kalanoski, D., & Bertrand, O. (2023). The competitive effects of financial and fiscal institutional arbitrage opportunities: evidence from cross-border M&As. *Long Range Planning*, 56(3), 102324.

Geraldi, J., Teerikangas, S., & Birollo, G. (2022). Project, program and portfolio management as modes of organizing: theorising at the intersection between mergers and acquisitions and project studies. *International Journal of Project Management*, 40(4), 439–453.

Goldstein, J. (1999). Emergence as a construct: history and issues. *Emergence*, 1(1), 49–72.

Graebner, M. (2004). Momentum and serendipity: how acquired leaders create value in the integration of technology firms. *Strategic Management Journal*, 25(8–9), 751–777.

Graebner, M. (2009). Caveat venditor: trust asymmetries in acquisitions of entrepreneurial firms. *Academy of Management Journal*, 52(3), 435–472.

Graebner, M., Heimeriks, K., Huy, Q., & Vaara, E. (2017). The process of postmerger integration: a review and agenda for future research. *Academy of Management Annals*, 11(1), 1–32.

Grégoire, D., & Cherchem, N. (2020). A structured literature review and suggestions for future effectuation research. *Small Business Economics*, 54, 621–639.

Haleblian, J., & Finkelstein, S. (1999). The influence of organizational acquisition experience on acquisition performance: a behavioral learning perspective. *Administrative Science Quarterly*, 44(1), 29–56.

Haspeslagh, P., & Jemison, D. (1991). *Managing Acquisitions: Creating Value through Corporate Renewal* (Vol. 416). New York: The Free Press.

Hitt, M., Hoskisson, R., Ireland, R., & Harrison, J. (1991). Effects of acquisitions on R&D inputs and outputs. *Academy of Management Journal*, 34(3), 693–706.

Homberg, F., Rost, K., & Osterloh, M. (2009). Do synergies exist in related acquisitions? A meta-analysis of acquisition studies. *Review of Managerial Science*, 3, 75–116.

Jemison, D., & Sitkin, S. (1986). Corporate acquisitions: a process perspective. *Academy of Management Review*, 11(1), 145–163.

King, D., Dalton, D., Daily, C., & Covin, J. (2004). Meta-analyses of post-acquisition performance: indications of unidentified moderators. *Strategic Management Journal*, 25(2), 187–200.

King, D., Schriber, S., Bauer, F., & Amiri, S. (2018). Acquisitions as corporate entrepreneurship. In S. Finkelstein & C. L. Cooper (eds.), *Advances in Mergers and Acquisitions* (Advances in Mergers and Acquisitions, Vol. 17) (pp. 119–144). Bingley: Emerald Publishing.

King, D., Shijaku, E., & Urtasun, A. (2023). Are acquirers different? Identifying firm precursors to acquisitions. *Journal of Strategy and Management*. https://doi.org/10.1108/JSMA-07-2022-0126.

King, D., Slotegraaf, R., & Kesner, I. (2008). Performance implications of firm resource interactions in the acquisition of R&D-intensive firms. *Organization Science*, 19(2), 327–340.

King, D., Wang, G., Samimi, M., & Cortes, A. (2021). A meta-analytic integration of acquisition performance prediction. *Journal of Management Studies*, 58(5), 1198–1236.

Kusewitt, J. (1985). An exploratory study of strategic acquisition factors relating to performance. *Strategic Management Journal*, 6(2), 151–169.

Larsson, R., & Finkelstein, S. (1999). Integrating strategic, organizational, and human resource perspectives on mergers and acquisitions: a case survey of synergy realization. *Organization Science*, 10(1), 1–26.

Maas, A., Heugens, P., & Reus, T. (2019). Viceroys or emperors? An institution-based perspective on merger and acquisition prevalence and shareholder value. *Journal of Management Studies*, 56(1), 234–269.

Madhok, A., & Keyhani, M. (2012). Acquisitions as entrepreneurship: asymmetries, opportunities, and the internationalization of multinationals from emerging economies. *Global Strategy Journal*, 2(1), 26–40.

McMullen, J., & Dimov, D. (2013). Time and the entrepreneurial journey: the problems and promise of studying entrepreneurship as a process. *Journal of Management Studies*, 50(8), 1481–1512.

Meglio, O. (2015). The acquisition performance game: a stakeholder approach. In A. Risberg, D. R. King, & O. Meglio (eds.), *The Routledge Companion to Mergers and Acquisitions* (pp. 187–200). New York: Routledge.

Meglio, O. (2022). Reshaping M&A research: strategies and tactics for a new research agenda. *European Management Journal*, 40(6), 823–831.

Meglio, O., King, D., & Risberg, A. (2015). Improving acquisition outcomes with contextual ambidexterity. *Human Resource Management*, 54(S1), s29–s43.

Meglio, O., King, D., & Shijaku, E. (2023). Addressing information asymmetry in acquisitions: the role of social ties. In S. Cooper & S. Finkelstein (eds.), *Advances in Mergers and Acquisitions* (Vol. 22) (pp. 1–17). Bingley: Emerald Group Publishing.

Meglio, O., & Risberg, A. (2010). Mergers and acquisitions: time for a methodological rejuvenation of the field? *Scandinavian Journal of Management*, 26(1), 87–95.

Meglio, O., & Risberg, A. (2012). Are all mergers and acquisitions treated as if they were alike? A review of empirical literature. *Advances in Mergers and Acquisitions*. https://doi.org/10.1108/S1479-361X(2012)0000010004.

Meyer, C. (2008). Value leakages in mergers and acquisitions: why they occur and how they can be addressed. *Long Range Planning*, 41(2), 197–224.

Napier, N. (1989). Mergers and acquisitions, human resource issues and outcomes: a review and suggested typology. *Journal of Management Studies*, 26(3), 271–290.

Öberg, C. (2015). Acquisitions as an adaptation strategy. In A. Risberg, D. King, & O. Meglio (eds.), *The Routledge Companion to Mergers and Acquisitions* (pp. 27–39). Abingdon: Routledge.

Osmani, J. (2017). Heuristics and cognitive biases: can the group decision-making avoid them? *Academic Journal of Interdisciplinary Studies*, 5(3 S1), 225–232.

Park, K., & Meglio, O. (2019). Playing a double game? Pursuing innovation through ambidexterity in an international acquisition program from the Arabian Gulf Region. *R&D Management*, 49(1), 115–135.

Park, K., Meglio, O., Bauer, F., & Tarba, S. (2018). Managing patterns of internationalization, integration, and identity transformation: the post-acquisition metamorphosis of an Arabian Gulf EMNC. *Journal of Business Research*, 93, 122–138.

Parvinen, P., & Tikkanen, H. (2007). Incentive asymmetries in the mergers and acquisitions process. *Journal of Management Studies*, 44(5), 759–787.

Patel, P., & King, D. (2016). Interaction of cultural and technological distance in cross-border, high-technology acquisitions. In S. Finkelstein & C. L. Cooper (eds.), *Advances in Mergers and Acquisitions*. Leeds: Emerald Publishing. https://doi.org/10.1108/S1479-361X20160000015007.

Puranam, P., Singh, H., & Zollo, M. (2006). Organizing for innovation: managing the coordination-autonomy dilemma in technology acquisitions. *Academy of Management Journal*, 49(2), 263–280.

Ragozzino, R., & Reuer, J. J. (2010). The opportunities and challenges of entrepreneurial acquisitions. *European Management Review*, 7(2), 80–90.

Ranft, A. L., & Lord, M. D. (2002). Acquiring new technologies and capabilities: a grounded model of acquisition implementation. *Organization Science*, 13(4), 420–441.

Reus, T., & Lamont, B. (2009). The double-edged sword of cultural distance in international acquisitions. *Journal of International Business Studies*, 40(8), 1298–1316.

Risberg, A., King, D. R., & Meglio, O. (eds.) (2015). *The Routledge Companion to Mergers and Acquisitions*. Abingdon: Routledge.

Rogan, M., & Sorenson, O. (2014). Picking a (poor) partner: a relational perspective on acquisitions. *Administrative Science Quarterly*, 59(2), 301–329.

Rouzies, A., Colman, H., & Angwin, D. (2019). Recasting the dynamics of post-acquisition integration: an embeddedness perspective. *Long Range Planning*, 52(2), 271–282.

Sarasvathy, S. (2001). Causation and effectuation: toward a theoretical shift from economic inevitability to entrepreneurial contingency. *Academy of Management Review*, 26(2), 243–263.

Sarasvathy, S., & Dew, N. (2005). New market creation through transformation. *Journal of Evolutionary Economics*, 15, 533–565.

Schriber, S., Bauer, F., & King, D. (2019). Organisational resilience in acquisition integration: organisational antecedents and contingency effects of flexibility and redundancy. *Applied Psychology*, 68(4), 759–796.

Schweizer, L. (2005). Organizational integration of acquired biotechnology companies into pharmaceutical companies: the need for a hybrid approach. *Academy of Management Journal*, 48(6), 1051–1074.

Seth, A., Song, K., & Pettit, R. (2002). Value creation and destruction in cross-border acquisitions: an empirical analysis of foreign acquisitions of US firms. *Strategic Management Journal*, 23(10), 921–940.

Spedale, S., Van Den Bosch, F., & Volberda, H. (2007). Preservation and dissolution of the target firm's embedded ties in acquisitions. *Organization Studies*, 28(8), 1169–1196.

Stensaker, I., Colman, H., & Grøgaard, B. (2023). The dynamics of union-management collaboration during postmerger integration. *Long Range Planning*, 56(6), 102326.

Teerikangas, S., Vèry, P., & Pisano, V. (2011). Integration managers' value-capturing roles and acquisition performance. *Human Resource Management*, 50(5), 651–683.

Thanos, I., Angwin, D., Bauer, F., & Teerikangas, S. (2022). Reshaping M&A scholarship: broadening boundaries of M&A research. *European Management Journal*, 40(6), 819–822.

Trautwein, F. (1990). Merger motives and merger prescriptions. *Strategic Management Journal*, 11(4), 283–295.

Tuch, C., & O'Sullivan, N. (2007). The impact of acquisitions on firm performance: a review of the evidence. *International Journal of Management Reviews*, 9(2), 141–170.

Vuori, N., Laamanen, T., & Zollo, M. (2023). Capability development in infrequent organizational processes: unveiling the interplay of heuristics and causal knowledge. *Journal of Management Studies*, 60(5), 1341–1381.

Walter, G., & Barney, J. (1990). Research notes and communications management objectives in mergers and acquisitions. *Strategic Management Journal*, 11(1), 79–86.

Welch, X., Pavićević, S., Keil, T., & Laamanen, T. (2020). The pre-deal phase of mergers and acquisitions: a review and research agenda. *Journal of Management*, 46(6), 843–878.

Wiltbank, R., Dew, N., Read, S., & Sarasvathy, S. (2006). What to do next? The case for non-predictive strategy. *Strategic Management Journal*, 27(10), 981–998.

Zaheer, A., Castañer, X., & Souder, D. (2013). Synergy sources, target autonomy, and integration in acquisitions. *Journal of Management*, 39(3), 604–632.

9 M&A failure: an interdisciplinary, systematic review

Timo Paumen, David Kroon and Svetlana N. Khapova

Introduction

Merger and acquisition (M&A) activity continues to set new records. Despite an increase in M&A activity, at least 50 percent of M&As continue to fail (Healy, 2016). Unsurprisingly, years and vast amounts of money have been spent researching M&A transactions (Renneboog and Vansteenkiste, 2019). Although research has offered a wealth of insights on solutions to mitigate M&A failure (Calipha, Tarba and Brock, 2010), M&A performance has not improved (Dao and Bauer, 2021). Studies on M&A failure have adopted a plenitude of theoretical perspectives, leading to a fragmentation of the field (King et al., 2021). Moreover, existing studies mostly treat the M&A process as static to cover one phase of the M&A process, such as the pre-M&A phase (Welch et al., 2020) or the post-M&A integration phase (Graebner et al., 2017; Henningsson, Yetton and Wynne, 2018; Steigenberger, 2017). King et al. (2021) explicitly argue that we need more research examining the overall M&A process.

Therefore, we perform a systematic literature review of M&A failure research. In our review, we propose that M&A failure is a multi-disciplinary phenomenon that can occur at different stages of the M&A's timeline, including the (a) pre-M&A phase, (b) acquisition or merger itself, and (c) post-M&A phase (Banal-Estañol and Seldeslachts, 2011). To further understand M&A failure, we were guided by the following sub-questions:

1. How is M&A failure defined?
2. By taking a multi-disciplinary perspective, how is M&A failure induced, and how is it mitigated along the three stages of an M&A?
3. What guidance needs to be provided for future research?

Our study makes three main contributions. First, we accumulate and synthesize the body of knowledge on the phenomenon of M&A failure. By structuring the existing literature, we provide a taxonomy based on a classification of different scholarly disciplines throughout different phases of a merger or acquisition. We have identified blind spots which point toward further needed research within the processual perspective (Graebner et al., 2017). We encourage scholars to examine the influences of interconnected processes and operations among all three phases of an M&A. Finally, we provide more clarity on the definition and operationalization of M&A failure.

Methodology

Our systematic literature review covers articles on M&A failure published in academic journals between 1995 and February 2022. Our methodology follows the approach of previous systematic reviews on single M&A perspectives, such as culture and post-M&A integration (Dauber, 2012; Friedman et al., 2016; Steigenberger, 2017). We cover peer-reviewed scholarly journals, selected book chapters, and working papers. Our article selection process used four stages. Starting with the relevant article identification, we used Clarivate Analytics' Web of Science (WoS). This website provides subscription-based access to multiple databases that provide comprehensive citation data for different academic disciplines. In WoS, we selected the Core Collection database, applying the following search function of keywords to determine a relevant set of articles for this systematic review: "Mergers and acquisitions failure" and "M&A failure." We searched keywords in All fields, including the Topic, Title, and Publication name, to prevent missing any relevant articles. We set the period from 1995 to 2022. This search process led to a sample of 6,291 articles. To only include relevant articles, we set the following filters regarding the categorization of the papers: Management, Business, Economics, Business Finance, Operations Research, and Management Science. After neglecting duplicates, we identified a total sample of 213 articles.

In selecting relevant papers, we read 213 abstracts. We excluded papers that included the determined search keywords but did not directly examine M&A failure from the final sample. In these papers, the authors gave M&A failure secondary attention, so they did not fit the purpose of the current systematic literature review. The sample size of relevant articles amounted to 97 eligible papers. While closely evaluating the eligible papers, we applied snowball sampling (Steigenberger, 2017) and identified 16 additional relevant papers. Selection criteria, as described above, are necessary to find a relevant

Table 9.1   Paper selection process

Stage	Selection Process	No. of papers
I	Web of Science keywords: "mergers and acquisitions failure" *and* "M&A failure"	6,291
II	Filter application	253
III	Duplicate neglection	213
IV	Abstract examination	97
V	Snowball sampling	+ 16
Σ	Final sample size	113

set of articles to focus on certain constructs and present a feasible scope of research. However, it risks excluding valuable contributions to the field (Dauber, 2012). Therefore, after reading the articles in detail, studies they frequently cited were included in this review. Table 9.1 summarizes the selection process and displays how we reached the final sample size of 113 articles.

Next, we coded each article in line with commonly used procedures for qualitative content analysis. Specifically, we coded the operationalization of M&A failure in values of 1 to 6 representing the different clusters "Deal completion," "Divesture/non-survival," "Employee satisfaction," "Shareholder value/Financial performance," "Strategic goal accomplishment," and "Other." Following this study's aim to identify research gaps within the M&A literature, we coded the documents against the different examined phases. Finally, we coded papers for different M&A perspectives. We applied the clustering of theoretical perspectives in line with Dao and Bauer (2021).

We read the identified articles carefully, and we built an extensive Excel file that supported the data's organization (Steigenberger, 2017). Further, we determined key messages and constructs. While coding the relevant information, its interconnections became clear, and links between topics emerged throughout this iterative process. Therefore, by synthesizing the results from different articles, we created the theoretical framework presented in the following sections.

Findings

Definitions, operationalizations, and perspectives of M&A failure

Based on the current study's underlying sample of articles, there are five dominant proxies of M&A failure operationalized by various constructs. Largely, they are connected to the M&A phase the study examines. Moreover, in line with Dao and Bauer's (2021) findings, there are four dominant theoretical perspectives in the M&A failure literature – the strategic, the organizational, the human, and the processual perspective. The definition of M&A failure is also dependent on the study's perspective and academic discipline. However, each scholarly discipline does not follow only one single definition. There might be a concentration around a certain definition, but some researchers use "uncommon" ones (Chu, 2015; Craninckx and Huyghebaert, 2011; Daniliuc, Bilson and Shailer, 2014; Friedman et al., 2016).

The most common proxy for M&A failure is a loss of shareholder value or negative financial performance (James, Georghiou and Metcalfe, 1998). In total, nearly half of the sample of reviewed studies (n=44) focuses on shareholder value and financial performance, measured by multiple constructs, such as profits, returns, and share prices.

The second most used proxy for M&A failure (n=23) concerns strategic goal accomplishment. Scholars examining the pre-M&A or post-M&A phase refer to shortcomings in the goal definition or poor execution in the post-M&A integration process (Ariño, 2003; Kar and Kar, 2017; Lovallo and Kahneman, 2003).

Third, 18 studies define M&A failure as deal incompletion (Aktas, De Bodt and Roll, 2013). The termination of M&A deals is often operationalized as a binary variable containing information whether a transaction was legally closed or not.

In addition, M&A failure is defined as employee dissatisfaction (Kroon and Noorderhaven, 2018; Zhou, Xie and Wang, 2016). In total, seven relevant studies from the underlying sample examined the effects of M&As on employee satisfaction in the post-M&A phase.

Finally, three studies from our sample define M&A failure as divesture or non-survival of the entire operation (Allred, Boal and Holstein, 2005; Bergh, 2001; Vulanovic, 2017). With a better understanding of the respective

M&A failure definitions and operationalizations, we can now synthesize the antecedents of M&A failure throughout the different M&A phases.

Pre-M&A phase: strategic discipline

In this phase, most studies operationalize M&A failure by financial performance losses.

M&A motives: efficiency theory vs. managerial economics

It is strategically important to understand the M&A motive in the pre-M&A phase because it can determine failure or success (Sherman, 2002). Value-maximizing motives (e.g., synergies, speed, and market share) are mostly seen as the origin of M&As (Barkema and Schijven, 2008). However, throughout the years of M&A research, scholars have also identified non-value-maximizing M&A motives (Rozen-Bakher, 2018a). Brooks and Ritchie (2005) and Eschen and Bresser (2005) highlight the two essential theories of M&A motives.

Efficiency theory is based on value-maximizing motives. The most prevalent M&A motives are creating economies of scope and scale (Christensen et al., 2011). Companies cut costs on either the production of various products or on a single product (Brooks and Ritchie, 2005).

While purely value-maximizing motives in the pre-M&A phase drive M&A success, the literature on managerial economics illustrates that non-value-maximizing motives induce M&A failure. By adopting an agency theoretical perspective (Eschen and Bresser, 2005), the main argument is that managers have substantial freedom in their companies, often misused for personal interests, harming the company's shareholder value (Jensen and Meckling, 1976). Quek (2011) associates the so-called managerial hubris with value-destroying motives.

Firm characteristics

Rozen-Bakher (2018a) points to the influence of relatedness between acquirer and target on M&A success or failure. This refers to the so-called economies of sameness, emerging from expanding similar operations and technologies or economies of fitness resulting from similar products, markets, and knowledge (Larsson and Finkelstein, 1999). Pre-M&A performance of both the acquirer and target can be another antecedent of M&A performance (Rozen-Bakher, 2018a).

Pre-M&A phase: organizational discipline

Most of the studies in this field understand M&A failure in this phase as failed deal completion or the termination of M&A processes.

Organizational fit

The organizational discipline emphasizes the importance of organizational distance and similarity, or 'fit,' during the pre-M&A phase (Ang, Knill and Mauck, 2017). Organizational distance is an umbrella term for external and internal distance. External distance describes the physical distance and length of communication paths between involved parties. On the other hand, internal distance describes differences in values, norms, and goals between the organizations involved. A misfit of the parties involved in the transaction in terms of external or internal organizational distance leads to conflicts and lowers the longevity of relationships (Meirovich, 2017).

Type of shareholder

Organizational scholars found evidence that M&A's failure rate in terms of deal completion and valuation is dependent on the type of shareholder. For example, we can distinguish between strategic (vertical/horizontal), financial, or unrelated shareholders. The target pricing can be dominant when the buyer and target have different types of investors/shareholders (Sedlacek and Valouch, 2018). Thus, the target or buyer selection can be adapted in the pre-M&A phase to reduce potential deal failure risks.

Pre-M&A phase: human discipline

Many of the respective studies in this field operationalize M&A failure in this phase by failed deal completion. Dao and Bauer (2021) cluster these studies, focusing on human and cultural integration, as one stream of literature and detach it from the strategic, organizational, and processual disciplines.

Micro level: relationships

Within the human discipline of M&A failure research, scholars found that M&As are influenced by customer and supplier relationships (Anderson, Havila and Salmi, 2001). Business relationships are shaped by the interaction of actors, which may change over time in terms of content and strategy (Håkansson and Snehota, 1995). Anderson et al. (2001) point toward the importance of associating the target's business relationships in strategic evaluations in the pre-M&A phase because they may be weakened in a post-M&A phase and induce M&A failure. While many scholars focus solely on the acquirer and target, Öberg (2012) shifts her focus toward a network perspective, stating that neglecting other stakeholders can drive M&A failure.

Macro level: culture

Alongside the micro level, a human perspective on the macro level is applied to the pre-M&A phase. Dauber (2012) provides evidence of the influence of cultural differences on M&A failure. Multiple concepts of culture, such as organizational (cf., previous section), national, industry, and team culture have been revealed (Dauber, 2012). Based on all these concepts, M&A failure rates rise if cultural values result in lower levels of acculturation (Björkman, Stahl and Vaara, 2007) and prevent high degrees of human integration (Stahl and Voigt, 2008). Therefore, it is necessary to evaluate the cultural differences in the target or buyer selection activity.

M&A phase: strategic discipline

Most studies in this field and phase understand M&A failure as failed deal completion.

Due diligence

The acquisition phase has also been subject to M&A failure studies in the strategic discipline. Cartwright and Schoenberg (2006) note that strategic fit should be evaluated during the due diligence review of a target firm. In this way, the acquiring firm can assess whether value creation strategies reliant on resource sharing (Capron and Pistre, 2002) or knowledge transfer (Ahuja and Katila, 2001) will be successful or not.

Valuation and negotiation

Strategic choices affect the target valuation during the acquisition phase. Capron, Mitchell and Swaminathan (2001) illustrate the influence of the relatedness between the target's and buyer's assets on the calculated synergies. Therefore, the intended strategy of divesting similar assets in a post-M&A phase influences valuation during the acquisition phase. Following the definition of financial value, this ultimately affects M&A success or failure, as asset divestitures induce effectiveness and profitability (Capron et al., 2001).

M&A phase: organizational discipline

Most studies in this field understand M&A failure in this phase as financial performance losses.

Corporate governance

As decision-making is critical to shareholder value creation in the acquisition phase, corporate governance mechanisms are usually implemented (Billings, Tilba and Wilson, 2016). Corporate governance is defined as a set of relationships between the board of directors and shareholders of a respective firm (Roe, 2005). To align the management's and shareholders' interests, internal and external governance mechanisms can be applied. Internal governance mechanisms may involve managerial share ownership (Jensen and Meckling, 1976) and the implementation of a supervisory board of directors (Baysinger and Butler, 1985). External governance mechanisms include managerial labor markets (Fama, 1980) and major external shareholder existence (Shleifer and Vishny, 1986). Weir, Laing and McKnight (2002) argue that the combination of internal and external governance mechanisms is effective in the acquisition phase, compensating for the CEO hubris phenomenon.

M&A phase: human discipline

Many of the studies in this field understand M&A failure in this phase as financial losses.

Employees and teams

Within the human discipline, the acquisition phase has also been examined in relation to M&A failure. Marks and Mirvis (2011) argue that employees or advisors performing due diligence reviews usually have financial positions and backgrounds. Thus, a financial mindset is applied to the evaluation of the target firm. The focus on "hard" factors may overrule the "soft" ones. Therefore, the authors promote including diverse teams from different departments in a due diligence process. M&A failure is also driven by the M&A teams' attitude toward quickly closing the respective deal (Ashkenas and Francis, 2000). Marks (2002) claims that M&A failure can be prevented by implementing merger sensitization workshops, role plays, and other experimental activities during the acquisition phase that help decision-makers empathize with the target's or buyer's employees.

Cultural evaluation

Cultural due diligence positively influences M&A outcomes (Marks and Mirvis, 2011). Moreover, acquirers who undertake behavioral due diligence regarding employees and managers of the target firm are often more successful (Anslinger and Copeland, 1996). Concerning cooperation, Zhang, Zhou and Ebbers (2011) point out the positive effect of similarity in terms of national and organizational culture on M&A outcomes.

Post-M&A phase: strategic discipline

Most studies in this field understand M&A failure in this phase as financial performance losses.

PMI strategy development

Analyzing the post-M&A phase through a strategic lens, Lahovnik (2005) points toward a post-merger strategy as a necessity for M&A success. This high-level strategy development often results from the M&A type defined in the pre-M&A phase. In terms of post-merger performance, Rozen-Bakher (2018a) argues that different types of M&As have different outcomes based on two prevalent effects. M&A failure occurs less in conglomerate transactions when the integration stage is less complicated. However, regarding synergies, vertical and horizontal acquisitions offer more potential for cutting costs. High-level strategy development should therefore include Lahovnik's (2011) suggestion to focus on one strategy.

Synergy realization

To capture synergies in a post-M&A phase, the parties need to have similar assets and be able to combine them (Meyer and Altenborg, 2008). Rozen-Bakher (2018c) points toward the importance of synergy and efficiency. First, the more synergies are captured by reducing the workforce within the post-merger phase, the more efficient the merged company operates until this effect reverses, and more synergies will result in downscaling efficiency levels. Thus, an optimal trade-off is needed and should be considered during the post-M&A integration strategy development. In a later study, Rozen-Bakher (2018b) re-examines this effect and argues that the efficiency increase is based on productivity spillovers from one acquisition party to the other.

Post-M&A phase: organizational discipline

Most of the studies in this field understand M&A failure in this phase as financial performance losses and a failed strategic goal accomplishment.

Ownership and other organizational characteristics

Scholars in the organizational discipline have been investigating agency conflicts in companies and their impact on M&A failure for a long time (Shleifer and Vishny, 1988). Organizational change (of which M&As are a prominent example) has been problematized due to tight and rigid target companies with often high levels of bureaucracy (Tannenbaum and Davis, 1969). In explaining the outcomes of post-M&A projects, several elements toward overcoming corporate inertia by positive strategy adaption have been identified (Sull, 1999). In this regard, financial conservatism, sensitivity to the external world, awareness of the firm's identity, and tolerance of new ideas are key success factors for M&As (Edwards, 2018).

Selective and comprehensive integration

Because a comprehensive integration is costly and not always beneficial, an alternative leverage point against M&A failure is to only selectively integrate when the acquisition is based on economies of scope as motivation and comprehensively integrate when the motivation is economies of scale (Vestring, Rouse and Rovit, 2004). Comprehensively integrated organizations share many characteristics with stepfamilies, such as high stress levels, culture shocks, role ambiguity, and limited shared history. Therefore, Allred et al. (2005) note that a clear focus on the organizational and human relationships and processes should be applied to M&A research.

Post-M&A phase: human discipline

Many of the studies in this field understand M&A failure in this phase as financial losses and employee dissatisfaction.

Project definition

When looking into the activity of project definition after a high-level strategy development, it has been suggested that M&A success can be driven by preserving the specificities of a firm and pooling its capabilities (Thelisson et al., 2019). However, regarding pooling capabilities, (de-)centralization has not been consistently indicated to drive post-merger integration outcomes within the human discipline. For example, Alharbi et al. (2016) suggest reducing agency costs within the post-M&A phase through a mix of implicit (e.g., cultural control) and explicit (e.g., bureaucracy) control. However, at the same time, the authors state that too much control could also drive M&A failure.

Synergy realization

During the post-M&A stage, a focus on managing processes and operational planning, key factors in synergy realization, positively influence M&A performance (Daniliuc et al., 2014). Although synergy realization is a strategic motivation, many indicators are also examined by scholars from the human discipline. For example, the involvement of middle management in a constructive role in operational integration planning is considered vital because it can induce neglected inertia (Meyer, 2006). Moreover, integrating certain management functions (e.g., human resources), can be a source of failure if not planned well. A successful plan of department integration includes open communication and less radical staffing reallocations (Łupina-Wegener, 2013).

Stakeholders

Not only managers are affected by M&As; other stakeholders, such as suppliers, also need to be included in knowledge transfer. For instance, they need to adapt to changing production requirements (Öberg, 2017). Further, customers cannot be neglected, as purchase decisions are emotional decisions. When comprehensive integration is part of the overall M&A strategy, the risk of reducing customer loyalty is present (Heinberg, Ozkaya and Taube, 2016). Thus, it has been suggested that strong brands should be kept independent instead of fully integrating them into another brand.

In addition to external stakeholders, internal stakeholders (e.g., managers and employees) are also emotionally affected (Cartwright and Cooper, 1990). As employees' negative emotions can influence the post-M&A integration and harm M&A success, Gunkel et al. (2015) suggest multiple solutions, such as preparing employees through managerial communication (Irrmann, 2005). Kroon and Noorderhaven (2018) study employee satisfaction in a post-M&A phase and suggest that occupational and organizational identification positively affect employees' willingness to cooperate, ultimately driving post-merger success. Their findings imply that managers should focus on their employees' identification through effective communication.

Processual discipline

Most studies in this field define M&A failure as financial performance losses or failed deal completion. Studies from the processual discipline cannot be assigned to one of the three phases in the process of a merger or acquisition. In contrast, they shed light on M&A failure by looking through a phase-overlapping lens. Friedman et al. (2016) point toward the importance of a processual view on M&As.

Deal characteristics

Certain deal characteristics can influence M&A outcomes during all stages of the transaction. One prominent example is the nature of the transaction, whether it is a friendly or a hostile takeover attempt (Caiazza and Pozzolo, 2016). Moreover, Koska and Stahler (2014) suggest a competition effect, meaning multiple bidders involved in a sell-side transaction positively influence deal completion rates. However, after failed takeover attempts, there is usually a higher takeover activity in the respective market (Malmendier, Opp and Saidi, 2016). In this regard, Aktas et al. (2013) call for more studies on failed takeover attempts as they rarely appear in large sample studies.

Executives

Applying a micro-level perspective, processual scholars have been examining acquisitions as dynamic processes, focusing on the significant influence of teams of executives (Very and Schweiger, 2001). As managerial self-interest and hubris are prevalent, executives, particularly the CEO, can induce agency conflicts that might harm future M&A success (Bhimani, Ncube and Sivabalan, 2015; Neyland and Shekhar, 2018). Further, managerial overconfidence and the so-called confirmation bias, based on positive experiences, can mislead managers in their decision-making (Bogan and Just, 2009).

Finally, processual scholars identify learning as valuable during all transaction stages and a key source of M&A success/failure (Doan, Sahib and van Witteloostuijn, 2018). Zollo (2009) states that learning in acquisitions is successful when experience accumulation does not lead to overconfidence.

Discussion

Years and vast amounts of money have been spent researching M&A trans-actions (Renneboog and Vansteenkiste, 2019). Still, this mature academic field remains fragmented and fails to provide conclusive answers on recurring M&A failures. Therefore, we accumulate and synthesize evidence retrieved from the existing body of knowledge on M&A failure to shed light on the blind spots of this complex field. Based on our systematic literature review, we provide a comprehensive framework for M&A failure capturing the various determinants of M&A failure (Figure 9.1). Our framework integrates different scholarly disciplines and M&A phases.

Our framework maps how different perspectives identify predictors in light of the different phases within an acquisition's timeline. Studies use different proxies for M&A failure, including financial performance, strategic goal accomplishment, deal completion, employee satisfaction, and divesture or non-survival of the entire operation as indicated by coloring within the framework. The existence of five dominant definitions of M&A failure leads to ambiguity when trying to understand what variables drive M&A failure. This conclusion is in line with Meglio and Risberg (2011), who distinguished between financial, non-financial, and mixed definitions of M&A performance.

Moreover, some scholars argue that deal incompletion or termination of an M&A process does not necessarily imply M&A failure. Withdrawing from M&A processes can also be reasoned from the perspective of risk management (Amiri et al., 2022), especially after the due diligence indicated major risks (Thompson and Kim, 2020). In addition, while scholars used to take divesture as a proxy for M&A failure, recent studies point out that divesture in a broader strategic context is rather motivated by a resource/capability allocation specif-ically regarding innovation/transformation processes (Eklund and Feldman, 2020). Based on the findings of the current systematic review, we identify the first blind spot as:

Blind spot 1: There is still ambiguity in the definition of M&A failure in respec-tive M&A contexts.

We suggest that scholars clearly define the scope of M&A failure construct measurement. As a workable definition of M&A failure, we propose the following: *M&A failure is the state of a significant and unfavorable mismatch between reality and predefined expectations of relevant stakeholders at different points in the acquisition's timeline.* This proposed definition leaves room for

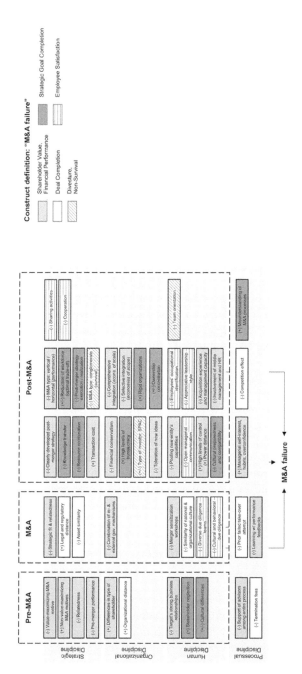

Figure 9.1   M&A failure from a phase-oriented and multi-disciplinary perspective

M&A's multifacetedness and to examine the different phases of a transaction. This definition is in line with Meglio (2020), who suggests a pluralism of measures and an umbrella construct perspective in which a new definition replaces too specific conceptualizations of M&A failure (e.g., stock performance).

We also observe room for intersections between different scholarly disciplines. For example, both the organizational (Ahern, Daminelli and Fracassi, 2015) and human disciplines (Dauber, 2012) study the influence of culture. While the concept of culture within the organizational discipline is understood from a meso-level perspective, the human discipline elaborates on the employees or teams that constitute the corporate culture. However, the boundaries between disciplines become weak and flow into one another. Learning is another example of a predictor of M&A failure with significant intersections with all theoretical disciplines, leading us to identify the second blind spot:

Blind spot 2: Studies are mostly conducted in isolation, leaving little room for integration across disciplines.

Hence, we suggest more integration across different disciplines to explain M&A failure. A good example of integration is the recent study by Li et al. (2020), who merged the organizational and strategic discipline by examining institutional distance and cross-border M&A performance. Notably, they found new insights from this interdisciplinary inquiry by combining two prevalent constructs.

We further observed that M&A failure is often examined at separate stages of the M&A process. We therefore identify the third blind spot as:

Blind spot 3: Studies mostly adopt a within-phase analysis, and there is an unequal weight of attention across different M&A phases.

Thus, we argue that taking a temporal/processual perspective across phases (instead of a within-phase analysis) is essential to explain M&A failure. From a human perspective, tolerance to new ideas (Edwards, 2018), open managerial communication (Vuori, Vuori and Huy, 2018), and managerial ambition (Thomson and McNamara, 2001) could be applied beyond the post-M&A phase to also include the pre-merger and M&A phase. Following other scholars, we suggest comprehensively studying M&A processes from a temporal perspective and taking a more holistic view instead of analyzing each phase of an M&A in isolation (Haleblian et al., 2009; Holland and Scullion, 2021; King et al., 2021; Rodríguez-Sánchez, Mora-Valentín and Ortiz-de-Urbina-Criado, 2018).

Another finding based on our systematic literature review is that the strategic and human disciplines suggest significantly more determining factors on M&A success/failure than studies within the organizational and processual field. Moreover, we noticed a significant imbalance between studies focusing on the post-M&A phase compared to those addressing pre-M&A and acquisition stages. Our gathered insights and framework allow for the development of a clear research focus.

To conclude, M&As continue to be a prominent business decision demanding clear understanding. The reasons for the success and failure of M&As remain highly relevant. As failed M&As bear the risk of value destruction and employee dissatisfaction, research should integrate academic disciplines and construct longitudinal designs that consider all phases of the M&A process.

References (references with an asterisk are part of the review's sample)

*Ahern, K., Daminelli, D., & Fracassi, C. (2015). Lost in translation? The effect of cultural values on mergers around the world. *Journal of Financial Economics*, 117(1), 165–189.

Ahuja, G., & Katila, R. (2001). Technological acquisitions and the innovation performance of acquiring firms: a longitudinal study. *Strategic Management Journal*, 22(3), 197–220.

*Aktas, N., De Bodt, E., & Roll, R. (2013). MicroHoo: deal failure, industry rivalry, and sources of overbidding. *Journal of Corporate Finance*, 19, 20–35.

*Alharbi, J., Gelaidan, H., Al-Swidi, A., & Saeed, A. (2016). Control mechanisms employed between headquarters and subsidiaries in multinational enterprises (MNEs): an empirical study. *Review of International Business and Strategy*, 26(4), 493–516.

*Allred, B., Boal, K., & Holstein, W. (2005). Corporations as stepfamilies: a new metaphor for explaining the fate of merged and acquired companies. *Academy of Management Executive*, 19(3), 23–37.

Amiri, S., King, D., DeMarie, S., & Brown, J. (2022). Predicting the divestment of prior acquisitions. *British Journal of Management*, 33(4), 1803–1819.

*Anderson, H., Havila, V., & Salmi, A. (2001). Can you buy a business relationship? On the importance of customer and supplier relationships in acquisitions. *Industrial Marketing Management*, 30(7), 575–586.

*Ang, J., Knill, A., & Mauck, N. (2017). Cross-border opportunity sets: an international empirical study based on ownership types. *Global Finance Journal*, 33, 1–26.

Anslinger, P., & Copeland, T. (1996). Growth through acquisitions: a fresh look. *The McKinsey Quarterly*, 2, 96–97.

Ariño, A. (2003). Measures of strategic alliance performance: an analysis of construct validity. *Journal of International Business Studies*, 34(1), 66–79.

Ashkenas, R., & Francis, S. (2000). Integration managers: special leaders for special times. *Harvard Business Review*, 78(6), 108–116.

*Banal-Estañol, A., & Seldeslachts, J. (2011). Merger failures. *Journal of Economics & Management Strategy*, 20(2), 589–624.

Barkema, H., & Schijven, M. (2008). Toward unlocking the full potential of acquisitions: the role of organizational restructuring. *Academy of Management Journal*, 51(4), 696–722.

Baysinger, B., & Butler, H. (1985). Corporate governance and the board of directors: performance effects of changes in board composition. *Journal of Law, Economics, & Organization*, 1(1), 101–124.

*Bergh, D. (2001). Executive retention and acquisition outcomes: a test of opposing views on the influence of organizational tenure. *Journal of Management*, 27(5), 603–622.

*Bhimani, A., Ncube, M., & Sivabalan, P. (2015). Managing risk in mergers and acquisitions activity: beyond "good" and "bad" management. *Managerial Auditing Journal*, 30(2), 160–175.

*Billings, M., Tilba, A., & Wilson, J. (2016). "To invite disappointment or worse": governance, audit and due diligence in the Ferranti-ISC merger. *Business History*, 58(4), 453–478.

*Björkman, I., Stahl, G., & Vaara, E. (2007). Cultural differences and capability transfer in cross-border acquisitions: the mediating roles of capability complementarity, absorptive capacity, and social integration. *Journal of International Business Studies*, 38(4), 658–672.

*Bogan, V., & Just, D. (2009). What drives merger decision making behavior? Don't seek, don't find, and don't change your mind. *Journal of Economic Behavior & Organization*, 72(3), 930–943.

*Brooks, M., & Ritchie, P. (2005). Trucking mergers and acquisitions in Canada and the US since NAFTA. *Transportation Journal*, 44(3), 23–38.

*Caiazza, S., & Pozzolo, A. (2016). The determinants of failed takeovers in the banking sector: deal or country characteristics? *Journal of Banking & Finance*, 72, S92–S103.

Calipha, R., Tarba, S., & Brock, D. (2010). Mergers and acquisitions: a review of phases, motives, and success factors. In C. L. Cooper & S. Finkelstein (eds.), *Advances in Mergers and Acquisitions* (pp. 1–24). Bingley: Emerald Group Publishing.

*Capron, L., Mitchell, W., & Swaminathan, A. (2001). Asset divestiture following horizontal acquisitions: a dynamic view. *Strategic Management Journal*, 22(9), 817–844.

Capron, L., & Pistre, N. (2002). When do acquirers earn abnormal returns? *Strategic Management Journal*, 23(9), 781–794.

Cartwright, S., & Cooper, C. (1990). The impact of mergers and acquisitions on people at work: existing research and issues. *British Journal of Management*, 1(2), 65–76.

*Cartwright, S., & Schoenberg, R. (2006). Thirty years of mergers and acquisitions research: recent advances and future opportunities. *British Journal of Management*, 17, 1–5.

*Christensen, C., Alton, R., Rising, C., & Waldeck, A. (2011). The new M&A playbook. *Harvard Business Review*, 89(3), 4–11.

Chu, K. H. (2015). Bank consolidation and stability: the Canadian experience, 1867–1935. *Journal of Financial Stability*, 21, 46–60.

*Craninckx, K., & Huyghebaert, N. (2011). Can stock markets predict M&A failure? A study of European transactions in the fifth takeover wave. *European Financial Management*, 17(1), 9–45.

*Daniliuc, S., Bilson, C., & Shailer, G. (2014). The interaction of post-acquisition integration and acquisition focus in relation to long-run performance. *International Review of Finance*, 14(4), 587–612.

Dao, M., & Bauer, F. (2021). Human integration following M&A: synthesizing different M&A research streams. *Human Resource Management Review*, 31(3), 100746.

*Dauber, D. (2012). Opposing positions in M&A research: culture, integration and performance. *Cross Cultural Management: An International Journal*, 19(3), 375–398.

*Doan, T., Sahib, P., & van Witteloostuijn, A. (2018). Lessons from the flipside: how do acquirers learn from divestitures to complete acquisitions? *Long Range Planning*, 51(2), 252–266.

*Edwards, P. (2018). The contingencies of corporate failure: the case of Lucas industries. *Management & Organizational History*, 13(3), 220–235.

Eklund, J., & Feldman, E. (2020). Understanding the relationship between divestitures and innovation: the role of organization design. https:// mackinstitute .wharton .upenn.edu/wp-content/uploads/2019/02/FP0410_WP_2019Sept.pdf.

*Eschen, E., & Bresser, R. (2005). Closing resource gaps: toward a resource-based theory of advantageous mergers and acquisitions. *European Management Review*, 2(3), 167–178.

Fama, E. (1980). Agency problems and the theory of the firm. *Journal of Political Economy*, 88(2), 288–307.

*Friedman, Y., Carmeli, A., Tishler, A., & Shimizu, K. (2016). Untangling micro-behavioral sources of failure in mergers and acquisitions: a theoretical integration and extension. *The International Journal of Human Resource Management*, 27(20), 2339–2369.

Graebner, M., Heimeriks, K., Huy, Q., & Vaara, E. (2017). The process of postmerger integration: a review and agenda for future research. *Academy of Management Annals*, 11(1), 1–32.

*Gunkel, M., Schlaegel, C., Rossteutscher, T., & Wolff, B. (2015). The human aspect of cross-border acquisition outcomes: the role of management practices, employee emotions, and national culture. *International Business Review*, 24(3), 394–408.

Håkansson, H., & Snehota, I. (1995). *Developing Relationships in Business Networks*. London: Routledge.

Haleblian, J., Devers, C., McNamara, G., Carpenter, M., & Davison, R. (2009). Taking stock of what we know about mergers and acquisitions: a review and research agenda. *Journal of Management*, 35(3), 469–502.

*Healy, P. (2016). Reflections on M&A accounting from AOL's acquisition of Time Warner. *Accounting and Business Research*, 46(5), 528–541.

*Heinberg, M., Ozkaya, H., & Taube, M. (2016). A brand built on sand: is acquiring a local brand in an emerging market an ill-advised strategy for foreign companies? *Journal of the Academy of Marketing Science*, 44(5), 586–607.

Henningsson, S., Yetton, P., & Wynne, P. (2018). A review of information system integration in mergers and acquisitions. *Journal of Information Technology*, 33(4), 255–303.

Holland, D., & Scullion, H. (2021). Towards a talent retention model: mapping the building blocks of the psychological contract to the three stages of the acquisition process. *The International Journal of Human Resource Management*, 32(13), 2683–2728.

*Irrmann, O. (2005). Communication dissonance and pragmatic failures in strategic processes: the case of cross-border acquisitions. *Strategy Process*, 22, 251–266.

*James, A., Georghiou, L., & Metcalfe, J. (1998). Integrating technology into merger and acquisition decision making. *Technovation*, 18(8–9), 563–573.

Jensen, M., & Meckling, W. (1976). Theory of the firm: managerial behavior, agency costs and ownership structure. *Journal of Financial Economics*, 3(4), 305–360.

*Kar, R., & Kar, M. (2017). Cross-cultural issues in M&As: experiences and future agenda from Asia-Pacific deals. *Transnational Corporations Review*, 9(3), 140–149.

King, D., Wang, G., Samimi, M., & Cortes, A. (2021). A meta-analytic integration of acquisition performance prediction. *Journal of Management Studies*, 58(5), 1198–1236.

*Koska, O., & Stahler, F. (2014). Optimal acquisition strategies in unknown territories. *Journal of Institutional and Theoretical Economics/Zeitschrift Fur Die Gesamte Staatswissenschaft*, 170(3), 406–426.

*Kroon, D., & Noorderhaven, N. (2018). The role of occupational identification during post-merger integration. *Group & Organization Management*, 43(2), 207–244.

*Lahovnik, M. (2005). Strategic factors underlying acquisition performance in a post-communist economy: experience from Slovenia. *Post-Communist Economies*, 17(4), 503–521.

Lahovnik, M. (2011). Strategic fit between business strategies in the post-acquisition period and acquisition performance. *Journal for East European Management Studies*, 16(14), 358–370.

Larsson, R., & Finkelstein, S. (1999). Integrating strategic, organizational, and human resource perspectives on mergers and acquisitions: a case survey of synergy realization. *Organization Science*, 10(1), 1–26.

Li, W., Wang, C., Ren, Q., & Zhao, D. (2020). Institutional distance and cross-border M&A performance: a dynamic perspective. *Journal of International Financial Markets, Institutions and Money*, 66, 101207.

*Lovallo, D., & Kahneman, D. (2003). Delusions of success: how optimism undermines executives' decisions. *Harvard Business Review*, 81(7), 1–10.

*Łupina-Wegener, A. (2013). Human resource integration in subsidiary mergers and acquisitions: evidence from Poland. *Journal of Organizational Change Management*, 26(2), 286–304.

*Malmendier, U., Opp, M., & Saidi, F. (2016). Target revaluation after failed takeover attempts: cash versus stock. *Journal of Financial Economics*, 119(1), 92–106.

Marks, M. (2002). *Charging Back Up the Hill: Workplace Recovery After Mergers, Acquisitions and Downsizings*. Hoboken, NJ: John Wiley & Sons.

*Marks, M., & Mirvis, P. (2011). Merge ahead: a research agenda to increase merger and acquisition success. *Journal of Business and Psychology*, 26(2), 161–168.

Meglio, O. (2020). Construct measurement in strategic management: key issues and debate. In O. Meglio, & S. Schriber (eds.), *Mergers and Acquisitions: Rethinking Key Umbrella Constructs* (pp. 3–26). Cham: Springer.

Meglio, O. & Risberg, A. (2011). The (mis) measurement of M&A performance: a systematic narrative literature review. *Scandinavian Journal of Management*, 27(4), 418–433.

Meirovich, G. (2017). External and internal organizational distance: distinction and relationship. *American Journal of Management*, 17(5), 67–80.

*Meyer, C. (2006). Destructive dynamics of middle management intervention in post-merger processes. *Journal of Applied Behavioral Science*, 42(4), 397–419.

*Meyer, C., & Altenborg, E. (2008). Incompatible strategies in international mergers: the failed merger between Telia and Telenor. *Journal of International Business Studies*, 39(3), 508–525.

*Neyland, J., & Shekhar, C. (2018). How much is too much? Large termination fees and target distress. *Journal of Banking & Finance*, 88, 97–112.

*Öberg, C. (2012). Mergers and acquisitions as embedded network activities. *European Journal of International Management*, 6(4), 421–441.

*Öberg, C. (2017). Transferring acquisition knowledge: sources, directions and outcomes. *Management Research: Journal of the Iberoamerican Academy of Management*, 15(1), 28–46.

*Quek, M. (2011). Comparative historical analysis of four UK hotel companies, 1979-2004. *International Journal of Contemporary Hospitality Management*, 23(2), 147–173.

*Renneboog, L., & Vansteenkiste, C. (2019). Failure and success in mergers and acquisitions. *Journal of Corporate Finance*, 58, 650–699.

Rodríguez-Sánchez, J.-L., Mora-Valentín, E.-M., & Ortiz-de-Urbina-Criado, M. (2018). Successful human resources management factors in international mergers and acquisitions. *Administrative Sciences*, 8(3), 45.

Roe, M. (2005). The institutions of corporate governance. In C. Menard & M. M. Shirley (eds.), *Handbook of New Institutional Economics* (pp. 371–399). Boston, MA: Springer.

*Rozen-Bakher, Z. (2018a). Comparison of merger and acquisition (M&A) success in horizontal, vertical and conglomerate M&As: industry sector vs. services sector. *The Service Industries Journal*, 38(7–8), 492–518.

*Rozen-Bakher, Z. (2018b). Labour productivity in M&As: industry sector vs. services sector. *The Service Industries Journal*, 38(15–16), 1043–1066.

*Rozen-Bakher, Z. (2018c). The trade-off between synergy success and efficiency gains in M&A strategy. *Euromed Journal of Business*, 13(2), 163–184.

*Sedlacek, J., & Valouch, P. (2018). Mergers of corporations and causes of their failure. *Inzinerine Ekonomika/Engineering Economics*, 29(4), 397–404.

Sherman, A. (2002). Structuring M&A deals in 2002 and beyond. *AFP Exchange*, 22(3), 6–15.

Shleifer, A., & Vishny, R. (1986). Large shareholders and corporate control. *Journal of Political Economy*, 94(3, Part 1), 461–488.

Shleifer, A., & Vishny, R. (1988). Value maximization and the acquisition process. *Journal of Economic Perspectives*, 2(1), 7–20.

Stahl, G., & Voigt, A. (2008). Do cultural differences matter in mergers and acquisitions? A tentative model and examination. *Organization Science*, 19(1), 160–176.

*Steigenberger, N. (2017). The challenge of integration: a review of the M&A integration literature. *International Journal of Management Reviews*, 19(4), 408–431.

Sull, D. (1999). The dynamics of standing still: Firestone Tire & Rubber and the radial revolution. *Business History Review*, 73(3), 430–464.

Tannenbaum, R., & Davis, S. (1969). Values, man, and organizations. *IMR/Industrial Management Review*, 10(2), 67–86.

*Thelisson, A., Missonier, A., Guieu, G., & Luscher, L. (2019). A paradoxical approach symbiotic to postmerger integration: a French longitudinal case study. *European Business Review*, 31(2), 232–259.

Thompson, E., & Kim, C. (2020). Post-M&A performance and failure: implications of time until deal completion. *Sustainability*, 12(7), 2999.

*Thomson, N., & McNamara, P. (2001). Achieving post-acquisition success: the role of corporate entrepreneurship. *Long Range Planning*, 34(6), 669–697.

*Very, P., & Schweiger, D. (2001). The acquisition process as a learning process: evidence from a study of critical problems and solutions in domestic and cross-border deals. *Journal of World Business*, 36(1), 11–31.

*Vestring, T., Rouse, T., & Rovit, S. (2004). Integrate where it matters. *MIT Sloan Management Review*, 46(1), 15–19.

*Vulanovic, M. (2017). SPACs: post-merger survival. *Managerial Finance*, 43(6), 679–699.

*Vuori, N., Vuori, T., & Huy, Q. (2018). Emotional practices: how masking negative emotions impacts the post-acquisition integration process. *Strategic Management Journal*, 39(3), 859–893.

Weir, C., Laing, D., & McKnight, P. J. (2002). Internal and external governance mechanisms: their impact on the performance of large UK public companies. *Journal of Business Finance & Accounting*, 29(5–6), 579–611.

Welch, X., Pavićević, S., Keil, T., & Laamanen, T. (2020). The pre-deal phase of mergers and acquisitions: a review and research agenda. *Journal of Management*, 46(6), 843–878.

Zhang, J., Zhou, C., & Ebbers, H. (2011). Completion of Chinese overseas acquisitions: institutional perspectives and evidence. *International Business Review*, 20(2), 226–238.

*Zhou, C., Xie, J., & Wang, Q. (2016). Failure to complete cross-border M&As: "to" vs. "from" emerging markets. *Journal of International Business Studies*, 47(9), 1077–1105.

*Zollo, M. (2009). Superstitious learning with rare strategic decisions: theory and evidence from corporate acquisitions. *Organization Science*, 20(5), 894–908.

10 An ecosystem perspective of acquisition outcomes: a research agenda

Svante Schriber and Olimpia Meglio

Introduction

How acquisitions perform is a longstanding issue in acquisition research (King et al., 2004, 2021). A significant body of research tries to establish what explains or predicts acquisition performance (e.g., Datta, 1991; Datta, Pinches and Narayanan, 1992; Haleblian and Finkelstein, 1999; Loughran and Vijh, 1997; Rabier, 2017), and how best to measure performance (e.g., Oler, Harrison and Allen, 2008; Cording, Christmann and Weigelt, 2010). A common thread in this research is the tendency to operationalize performance as shareholder value, measured by share price data (Zollo and Meier, 2008; Meglio and Risberg, 2011). Today, shareholder value is broadly treated in research not only as a suitable operationalization of acquisition performance, but has morphed into the generally accepted aim of acquisitions (Meglio and Schriber, 2023).

However, a growing awareness of societal and environmental implications has led management scholars to question a one-sided focus on shareholder value (e.g., Lepak, Smith and Taylor, 2007; van der Linden and Freeman, 2017). Still, acquisition research has not yet directly analyzed how various singular effects from acquisitions intertwine and amount to more substantial consequences for a variety of constituents. We think of this broad variety of organizations, authorities, interest groups, informal collectives, or others surrounding acquisitions, as actors populating an ecosystem; each with their own considerations about what acquisition outcomes are desirable or not.

We contend that the centrality of financial value and the corresponding lack of attention to other outcomes hamper existing research for at least three intertwined reasons. First, research has given the environment surrounding acquisitions only scarce attention. This impedes the ability of research to understand the conditions in which acquisitions take place. Second, by limiting attention to shareholders, other actors affected by acquisitions are overlooked. Even if research has highlighted for instance customers following acquisitions (Kato and Schoenberg, 2014), many other constituents are left unnoticed. Third, acquisitions are complex and produce a multitude of consequences that can be hardly expressed in financial terms only (Meglio and Park, 2019). For instance, it is noteworthy that acquisition research largely has excluded social or environmental impacts that have come much to the fore in other research streams (e.g., Hosta and Zabkar, 2021; Liao, Hsu and Chiang, 2021). In sum, the environment surrounding acquisitions, those populating this environment, and the variety of outcomes these constituents experience, have been largely neglected in research.

Our analysis offers multiple contributions. First, we complement the dominating research on the financial value of acquisitions, thus joining recent conversations in business research (Smith and Rönnegard, 2016). Second, we innovate acquisition research by building on the idea of business ecosystems to develop an integrative framework that extends beyond the involved firms to illuminate a variety of actors outside of the acquisition. Third, we identify outcomes that have remained surprisingly unnoticed in acquisition research, such as effects on the natural environment. Fourth, we offer a research agenda to inspire future research on acquisition impact.

Applying ecosystems to acquisitions

The concept of business ecosystems has remained relatively unnoticed in acquisition research, and we believe it holds potential to further a systematic understanding of acquisition outcomes. The term ecosystem is a metaphor from the natural sciences, where it signifies a set of organisms that exist in a physical environment. In business research the term denotes a set of organizations, how they interact, compete, influence, and depend on each other. Compared to similar terms, like industry or markets, the metaphor highlights that firms can entertain various relations with other actors. For example, firms can be competitors in an industry, suppliers and customers in a market with more distant or less direct interactions, or be in unarticulated and non-contractual co-dependence relations, including virtual networks (Iyer, Lee and Venkatraman, 2006). The ecosystem concept thus also partly aligns with how networks have been studied in acquisition research (e.g., Degbey and Hassett, 2016); however, it takes a broader scope to also include actors beyond the immediate relations of a particular firm. In short, the ecosystem concept includes actors with transactional (e.g., markets), competitive (e.g., industries), partly cooperative (e.g., coopetitive) relations (Nalebuff and Brandenburger, 1996; Porter, 1980; Ritter, Wilkinson and Johnston, 2004), and other, more distant actors affecting or being affected by a particular firm.

Research on ecosystems has gained increasing interest, emphasizing for instance innovation and the contribution of up- and downstream actors (Masucci, Brusoni and Cennamo, 2020), or the collaborative environment, typically around technical platforms, to produce value to customers (Gawer and Cusumano, 2008). We build on Teece (2007, p. 1325) who describes an ecosystem as a "community of organizations, institutions, and individuals that impact the enterprise and the enterprise's customers and supplies. The relevant community therefore includes complementors, suppliers, regulatory authorities, standard-setting bodies, the judiciary, and educational and research institutions." This definition offers the benefit of spanning a variety of actors, intentional as well as non-intentional interaction, and opening up to effects beyond financial gains.

An important starting point for our analysis is that acquisitions can have a wide range of effects that can differ significantly. Some effects can be described as relatively tangible (e.g., layoffs, or the construction of a new factory), other effects less so (e.g., expectations of new career paths, founded or unfounded anxiety over the risk of losing one's job). Moreover, effects can be known or unknown to those affected, such as a reduced product range which is not communicated to customers, or drinking water polluted because of a laxer compliance with environmental regulations following an acquisition. Embracing a variety of acquisition effects across the ecosystem also opens up to the consideration that outcomes can be symbiotic (Meglio and Schriber, 2023) rather than conflicting, as is often assumed in financially centered outcome studies of acquisitions (Selden and Colvin, 2003).

We use the term "actor" for the variety of players in an ecosystem. This term suggests a more inclusive role than target (Lepak et al., 2007), which invokes a rather static idea of an effect on an actor, while we consider effects as constantly evaluated and re-evaluated, or dynamic. Relatedly, an actor represents a subject with agency, exceeding connotations of a passive target, as one outcome can be perceived differently depending on an actor's circumstances, experiences, or preferences (Livengood and Reger, 2010). While the term stakeholder, drawn on by Meglio and Schriber (2023), allows for a more fluid understanding of outcomes than a mere zero-sum game, the term is generally limited to actors most closely related to a focal firm (van der Linden and Freeman, 2017), while we wish to expand the understanding of outcomes and actors at societal, organizational, or individual levels, also including non-humans, beyond the immediate surrounding of acquisitions.

Not all actors in the ecosystem will necessarily be affected by the same outcomes following an acquisition. Suppliers may notice little difference from an acquisition; customers experience a need to adapt to new products; the environment can suffer from increased pollution, and a local community can suffer from more traffic. Moreover, several minor effects of different sorts can amount to something more substantial that, collectively, may be thought of as an outcome. This view on acquisition outcomes broadens the set of considered outcomes in comparison to the traditional focus on financial performance in two complementary ways. On the one hand, it supports scholars in recognizing a wider range of outcomes appearing "between the lines" in extant acquisition research; on the other, it assists in identifying outcomes previously not considered in research. Our view of the acquisition ecosystem is portrayed in Figure 10.1.

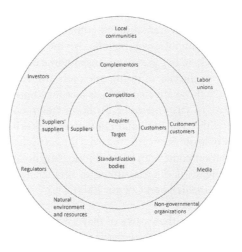

Figure 10.1   The acquisition ecosystem

We represent the ecosystem as a layered system of actors, starting with the involved firms, gradually adding actors which in literature are generally either overlooked or placed into minor, passive roles (Bauer et al., 2018; Meglio and Schriber, 2023; Rouzies, Colman and Angwin, 2019; Schriber, King and Bauer, 2022). The layers help to distinguish the proximity between the acquisition and particular actors, although this distinction is conceptual and can differ in practice. For instance, regulating bodies (in the outer layer in our figure) may not always have daily interactions with a focal acquisition (such as, e.g., customers depicted in the first layer), but can still have intense interactions with the acquisition. Moreover, actor categories are analytic and may in reality span different subcategories. For instance, target employees who are very much inside of an acquisition may simultaneously be members of labor unions, visualized in the outer layers. Rather than problematic, we see this as useful as it may help uncover additional outcomes from acquisitions. Taken together, an ecosystem lens can assist in balancing the emphasis on financial value in acquisition research, and thereby in structuring actors surrounding acquisitions, identify related outcomes, and illuminate acquisition outcomes for the ecosystem as such.

Drawing on acquisition research reviews (e.g., Barkema and Schijven, 2008; Graebner et al., 2017; Haleblian et al., 2009; Steigenberger, 2017), our effort is illustrative and not exhaustive and it is intended to ignite and direct future research. Next, we address how ecosystems help increase the scope of considered acquisition outcomes.

Broadening acquisition outcomes through an acquisition ecosystem lens

With ecosystems surrounding acquisitions as starting point, our reading of acquisition research suggests that outcomes appear in three broad categories. First, research on the ecosystem closest to the acquisition has focused on financial outcomes; however, largely under a different guise. Second, financial value dominates acquisition research on actors in the proximity of acquisitions such as competitors, suppliers, and so on, while other outcomes have remained largely unnoticed. Third, although surprisingly sparse, research on the outer parts of the ecosystem has focused on the financial outcomes, leaving much room for considering other outcomes. We elaborate these patterns below, also summarized in Table 10.1.

The acquirer–target constellation

The buyer and seller firms has been the natural starting point for acquisition research, and here, a focus primarily on shareholder value dominates, albeit under a slightly different guise. As Table 10.1 displays, research in this part of the ecosystem largely has emphasized employee well-being; however, typically it has had expressed aim to avoid insufficient financial acquisition performance. That is, while the empirical focus is on employees, the perspective is

Table 10.1   Outcomes across the acquisition ecosystem

Ecosystem category	Definition	Studied actors	Highlighted outcomes	Implied/understudied actors	Implied/understudied outcome
The acquirer–target constellation	Organizational and individual actors involved in a focal acquisition	• Managers • Employees	• Employee well-being	• Middle managers • Labor unions	• Ethical concerns • Financial and other gains to employees
The nearby ecosystem	Actors in transactional or other direct relationships with a focal acquisition	• Competitors • Customers	• Financial wealth • Network relations and stability • Product quality	• Suppliers	• Innovation effects on environmental and social concerns • Changes in choice or discretion

Ecosystem category	Definition	Studied actors	Highlighted outcomes	Implied/understudied actors	Implied/understudied outcome
The wider ecosystem	Actors not in transactional or other direct relationships with a focal acquisition	• Investors (acquiring owners and target owners) • Customers' customers	• Financial wealth	• Suppliers' suppliers • Complementors • Regulators • Standardization bodies • Natural environment and resources • Regulators • Local communities • Labor unions • Media • Non-governmental organizations • Substitute providers	• Environmental impact • Social impact • Ethical concerns

that of shareholders. In so doing, research shows acquisitions often strive to create profits through cost-cutting and staff reductions, with negative effects on job security and general employee welfare (Siegel and Simons, 2010). As a consequence, employee physical and psychological security is often at risk (Buono and Lewis, 1985). Anxiety and stress can result from fear of losing one's job, changed work conditions, or challenges to organizational culture or identity (Seo and Hill, 2005). Bansal and King (2022) draw on data from Indian acquisitions to show that communication can help successfully achieving both employee well-being and financial value creation. Despite research demonstrating that acquisitions can also benefit employees (Teerikangas, 2012), positive effects on employee well-being have not consistently been recognized as an outcome.

Also, managers suffer from similar negative effects. For example, research shows that turnover in acquisitions is higher among managers than other personnel categories (Kesner and Dalton, 1994). While managers in the top echelons are sometimes cushioned from the purely financial effects (e.g., golden parachutes), this rarely applies to other levels of the managerial hierarchy (Bebchuk, Cohen and Wang, 2014). Instead, research has pointed to the risk that managers become squeezed in acquisitions; forced to work more than usual to manage the integration process, while at the same time suffering an increased risk of losing one's job because of the integration (Schriber, 2012), and more research on how acquisitions affect managers is needed.

The nearby ecosystem

The next category of studies relates to ecosystem actors adjacent to an acquisition and includes customers, suppliers, and competitors. Most of these actors are covered in traditional industry frameworks (Porter, 1980), and appear to different extents in acquisition research, and with different outcomes.

The profit margin, or financial wealth, has stood at the forefront when considering competitors, as visible in the dominating view of acquisitions as moves to outmaneuver competitors. A stream of literature has grown around how acquisitions threaten to reduce competitor profits, and how these competitors may react (Schriber, King and Bauer, 2022; Uhlenbruck et al., 2017). However, acquisitions also can result in increased competitor profits (Clougherty and Duso, 2009). Despite these recent efforts, more research on how competitors are affected, and when they consider acquisitions reason for retaliating, is needed.

Acquisition outcomes for customers have received relatively more attention. Studies drawing on network theory show that acquisitions can threaten even established ties to customers, as the acquisition can reduce the customer's trust or lead to suspicion of information leakage (Rogan, 2014). While there clearly is also an underlying tension over profit distribution between acquirers, suppliers, and customers (Kato and Schoenberg, 2014), customers can be assumed to be affected by reduced stability in demand and disturbed network relations. Hence, even if rarely expressed as an outcome, network relation stability or instability is an acquisition outcome. Surprisingly, research on acquisition effects on suppliers is more limited (Anderson, Havila and Salmi, 2001; Kato and Schoenberg, 2014), and more research is needed in this area.

However, customers can also benefit from acquisitions, such as through improved products. Ahuja and Katila (2001) found that acquisitions can lead to improved innovative capability, although more recent research suggests the effects of acquisitions on innovation depends on a variety of factors (Wu, Yu and Khan, 2023). Beyond this, customers may experience greater dependence and reduced bargaining power as the number of suppliers is reduced following horizontal acquisitions (Porter, 1980). The resulting outcome can be considered a reduction in choice, discretion, or freedom; and how this affects actors in the ecosystem merits more research attention.

The wider ecosystem

The wider ecosystem spans several actors, mainly without a continuous and direct relationship with the focal firms (see Ranjan and Read, 2021). These involve complementors, customers' customers, suppliers' suppliers, substitute providers, and also local communities, standardization bodies, labor unions, media, non-governmental organizations, the natural environment, regulators, and investors. Investors are considered actors in the outer parts of our framework, as they are distanced from a focal firm (e.g., pension funds, individual savings). Despite the number and width of actors, acquisition research has given the broader ecosystem scant attention, and then mainly attending to financial outcomes, leaving room for much future research.

The focus on financial outcomes of acquisitions to investors is reflected here, too. For instance, it appears in studies on how to avoid financial setbacks from overpaying. As an early example, Roll (1986) argued that any payment beyond the stock price was attributable to acquiring managers' hubris. Others have pursued how to avoid overpayment, such as Pavićević and Keil (2021), or who benefits financially (Kuvandikov, Pendleton and Higgins, 2020), showing that acquirers typically lose value, while target owners gain (King et al., 2004).

Relaxing the primacy of shareholder financial value, the way an acquisition is managed can influence several outcomes. Acquisitions typically strive to increase operational efficiency through economies of scale and scope (e.g., Larsson and Finkelstein, 1999) that are connected more broadly to the use of resources. Yet, limited attention has been paid to how acquisitions can offer a more efficient production, or more output per unit of input (King et al., 2021), and the resulting implications for the wider ecosystem, such as suppliers, as well as whether and how increased productivity also can benefit society (cf., Abramovitz, 1986). This is pertinent not least in light of a broadly increased attention to environmental impacts. Many natural resources, for instance for building electric vehicles, are in short supply and can only be retrieved with negative effects on sometimes fragile ecological systems and on local communities. More research is needed on the relation between acquisitions and such outcomes on the environment and society.

A similar argument can be made for innovation outcomes touched upon earlier. In general, acquisitions offer an alternative to organic innovation, achieving faster innovation that in turn can impact green technologies. In turn, acquisitions can be related to innovation that may eventually lead to reduced pollution, improved quality of life, or other environmental and social outcomes. Still, innovation outcomes of an acquisition are subject to managerial intervention (McCarthy and Aalbers, 2016), and how acquisitions and integration management affect such outcomes deserves more research.

Location decisions also likely produce social outcomes. Acquisitions typically play an important role in the rationalization of entire industries (Breinlich, 2008). Beyond the effects on the involved organizations, this also can have very tangible effects on society. While dynamism and dislocation of work opportunities are a natural part of economic activity and can provide a wide range of benefits, they, too, can mean uprooting livelihoods with negative effects on social outcomes such as ties to family and friends. More research is needed on the social outcomes of acquisitions.

Complementors (actors whose products or services are required for the use of the products or services of a focal firm) are given almost no explicit attention in acquisition research. An exception is Staub and colleagues (2021) who point to profit gains from acquiring complementors. Also customers' customers to acquisitions are rarely studied, but often silently equated to consumers primarily striving for lower prices, in financial and economics research equated to welfare to society (Jensen, 2010). Against this background reduced competition through acquisitions constitutes a risk. Indeed, antitrust law was one of the earliest legal concerns surrounding acquisitions, manifested in the Interstate Commercial Act of 1887 relating to railroads, followed by the broader Sherman Act of 1990 (Dobbin and Dowd, 2000). Still, more research on outcomes from acquisitions for customers' customers is clearly needed.

Relatedly, while traditional economic theory regards a well-functioning competition as a precondition for economic welfare, reduced competition, as a result of acquisitions, may also offer societal benefits. For instance, Claassen and Gerbrandy (2018) argue for a broadened understanding of what competition law can achieve, and what regulators should aim for, claiming that a narrow focus on economic gains should be broadened to also include ethical concerns, or what is considered morally right in a situation. More research on regulating bodies is needed. For instance, relaxing the assumption that authorities are neutral bodies, one pertinent topic is how decision-makers in antitrust authorities, including politicians, react to acquisitions in various industries and with different types of outcomes for consumers. Also research into providers of substitute product or services to those in an acquisition are left outside of mainstream acquisition research.

Although standardization bodies, labor unions, media and non-governmental organizations all can be assumed to play important roles in acquisitions, they are given scant attention in research. For instance, labor unions have been found to impact profit margins to owners (Levine, Lin and Shen, 2020). However, with few exceptions (e.g., Meyer, 2008), the impact from acquisitions on labor unions remains largely unstudied. A recent study highlights how collaboration of unions and management shapes the integration process through virtuous and vicious cycles (Stensaker, Colman and Grøgaard, 2023). Still, there is room for more research, such as more clearly distinguishing outcomes at the organizational and individual levels. For instance, while the individual members of labor unions can suffer from reduced well-being, acquisitions could benefit a union as an ecosystem actor through a boost in membership. Also media shape the landscape in which acquisitions take place (Hellgren et al., 2002), but more research on the mutual relation between media in constant search for news and acquisitions is needed.

Discussion

Our analysis of acquisition outcomes, from those already appearing in literature to those appearing only between the lines, or unexpressed consequences, provides a broader understanding of acquisitions, but also offers concrete guidance regarding the areas in need of further research. Further, management practice can benefit from acknowledging a variety of acquisition outcomes. To this end, we advance an acquisition ecosystem perspective to disentangle acquisition outcomes and identify actors surrounding acquisitions.

Broadening acquisition outcomes

Our starting point has been that acquisition outcomes remain underdeveloped in research, with an overwhelming and limiting emphasis on financial value to shareholders (Meglio and Schriber, 2023). We endorse joining a broader movement to consider more than financial outcomes (van der Linden and Freeman, 2017; van der Linden, Wicks and Freeman, 2023; Smith and Rönnegard, 2016). Research has given uneven attention to different outcomes, and our analysis reveals interesting patterns. Specifically, we find that different outcomes appear in different parts of the ecosystem surrounding acquisitions.

In focusing on the acquirer–target constellation (i.e., the center ring of our framework), the focus has largely been limited to employee well-being, corresponding to what has been called the organizational behavior school of acquisition research (Haspeslagh and Jemison, 1991). This means that the calls for more attention to research into the "human" side of acquisitions (Larsson and Finkelstein, 1999; Sarala, Vaara and Junni, 2019; Seo and Hill, 2005) have been answered. However, employee well-being has largely appeared as a vehicle to improve financial value, and research in this part of the ecosystem can be fruitfully extended to consider both acquisition outcome on employees in its own right, including potential positive outcomes, and other organizational outcomes.

Next, current research on outcomes to the actors appearing close to acquisitions largely reflects traditional industry analysis (Porter, 1980), where the dominating concern is over the distribution of industry profits. This interest mirrors the strategic management school (Haspeslagh and Jemison, 1991), and while studies also show a concern for customers (e.g., Kato and Schoenberg, 2014), a more varied understanding of outcomes for these actors and attention to suppliers is still missing.

Interestingly, financial outcomes mirroring the financial school (Haspeslagh and Jemison, 1991) dominate research focusing also on the wider ecosystem. This is surprising as this section spans a wide range of actors populating a broad part of the society surrounding acquisitions, and more research is required to fully grasp acquisition outcomes in this part of the ecosystem.

Considering acquisition ecosystems

We have introduced the concept of ecosystems as a useful approach to structure the understanding of the context of acquisitions. Compared to traditional industry analysis (Porter, 1980), an ecosystems approach allows a more holistic view of the actors surrounding acquisitions and their relations. While progress has been made in raising awareness of acquisitions as embedded in an organization-wide context (Rouzies et al., 2019), an ecosystem lens provides a more structured starting point for actors that typically surround acquisitions. For instance, rather than merely recording outcomes as they are perceived by actors, an ecosystem approach allows identifying also those actors that are not affected by a particular acquisition, as well as those unaware that they are affected. Moreover, the ecosystem structure illuminates how different parts of that context relate to a focal acquisition. Rather than considering the world outside of the firms involved in acquisitions as simply "out there," an ecosystem approach allows accounting for conceptual proximity. This complements studies that consider the role of national borders (Bauer et al., 2018), geographic (McCarthy and Aalbers, 2016) or psychic distance (Chikhouni, Edwards and Farashahi, 2017) in acquisitions, to consider both the ecosystem and its constituent actors.

The ecosystem view on acquisitions proposed here also assists in structuring how acquisitions affect the environment surrounding acquisitions. Ecosystems involve various actors, but are also entities in their own right. An ecosystem view also illuminates existing and potential benefits and costs accruing to various actors that complement traditional strategic management industry profit distribution analysis. For instance, the financial benefits to complementors are generally considered to mirror those of a focal firm, while the contrary is true for competitors. However, an ecosystem perspective highlights also coopetitive gains (Nalebuff and Brandenburger, 1996), where increased success of one firm can benefit also competitors through a shared technical standard.

In the same way, while standard strategy research emphasizes the benefits to singular firms from proprietary knowledge and innovation (Barney, 1991), taking an ecosystem approach highlights that copied, non-proprietary knowledge and innovation can also benefit competitors, suppliers, and customers. As a result, outcomes are not necessarily objective or mutually exclusive. For example, relationships can also be symbiotic (vs. antagonistic), growing (vs. finite) to echo Meglio and Schriber (2023). Clearly, more research is needed on how various acquisition outcomes are dispersed and shared. For instance, what ecosystem actors stand to gain or lose from acquisitions? What ecosystem characteristics define whether and what actors are affected by various outcomes?

Contextualizing acquisitions with actors

Our framework highlights that outcomes differ depending on perspective. This extends the understanding of relevant actors beyond Porter's Five Forces framework (Porter, 1980) or network analysis, and embraces a wider variety of actors that are affected by acquisitions. Moreover, we have emphasized actors subjectively interpret acquisition outcomes, and that these interpretations, in extension, help explain how actors react to acquisitions. This bears potential to complement research on reactions to acquisitions that so far has focused almost solely on competitors (e.g., Uhlenbruck et al., 2017).

Still, more research is needed to illuminate, also empirically, the relations between acquisitions and individual actors, as well as potential interaction effects. For instance, how do various circumstances (e.g., different levels of industry growth, product maturity, top management team interlocks) affect actors' interpretations of acquisitions? Answers to such questions would enrich the field by producing empirically grounded, novel research on outcomes in acquisitions in an approach that can be described as "bottom-up." Second, research can consider ecosystem outcomes. Ecosystems are phenomena in themselves, and more research is needed in how they are influenced by acquisitions and temporal patterns for when such influence takes place. Not least, we have proposed considering actors so far rarely considered in acquisition research. Connecting to ideas in research on corporate social responsibility and ethics (e.g., van den Linden and Freeman, 2017), future research could address environmental and social outcomes of acquisitions, positive as well as negative.

Limitations

Our coverage of this topic begins to unravel outcomes attributed to each ecosystem actor but comes with limitations. Our analysis of outcomes in current acquisition research is illustrative rather than exhaustive. Although arguably covering the most common outcomes, we welcome future studies revealing additional ones. Moreover, we actively avoided extending the analysis to infinity where a "butterfly effect" is impossible to predict. Despite these limitations, our study clearly advocates considering outcomes for a broader set of actors within an ecosystem. Our analysis is a step towards this aim, and we have focused on what broadly can be considered the most important and obvious actors and outcomes. This implies there is more work to do (e.g., confirming, falsifying, or nuancing) the topics we cover, as well as extending beyond them to produce new insights.

Conclusion

Oscar Wilde famously wrote that a cynic is a person who knows the price of everything and the value of nothing. This appears an apt description of current acquisition research and its persistent emphasis on financial outcomes. We establish ecosystems as a useful lens for regarding acquisition outcomes and thereby contribute to an extended, structured, and embedded view of acquisitions. In so doing, we broaden research to consider additional intertwined, subjective, and active actors that are affected by acquisition outcomes. This forms an important complement to traditional research on industry competition, industry profit distribution, and networks surrounding acquisitions. Throughout, we have produced a research agenda, and hope this can contribute to an even broader understanding of acquisition outcomes.

References

Abramovitz, M. (1986). Catching up, forging ahead, and falling behind. *Journal of Economic History*, 46(2), 385–406.

Ahuja, G., & Katila, R. (2001). Technological acquisitions and the innovation performance of acquiring firms: a longitudinal study. *Strategic Management Journal*, 22(3), 197–220.

Anderson, H., Havila, V., & Salmi, A. (2001). Can you buy a business relationship? On the importance of customer and supplier relationships in acquisitions. *Industrial Marketing Management*, 30(7), 575–586.

Bansal, A., & King, D. (2022). Communicating change following an acquisition. *International Journal of Human Resource Management*, 33(9), 1886–1915.

Barkema, H., & Schijven, M. (2008). How do firms learn to make acquisitions? A review of past research and an agenda for the future. *Journal of Management*, 34(3), 594–634.

Barney, J. (1991). Firm resources and sustained competitive advantage. *Journal of Management*, 17(1), 99–120.

Bauer, F., Schriber, S., Degischer, D., & King, D. (2018). Contextualizing speed and cross-border acquisition performance: labor market flexibility and efficiency effects. *Journal of World Business*, 53(2), 290–301.

Bebchuk, L., Cohen, A., & Wang, C. (2014). Golden parachutes and the wealth of shareholders. *Journal of Corporate Finance*, 25, 140–154.

Breinlich, H. (2008). Trade liberalization and industrial restructuring through mergers and acquisitions. *Journal of International Economics*, 76(2), 254–266.

Buono, A., & Lewis, J. (1985). When cultures collide: the anatomy of a merger. *Human Relations*, 38(5), 477–500.

Chikhouni, A., Edwards, G., & Farashahi, M. (2017). Psychic distance and ownership in acquisitions: direction matters. *Journal of International Management*, 23(1), 32–42.

Claassen, R., & Gerbrandy, A. (2018). Doing good together: competition law and the political legitimacy of interfirm cooperation. *Business Ethics Quarterly*, 28(4), 401–425.

Clougherty, J., & Duso, T. (2009). The impact of horizontal mergers on rivals: gains to being left outside a merger. *Journal of Management Studies*, 46(8), 1365–1395.

Cording, M., Christmann, P., & Weigelt, C. (2010). Measuring theoretically complex constructs: the case of acquisition performance. *Strategic Organization*, 8(1), 11–41.

Datta, D. (1991). Organizational fit and acquisition performance: effects of post-acquisition integration. *Strategic Management Journal*, 12(4), 281–297.

Datta, D., Pinches, G., & Narayanan, V. (1992). Factors influencing wealth creation from mergers and acquisitions: a meta-analysis. *Strategic Management Journal*, 13(1), 67–84.

Degbey, W., & Hassett, M. (2016). Creating value in cross-border M&As through strategic network. In H. Tüselmann, S. Buzdugan, Q. Cao, D. Freund, & S. Golesorkhi (eds.), *Impact of International Business: Challenges and Solutions for Policy and Practice* (pp. 158–177). London: Palgrave Macmillan.

Dobbin, F., & Dowd, T. (2000). The market that antitrust built: public policy, private coercion, and railroad acquisitions, 1825 to 1922. *American Sociological Review*, 65(5), 631–657.

Gawer, A., & Cusumano, M. A. (2008). How companies become platform leaders. *MIT Sloan Management Review*, 49(2), 28–35.

Graebner, M., Heimeriks, K., Huy, Q., & Vaara, E. (2017). The process of postmerger integration: a review and agenda for future research. *Academy of Management Annals*, 11(1), 1–32.

Haleblian, J., Devers, C., McNamara, G., Carpenter, M., & Davison, R. (2009). Taking stock of what we know about mergers and acquisitions: a review and research agenda. *Journal of Management*, 35(3), 469–502.

Haleblian, J., & Finkelstein, S. (1999). The influence of organizational acquisition experience on acquisition performance: a behavioral learning perspective. *Administrative Science Quarterly*, 44(1), 29–56.

Haspeslagh, P., & Jemison, D. (1991). *Managing Acquisitions*. New York: The Free Press.

Hellgren, B., Löwstedt, J., Puttonen, L., Tienari, J., Vaara, E., & Werr, A. (2002). How issues become (re)constructed in the media: discursive practices in the AstraZeneca merger. *British Journal of Management*, 13(2), 123–140.

Hosta, M., & Zabkar, V. (2021). Antecedents of environmentally and socially responsible sustainable consumer behavior. *Journal of Business Ethics*, 171(2), 273–293.

Iyer, B., Lee, C., & Venkatraman, N. (2006). Managing in a small world ecosystem: some lessons from the software sector. *California Management Review*, 48(3), 28–47.

Jensen, M. (2010). Value maximization, stakeholder theory, and the corporate objective function. *Journal of Applied Corporate Finance*, 22(1), 32–42.

Kato, J., & Schoenberg, R. (2014). The impact of post-merger integration on the customer–supplier relationship. *Industrial Marketing Management*, 43(2), 335–345.

Kesner, I., & Dalton, D. (1994). Top management turnover and CEO succession: an investigation of the effects of turnover on performance. *Journal of Management Studies*, 31(5), 701–713.

King, D., Dalton, D., Daily, C., & Covin, J. (2004). Meta-analyses of post-acquisition performance: indications of unidentified moderators. *Strategic Management Journal*, 25(2), 187–200.

King, D., Wang, G., Samimi, M., & Cortes, A. F. (2021). A meta-analytic integration of acquisition performance prediction. *Journal of Management Studies*, 58(5), 1198–1236.

Kuvandikov, A., Pendleton, A., & Higgins, D. (2020). The effect of mergers and acquisitions on employees: wealth transfer, gain-sharing or pain-sharing? *British Journal of Management*, 31(3), 547–567.

Larsson, R., & Finkelstein, S. (1999). Integrating strategic, organizational, and human resource perspectives on mergers and acquisitions: a case survey of synergy realization. *Organization Science*, 10(1), 1–26.

Lepak, D., Smith, K., & Taylor, M. (2007). Value creation and value capture: a multilevel perspective. *Academy of Management Review*, 32(1), 180–194.

Levine, R., Lin, C., & Shen, B. (2020). Cross-border acquisitions: do labor regulations affect acquirer returns? *Journal of International Business Studies*, 51, 194–217.

Liao, H., Hsu, C., & Chiang, H. (2021). How does green intellectual capital influence employee pro-environmental behavior? The mediating role of corporate social responsibility. *International Journal of Management Studies*, 28(2), 27–47.

Livengood, R., & Reger, R. (2010). That's our turf! Identity domains and competitive dynamics. *Academy of Management Review*, 35(1), 48–66.

Loughran, T., & Vijh, A. (1997). Do long-term shareholders benefit from corporate acquisitions? *Journal of Finance*, 52(5), 1765–1790.

Masucci, M., Brusoni, S., & Cennamo, C. (2020). Removing bottlenecks in business ecosystems: the strategic role of outbound open innovation. *Research Policy*, 49(1), 103823.

McCarthy, K., & Aalbers, H. (2016). Technological acquisitions: the impact of geography on post-acquisition innovative performance. *Research Policy*, 45(9), 1818–1832.

Meglio, O., & Park, K. (2019). *Strategic Decisions and Sustainability Choices*. London: Palgrave Macmillan.

Meglio, O., & Risberg, A. (2011). The (mis) measurement of M&A performance: a systematic narrative literature review. *Scandinavian Journal of Management*, 27(4), 418–433.

Meglio, O., & Schriber, S. (2023). Towards a more inclusive notion of values in acquisition research. *Long Range Planning*, 56(6), 102331.

Meyer, C. (2008). Value leakages in mergers and acquisitions: why they occur and how they can be addressed. *Long Range Planning*, 41, 197–224.

Nalebuff, B., & Brandenburger, A. (1996). *Co-opetition*. London: Profile Books.

Oler, D., Harrison, J., & Allen, M. (2008). The danger of misinterpreting short-window event study findings in strategic management research: an empirical illustration using horizontal acquisitions. *Strategic Organization*, 6(2), 151–184.

Pavićević, S., & Keil, T. (2021). The role of procedural rationality in debiasing acquisition decisions of overconfident CEOs. *Strategic Management Journal*, 42(9), 1696–1715.

Porter, M. (1980). *Competitive Strategy: Techniques for Analyzing Industries and Competitors*. New York: The Free Press.

Rabier, M. (2017). Acquisition motives and the distribution of acquisition performance. *Strategic Management Journal*, 38(13), 2666–2681.

Ranjan, K., & Read, S. (2021). An ecosystem perspective synthesis of co-creation research. *Industrial Marketing Management*, 99, 79–96.

Ritter, T., Wilkinson, I., & Johnston, W. (2004). Managing in complex business networks. *Industrial Marketing Management*, 33(3), 175–183.

Rogan, M. (2014). Too close for comfort? The effect of embeddedness and competitive overlap on client relationship retention following an acquisition. *Organization Science*, 25(1), 185–203.

Roll, R. (1986). The hubris hypothesis of corporate takeovers. *Journal of Business*, 59(2), 197–216.

Rouzies, A., Colman, H., & Angwin, D. (2019). Recasting the dynamics of post-acquisition integration: an embeddedness perspective. *Long Range Planning*, 52(2), 271–282.

Saarala, R., Vaara, E., & Junni, P. (2019). Beyond merger syndrome and cultural differences: new avenues for research on the "human side" of global mergers and acquisitions (M&As). *Journal of World Business*, 54(4), 307–321.

Schriber, S. (2012). Weakened agents of strategic change: negative effects of M&A processes on integration managers. *International Journal of Business and Management*, 7(12), 159–172.

Schriber, S., King, D., & Bauer, F. (2022). Retaliation effectiveness and acquisition performance: the influence of managerial decisions and industry context. *British Journal of Management*, 33(2), 939–957.

Selden, L., & Colvin, G. (2003). M&A needn't be a loser's game. *Harvard Business Review*, 81(6), 70–79.

Seo, M., & Hill, N. (2005). Understanding the human side of merger and acquisition: an integrative framework. *Journal of Applied Behavioral Science*, 41(4), 422–443.

Siegel, D., & Simons, K. (2010). Assessing the effects of mergers and acquisitions on firm performance, plant productivity, and workers: new evidence from matched employer–employee data. *Strategic Management Journal*, 31(8), 903–916.

Smith, N., & Rönnegard, D. (2016). Shareholder primacy, corporate social responsibility, and the role of business schools. *Journal of Business Ethics*, 134(3), 463–478.

Staub, N., Haki, K., Aier, S., Winter, R., & Magan, A. (2021). Acquisition of complementors as a strategy for evolving digital platform ecosystems. *MIS Quarterly Executive*, 20(4), 237–258.

Steigenberger, N. (2017). The challenge of integration: a review of the M&A integration literature. *International Journal of Management Reviews*, 19(4), 408–431.

Stensaker, I., Colman, H., & Grøgaard, B. (2023). The dynamics of union–management collaboration during postmerger integration. *Long Range Planning*, 56(6), 102326.

Teece, D. (2007). Explicating dynamic capabilities: the nature and microfoundations of (sustainable) enterprise performance. *Strategic Management Journal*, 28(13), 1319–1350.

Teerikangas, S. (2012). Dynamics of acquired firm pre-acquisition employee reactions. *Journal of Management*, 38(2), 599–639.

Uhlenbruck, K., Hughes-Morgan, M., Hitt, M., Ferrier, W., & Brymer, R. (2017). Rivals' reactions to mergers and acquisitions. *Strategic Organization*, 15(1), 40–66.

van der Linden, B., & Freeman, R. (2017). Profit and other values: thick evaluation in decision making. *Business Ethics Quarterly*, 27(3), 353–379.

van der Linden, B., Wicks, A., & Freeman, R. (2023). How to assess multiple-value accounting narratives from a value pluralist perspective? Some metaethical criteria. *Journal of Business Ethics*, 1–17. https://doi.org/10.1007/s10551-023-05385-1.

Wu, J., Yu, L., & Khan, Z. (2023). How do mutual dependence and power imbalance condition the effects of technological similarity on post-acquisition innovation performance over time? *British Journal of Management*, 34(1), 195–219.

Zollo, M., & Meier, D. (2008). What is M&A performance? *Academy of Management Perspectives*, 22(3), 55–77.

Index